Townlife in
Fourteenth-Century Scotland

In memory of
ROBERT GORDON AND ETHEL EWAN
and their love of Scotland and its history

Townlife in Fourteenth-Century Scotland

ELIZABETH EWAN

© Elizabeth Ewan 1990

Edinburgh University Press
22 George Square, Edinburgh

Set in Linotron Plantin by
by Koinonia, Bury, and
printed in Great Britain by
Page Bros Ltd
Norwich

British Library Cataloguing
 in publication data
Ewan, Elizabeth
 Townlife in Fourteenth-century
Scotland.
1. Scotland. Towns, history
I. Title
941.1009732

ISBN 0 7486 0128 7
 0 7486 0151 1 pbk

Contents

Preface

The writing of this book arose out of an interest in the life of the ordinary people of fourteenth-century Scotland, those who were not part of the aristocracy or the church. To my surprise, delight and trepidation, I discovered that there was more material than had hitherto been realised for a study of a smaller part of society, the townspeople. I had the good fortune to begin my work at a time when Scottish urban history was beginning to expand and have therefore benefited throughout the writing of this book from constant exposure to the new ideas and findings of those working in the field. Urban archaeology has also expanded in Scotland since the late 1970s and new evidence about medieval townlife is constantly appearing. This book attempts to present some conclusions based on the material which has appeared to date. Further excavation and discoveries should lead to the modification of some of the ideas put forward here, but it is hoped that a basis for future work has been presented. To the many historians and archaeologists with whom I have discussed this project over the years and who have encouraged me in my work, I owe a great debt of gratitude. The mistakes which remain are of course my own.

The first part of the research for this book was done in Edinburgh in 1980–5 as the work for a doctoral thesis. The enthusiasm of my teachers and fellow-students at the University of Edinburgh made it a joy to work there. They have continued to help me since then, easing the difficulties of trans-Atlantic research. I owe special thanks to my supervisor, Professor G.W.S.Barrow, who first sparked my interest in Scottish history when I was an undergraduate and who then gave unstintingly of his time and expertise when I decided to do graduate work, and to Dr Michael Lynch for his guidance and help in the field of medieval urban history. I am also grateful to many other friends, including David Sellar for discussions on Scots law and on the fortunes of individual burgesses, Pat Torrie for comparative material on other towns and the welcome corrective of detailed information on one of Scotland's smaller towns, David Ditchburn for discussions on medieval trade, and Geoffrey Stell of RCAHMS for information on urban buildings and architecture and for help with the illustrations.

Many people outside Edinburgh have also given me help. To Grant and Anne Simpson, I owe many thanks for their great encouragement and their hospitality on my research trips to Aberdeen, as well as for information about archaeological research and a host of contacts. The Scottish Medievalists' annual conferences at Pitlochry gave me the chance to exchange ideas with a wide number of Scottish medieval historians. I would also like to thank the many archaeologists who have given help to a historian trying to come to terms with archaeological evidence, especially Linda Blanchard, Michael Spearman, and Charles and Hilary Murray for their help with my early work in Perth and Aberdeen, Rose Stewart for access to the unpublished material on the Perth High Street excavations, and Philip Holdsworth and the staff of the Scottish Urban Archaeological Trust for information on recent urban excavation in Scotland and access to the resources of SUAT.

Much of the documentary material for this book is still in manuscript. My thanks go to the archival staff who helped me find my way through the resources of the Scottish Record Office, the National Library of Scotland, Aberdeen University Library, Aberdeen Town Archives, St Andrews University Library, Montrose Archives, Dundee Archives, Perth Sandeman Library, Perth Museum and Art Gallery and the British Library. For permission to reproduce illustrations, my thanks to Corpus Christi College, Cambridge, the Royal Commission on Ancient and Historical Monuments of Scotland, the National Library of Scotland, and the Scottish Urban Archaeological Trust. For her expert drawing of the maps, my thanks go to Marie Puddister.

I am grateful to the University of Edinburgh and the Social Sciences and Humanities Research Council of Canada who funded my doctoral research and to SSHRCC for funding the work necessary to continue that research for this book, and to the Universities of Western Ontario and Victoria for grants for research. I have also benefited from discussions with colleagues and students in the History departments at the Universities of Victoria, Western Ontario and Guelph, Medieval Studies at Victoria and Scottish Studies at Guelph. The guidance, help and patience of the people at Edinburgh University Press, especially Vivian Bone, has been greatly appreciated by a first-time author.

Finally, for help in innumerable ways including listening to me trying out ideas, proofreading, hospitality, soothing words when the computer ate a chapter at midnight, and encouragement and support through my years in Edinburgh and the first years of university teaching, I owe a special debt of gratitude to my parents, Maureen and George Ewan, Louise Howard, Tristram Clarke, Jean Ewan, Jean Dalgleish, Roger Emerson, Janice Helland, Marilyn Livingstone, and Morgen Witzel.

University of Guelph, Ontario
July, 1989

Introduction

The history of medieval Scotland is a colourful one, dominated by such heroes as Macbeth, St Margaret, Robert Bruce, and William Wallace. But increasingly those interested in Scotland's past have begun to ask about less well-known figures, about those people who were the ancestors of the majority of modern Scots. What were their lives like, how did they cope with the world around them, what were their achievements? It used to be felt that the sources for Scotland's early history were too scarce to allow historians even to begin to answer these questions. But in recent years people have looked at the sources afresh, and have produced new kinds of evidence. This book brings together the sources and the analyses of historians and archaeologists in order to examine one group from Scotland's past: the townspeople of the fourteenth century.

The origin of Scotland's towns is still a contentious issue, partly because of the way in which 'towns' are defined.[1] If they are defined as communities having special privileges conferred on them by a king or other overlord, then it could be argued that towns, or as they were known in Scotland, burghs, first appeared in the country in the early twelfth century. If, on the other hand, they are defined more broadly as settlements where a large proportion of the population spends all or a good part of its time in occupations which are not agricultural, and where the exchange of goods takes place, then archaeological evidence suggests that towns were known in Scotland before the twelfth century.[2] Some of these became burghs, others did not. Those that were successful were often aided by deliberate royal policy from the twelfth century on, as the Scottish kings granted them privileges and encouraged both domestic and foreign immigration. By the fourteenth century, such flourishing settlements were recognised as burghs, and it is on these which this study focuses. While it is not the purpose of this book to enter into the debate on burghal origins, the picture presented here may help to underline the fact that towns were not some strange new-fangled institutions introduced by the feudalising David I under Norman influence, but rather a form of settlement which fitted easily into, and complemented, the largely rural pattern of medieval Scotland. Indeed in

many ways life in the towns differed little from that in the countryside.

There were, however, certain privileges enjoyed by those who
lived in towns: for example, personal freedom, and the right to buy
and sell in the burgh market free of toll. Those who held burgh land,
for which they paid the burgh overlord an annual money rent, could
freely buy and sell it, apart from certain restrictions which protected
the rights of their heirs. Such landholders were admitted as burgesses
of the town and could have further privileges such as freedom from
toll on their merchandise throughout the kingdom, monopoly rights
on the trade in certain goods in a specified area surrounding the
burgh (known as the burgh's 'liberty'), and increasing degrees of
self-government.

All exports and imports were supposed to pass through the
burghs, creating valuable opportunities not just for enterprising
overseas merchants but also for craftsmen who gained easy access to
raw materials from home and abroad, for porters, captains and
sailors who loaded and sailed the ships, for those providing food and
drink for merchants and customers, and for a host of others. The
burghs were often the sites of religious institutions such as cathedrals
and abbeys, of secular centres of power such as castles, and of
important gatherings such as parliaments or courts of justice. All of
these provided employment to townsfolk.

During the thirteenth century, Scotland's townsfolk enjoyed a
period of prosperity, a time of increasing trade abroad, fuelled
especially by demand for Scottish wool in the cloth towns of
Flanders, and stability at home. But the death of Alexander III in
1286 ushered in a time of troubles. Over the next half century, people
lived through the increasing interference in and finally complete
takeover of Scottish affairs by Edward I of England from 1296 to
1307, the gradual recovery of the country's independence by Robert
Bruce from 1307 to 1329, more English interference in the 1330s
and the renewed recovery of Scottish autonomy by 1341. Several
towns suffered burning and devastation by invading armies.

English ambitions in Scotland were diverted by the start of the
Hundred Years War, but Bruce's heir, David II (1329-71) had the
ill fortune to be captured by the enemy when he led a raid on
northern England in 1346. His eventual release in 1357 was only
achieved after his subjects agreed to pay a huge ransom of 100,000
merks (£66,000). As much of the money was to be raised through
a tax on wool exports, the towns and their merchants came to play
an important role in the affairs of the kingdom, with the burgesses

winning political recognition as one of the three estates which made up the Scottish parliament. It is one of the signs of their strength that much of the ransom was paid off, even though the country had suffered the devastation of plague in 1349 and 1361.As a mark of their significance, many burghs were granted feu-ferme charters which replaced the various revenues owed to the king or burgh lord with a fixed yearly payment, giving official recognition to the townspeople's ability to run their own affairs.

Scotland enjoyed a period of peace and prosperity in the 1370s, but the last two decades of the century were marked by sporadic conflict with England, weak government under Robert II (1371-90) and Robert III (1390-1406), and declining markets for Scottish wool on the continent. But, as they had survived the troubles of the early century, the townspeople proved similarly resilient in its closing years. When James I came back from English captivity to claim his throne in 1424, he found in the towns a group of people who considered themselves to be an integral part of the wider community of the realm.

In the last fifteen years, there has been a growing interest in Scotland's medieval burghs. The subject has been approached from a number of perspectives — historical, archaeological, geographical, architectural. Some documentary sources have been used for the first time, while others have been re-examined. Since the mid-1970s, excavation has taken place in an increasing number of urban medieval sites. Town plans and the place of the town in the geography of the kingdom as a whole are being analysed. Burgh churches and the few other surviving medieval urban buildings, as well as old drawings and documentary references to structures, have been the subject of investigation. This work is now beginning to find its way into print, with the publication of two monographs on excavations in Aberdeen and Perth and more to come,[3] some surveys of Scotland's urban history,[4] a collection of essays on various aspects of the medieval burghs by contributors from a number of different disciplines,[5] and a monograph on urban architecture.[6] Work has been carried out over the last ten years by the Scottish Burgh Survey, which discusses the history of individual burghs and their potential for archaeological investigation in order to inform planners and those concerned with the future of their community of the remaining traces of its past.[7] Some individual towns have been the subject of detailed investigation, although the lack of extensive documentary evidence on any one town before 1400 makes it difficult to pursue such studies for periods any earlier than the fifteenth century.[8] As a result, this book looks at the fourteenth-century burghs as a group. The events and vicissitudes of the fourteenth century meant that the townspeople were often free to follow their own interests, as well as cope with their own problems. In many ways these years saw their coming of age, their full participation in the community of the realm. They gained political membership in the government of the country, they played an active part in the kingdom's commerce, adjusting their own economies to take cognizance of new economic conditions, and they forged new relationships with the world around them. Much of the strength they demonstrated in these years arose out of their sense of community, a sense of common purpose, which resulted in the mutual advantage of burgh and realm.

1 Life in the Burgh

By the fourteenth century the burgh was a familiar institution in Scotland. Granted privileges by the king or ecclesiastical or baronial overlords to stimulate trade, the burghs came to occupy a role in the economy and society of medieval Scotland out of all proportion to their size. For they were small – there was nothing in Scotland to compare to the great city-states of Italy, capitals such as London or Paris, or centres of European trade such as Bruges. Population data is scarce before the fifteenth century. Berwick, the leading town of Scotland at the end of the thirteenth century, a bustling port with a booming trade in wool exports and a prosperous hinterland, has eighty-two burgesses recorded in a list of 1291, while Perth, second or third in size after Berwick, has seventy-one, but these may not represent the total number of burgesses of these towns. We do not know what proportion of the townspeople were burgesses, nor, with one exception, are there any tax rolls to provide information on population until the mid-fifteenth century, but other evidence supports the picture of small settlements. Edinburgh in the 1380s was described as having 400 houses, while fourteenth-century Perth probably contained about 370 burgage plots, about 100 more than in the thirteenth century. A tax roll for Aberdeen in 1408 has about 350 names on it. These three towns were among the largest in late medieval Scotland, suggesting that the population of most burghs could be numbered in the hundreds rather than the thousands.[1]

The traveller on foot or by horse might find a burgh lying conveniently on a major highway or at the intersection of two or more roads, although the route to some towns might have to cross a river. Here he could take advantage of a ferry or a bridge usually maintained by the townspeople. The main revenues for the upkeep of the Tay Bridge at Perth in the fourteenth century came from the tolls paid by those using it, although if the traveller was a pauper, a religious or merely passing through, he was exempt. Bridges were expensive to maintain and sometimes royal help was given. Robert I and Robert III both made grants towards the upkeep of the Perth bridge, while in the thirteenth century Alexander II granted the burgh of Ayr a source of revenues to maintain its bridge and harbour. Other burghs benefited from the generosity of noble patrons such as Dervorguilla, wife of John Balliol and mother of King John, who provided a bridge at Dumfries. The Stirling ferry also gained from royal grants.[2] Bridges and ferries were important not only to local people but to the kingdom as a whole.

Foreign visitors, unless they came overland from England, usually made their first landfall at the harbour of a coastal or river burgh. David II, when he landed at Inverbervie on his return from France in 1341, promptly gave that settlement the privileges of a burgh. The majority of these burghs were in the eastern part of the country, reflecting the importance of trading links with the continent, although there was some trade on the west coast. Harbours also served water-borne commerce with other regions of the country. They ranged from simple beach landings to complex walls and quays. During the Middle Ages some burghs took steps to improve their harbour facilities, especially from the thirteenth century with the development of the large merchant ship, the cog, with its deeper draught.[3] The most detailed description of such work comes from Arbroath, where an agreement was made in 1394 between the abbot and the burgesses to build a harbour at the foot of the High Street, because of the losses suffered by the burgh (and undoubtedly by the abbot) for want of a port. The harbour was to be formed by the placing of coffers, probably either of stone or timber, filled with stones. The instructions suggest that a fairly large structure was contemplated. In 1398 Edinburgh gained permission from Sir Robert Logan of Restalrig, who held the lands around Leith, to expand the Leith harbourworks on to his lands, and to bring earth and sand to the site, probably as packing for a timbered quay-face. In the fifteenth century the Leith waterfront was extended outwards by dumping large amounts of rubbish on the beach. Similar schemes of land reclamation were common throughout medieval Europe and may have taken place elsewhere in Scotland, as the townspeople sought to provide extra room for warehouses, overcome silting, strengthen the waterfront or provide a deeper anchorage for ships tied up alongside the quay. Other towns established a new harbour altogether. Crail apparently had two harbours in 1371, the new one at Roome Bay probably being built in the fourteenth century.[4]

At Aberdeen, a 1398 reference to 'the Key' suggests the existence of harbourworks by the later fourteenth century, and this is supported by the French chronicler Jean Froissart's mention of an ashwood jetty some time between 1365 and 1383. An excavation, although it did not recover the earliest deposits at the site, revealed a stone-built late medieval wall whose smooth west face suggested that it was a quay wall. Nearby deposits and the construction method implied an early fifteenth century date. This wall may have succeeded the jetty described by Froissart, or it might have incorporated timber in its construction and be the one he described.[5]

Burghs not on the coast often had riverside harbours, with quays at which the ships could tie up. Perth probably had such a harbour, formed by wharves on the Watergate, the present Tay Street having been built at a later date. References to customs revenues suggest that some sort of harbour facilities existed from at least the time of David I. The wharf area may have been strengthened after the disastrous flood of 1209. Large jointed timbers uncovered in an excavation at the foot of the High Street were perhaps part of the medieval wharfage.[6] Inverness, Stirling and Kirkcudbright also had riverside harbours.

Some burghs enjoyed the advantage of natural harbours, which probably provided a major impetus to their first settlement. The original harbour of Ayr was the basin fed by the River Ayr, the river and the tides combining to scour away the sands. When the town shifted away from the exposed sand dunes to a gentle slope along the river, the plots on the riverside probably included wharves and warehouses. Montrose had an excellent natural harbour in the Montrose Basin, while the tidal estuary of the Kinness Burn provided shelter for ships at St Andrews.[7] Rock promontories, inshore islands, or a reef above the high-water mark, could also provide sheltered harbours. In many cases the natural harbour sufficed for the burgh's needs, with harbour works not being built until later. Blackness at Linlithgow was in use as a landing-place in 1304 and was granted to Linlithgow as a port in 1389, but permission for harbour works was not given until 1465. As elsewhere in Europe, many merchants probably built storehouses, boatsheds and other buildings on the beach, just above the high-water mark.[8]

Burghs not situated at a favourable harbour site were often granted nearby havens as their ports. Edinburgh carried on seaborne trade through Leith, Linlithgow through Blackness, Dunbar through Belhaven, and Haddington through Aberlady. The burgesses of Elgin were granted the use of the earl of Moray's harbour on the River Spey in 1393, but this was eight miles away and they seem to have made use of other sites as well, including (illegally) Spynie, which was controlled by the bishop of Moray.[9]

While ferries and harbours facilitated access to the burghs, they also helped to control entrance to the town. At the end of a bridge or on a quay, the burgh officials could collect market fees from merchants, keep out undesirables, or ceremonially welcome important visitors. In the parts of the town approached by road there may have been some sort of port, as at the West Port of St Andrews, although none of these survive from before the sixteenth century.But while some control was exercised over who came into the town, few Scottish burghs before the sixteenth century followed the continental and English fashion of surrounding themselves with walls. In the fifteenth century, Aeneas Sylvius, the future Pope Pius II, commented on the lack of walls in Scottish towns.[10] Gates at the foot of the closes opening on the burgh boundaries and fences or small walls at the back of individual properties probably formed the main defences of most burghs.

There has been much debate over the question of early urban defences in Scotland, with some historians maintaining that the towns must have had defensive works, pointing to continental parallels and the fourteenth-century references to the walls of Perth and Berwick as examples. In fact, these two towns form the exception rather than the rule. Both towns were occupied for extended periods by the English in the late thirteenth and early fourteenth centuries, and it was English military strategy which maintained their walls. Most towns relied on the neighbouring castle if there was one, or simply made do without proper military defences. In the twelfth century a fosse and palisade were planned for Inverness, a town on the very fringes of the area of royal control, but not much effort was put into maintaining it and the town was successfully attacked several times in the centuries which followed. The Scottish towns fell easy prey to the expeditions of the English kings during the Wars of Independence. Before this, most had few enemies to fear and no real need to raise defensive walls, nor did they hasten to build them in later years. A burgh law which made each burgess responsible for watch and ward may have been aimed as much at dealing with trouble within the burgh as with defence from dangers from outside.[11] Archaeological evidence from Aberdeen seems to support this picture, as no evidence of banks or walls has been found at the burgh boundaries. If some sort of enclosing fences were erected, they were not substantial enough to leave any traces. As was perhaps the case in many other burghs, the natural defences – in this case a loch, the sea, and steep slopes – were probably deemed sufficient.[12] Excavation of the perimeters of other burghs should help throw more light on the nature of whatever burgh defences did exist. On the whole, boundaries were used more to control trade and mark the limits of burgh jurisdiction and privileges than to guard against enemies. Boundary ditches could also have other uses, for instance as mill lades at Perth, and as a disposal site for rubbish at Inverness.

As he entered some towns, the traveller's eye might be caught by the castle of the royal or baronial overlord of the burgh or by the abbey or cathedral of its ecclesiastical overlord. However, although these buildings might appear to dominate the town, they were in fact outwith the burghal boundaries, both physically and legally. In times of trouble the castle could offer protection to the townspeople, sheltering them and their goods behind its walls, although in several cases during the Wars of Independence the garrison stood alone, independent of the town. In times of peace, it was quite separate. By the fourteenth century its officers had little jurisdiction over the town. In a few places such as Dundee the constable might retain some rights over the townsfolk but even here he gave up many of his special rights in the 1380s.[13] With cathedrals or abbeys the relationship was somewhat more complex as the head of the religious house was often overlord of the burgh as well. By the late Middle Ages, however, many burghs had won a good deal of autonomy in managing their affairs, and the abbeys and cathedrals played only a peripheral role in most townspeople's lives, except as a place of worship for those burghs which did not have churches of their own.

The traveller who had business to transact with the townspeople headed for the centre of the burgh, the market. On market days he would be joined by a steady stream of people bringing produce in from the countryside on horses or wagons or carrying it on their backs or their heads, foreign or local merchants transporting luxuries and other goods from abroad, craftsmen setting up stalls to sell their wares, entertainers, beggars and those who had come to buy. Burghs were generally granted a monopoly on trade in their hinterland, so that certain goods in the region had to be brought to the town for sale. Even on other days of the week, the market was a busy place. It was the centre of burgh life. Here were usually found any public buildings, the shops of merchants and craftsmen, and often the homes of the wealthiest families of the burgh, as a market frontage was considered to be a desirable property. The market cross was the symbol of the market privileges of the burgh, and a common place for making public royal proclamations and other important pronouncements. According to the chronicler Bower, the fair-minded Robert III, whenever he left a burgh, had his herald proclaim at the market cross that if any debts remained unpaid to people of the town, they were to inform him and they would be paid.[14]

The market area was often defined by the widening of the main street. At Ayr, 'the whole space was given a subtle double curve along its length so that when the frontages were built up the overlapping curved facades virtually closed the space.'[15] Occasionally the changing needs or the growth of the burgh led to a change in the location of the market. At St Andrews the cross was transferred in the 1190s, possibly from the east end of North Street near the cathedral, to its present location on Market Street. The Ayr marketplace was that burgh's second market. At Crail the market seems to have moved from the Nethergate to the High Street. In other cases the original market might survive an expansion or change of orientation of the burgh. The Perth market at the foot of the High Street was probably the focus of market activity when the main axis of the burgh was north-south along the Skinnergate, as well as in the later period when the axis had shifted to east-west along the High Street and South Street.[16]

As well as changing site, markets might grow in size. From at least the fifteenth century, and possibly earlier, a number of burghs had several markets at various sites, each specialising in different products. The extension of the market-place might be the first step in such a development. Excavations at Castle Street in Inverness have led to the suggestion that the street was a deliberately planned expansion of the market which occurred during the fourteenth century.[17] Perhaps as the market grew the various products offered for sale might be grouped together in separate sections, and later were offered at separate markets in different parts of the burgh.

The market could be affected in another way by burgh expansion. The centre of a wide market-place offered space for more buildings, especially if space elsewhere in the burgh was limited. In Dumfries in the late fourteenth century the New Wark, a large stone structure, was erected in the middle of the High Street, affecting the size of the market area. The Luckenbooths of Edinburgh, which were built in the High Street immediately in front of St Giles, may have been constructed as early as 1386. In Haddington the separation of the market area into two streets by 1425 can still be seen today. The street itself could be of sand and gravel, beach pebbles and large stones or cobbles.[18]

It was in or near the market that the tolbooth, symbol of the townspeople's rights of self-government, stood. The tolbooth or townhouse was the meeting-place for the burgh administration, and could also act as a toll-collecting centre and a prison. As the regulation of trade was one of the most important functions of the burgh government, the siting of its hall near the market was appropriate. The possession of a tolbooth was a mark of civic pride, a statement that the burgh had come of age. Several burghs erected them in the fourteenth century. Robert II's grant to Irvine of land in Market Street on which to build a tolbooth sums up the dual nature, practicality and prestige, of these buildings when it states that the people should erect a 'decent and fair house to hold public and secret councils that it might be a courthouse for the enhancement of the burgh.'[19]

Not all burghs had a tolbooth, however. Public meetings were often held in large open spaces within the town, frequently in churchyards. In 1272 the burgh of Elgin granted land to Pluscarden Abbey, the whole citizenry being gathered in the churchyard of St Giles to approve the action. In Inverness, the churchyard of the chapel of St Mary and the parish church were used. In Aberdeen in 1317, one sitting of the burgh court was held in a private house. A tolbooth was built here in the early fifteenth century, each citizen being ordered to contribute one day's work or 4d.[20]

The market was also the site of the tron or public weighbeam of the burgh. In 1364 David II ordered that a tron and the office of tronar be set up in each burgh. On 3 December 1364, two days earlier, David had granted land to the burgesses and community of Edinburgh in the High Street on which to build a new tron, to replace the old one. Payments to tronars appear in the custumars' accounts of many burghs from this time onwards, showing that the tron was used for weighing exports as well as market goods. Like the market cross, it was used as a place for public proclamations by individual townspeople. In 1399 Paul Crab, burgess of Aberdeen, gave a pledge to one of the bailies at the tron to pursue an action against another burgess over a land dispute.[21]

Another focus of community life was the parish church, especially if it was within the burgh, as it was in most towns. Unlike many English and continental towns, the small Scottish burghs were not divided into many different parishes but remained single-parish towns. Although the parish often extended beyond the burgh bounds, the kirk itself was usually identified most strongly with the townspeople, so much so that sometimes if the first parish church was outside the burgh, as at Cupar, it was later moved to a new site within the town. In Dundee the same object was achieved when the town expanded westwards, and embraced the site of St Mary's. Some burghs worshipped at an altar in the local cathedral or abbey church, but the majority had their own kirk. In some burghs such as

Perth it was situated away from the bustle of the market and was
reached by a side-street, while in others such as Elgin it was in the
centre of the High Street. Sometimes the parish church was put to
uses not intended by its founder. In 1299 Edward I used the tower
of Annan parish church to store supplies in case of attack by the
Scots, while the parish church of Linlithgow was incorporated in the
English king's defences there in the early fourteenth century.[22]

Religious houses of friars or canons were found in many burghs
– some prosperous towns such as Aberdeen had three friaries by the
fourteenth century. Generally, such institutions were established on
the outskirts of the burgh, helping to establish its limits at the time
of their founding. When the burgh later expanded beyond these
limits, the area around the friaries usually remained as open space.
The Greyfriars of Dumfries possessed almost all the lands north of
Friars' Vennel in the fourteenth century, and these were described
as still vacant in the sixteenth century. The area of the Green around
the Carmelite Friary of Aberdeen remained as garden for much of
the medieval period.[23] The friaries provided prayers for the townspeople, sustenance for the poor, accommodation for travellers, and
often schooling for the young. The street-name Schoolhill, near the
Dominican Friary in late fourteenth-century Aberdeen, suggests the
early establishment of a school there. Most burgh schools were
probably established by the church, but in the fifteenth century they
increasingly became a burgh concern. In 1479 the Aberdeen town
council began to collect £5 annually for the master of the grammar
school.[24]

Other religious foundations included chapels and hospitals. The
hospitals usually combined a number of functions, including caring
for the infirm and the old, and providing rest and lodging for the
traveller. They were founded by individual benefactors, often
members of the royal family, and endowed with funds for their
upkeep, commonly in the form of lands providing an annual rent.
The inmates were known as bedesmen, or 'those who are bound to
pray', and one of their duties was to offer prayers for the soul of the
founder. Special hospitals for lepers were founded outside the
burgh. One lepers' house was situated north of Aberdeen, another
near Elgin, and a third has recently been partially excavated outside
St Andrews.[25]

If the traveller did not put up at a religious house, he might be able
to find accommodation at a hostelry, although these probably only
existed in the larger towns. In 1427 Parliament tried to remedy this
situation by ordering that all burghs were to provide decent hostel-

ries for travellers. This was not only for the traveller's benefit; there was a certain mistrust of strangers and they could be watched more closely in a public inn than in a private house. Only if they were relations or close friends, and a burgess was willing to vouch for them, would they be permitted to stay in a private dwelling.[26]

The public buildings of the burgh reflected municipal pride, but it is the individual properties of the townspeople which reveal most about the experience of daily life in the town. For the burgess, member of the most privileged class of the burgh, the most important possession was the burgage, the piece of land which qualified him to enjoy the rights of burgess-ship. The burgages were generally long narrow rigs stretching back from either side of the main streets. Many can still be clearly seen in burghs such as Elgin, Forres, Montrose and Linlithgow. In single-street burghs, where the road widened in the middle for the market, the burgages often formed a herring-bone pattern. In other burghs the shape of the properties might be determined by the presence of rivers or hills, or by development of the lands on a parallel or connecting street when the backlands of the burgages would have to be divided between two sets of properties. Where later streets were built at right angles to earlier streets, short burgage plots might be carved out of a burgage or two fronting the earlier street. In some burghs an attempt was made to keep the burgages fairly uniform, but what really mattered was the breadth of the frontage. According to the early burgh laws a burgess was to possess a burgage of twenty feet in width. Burgh officials called liners were appointed to supervise the burgage widths, indicating the importance placed on the property qualification.[27]

Excavations, town plan analysis, and modern property lines, which often preserve the medieval boundaries, show that many burgages were between five and six metres in width, thereby conforming roughly to the recommended size. However, the case of St Andrews, where the rigs were between nine and eleven metres wide, shows the danger of assuming too great a similarity between the burghs. Here many of the burgages were about ten paces in width, a measurement common in Europe and England. The burgh was first laid out by Mainardus the Fleming, a burgess of Berwick, and it has been suggested that his planning of the town may have reflected the situation there. There was also variation between different parts of some burghs.[28]

Sometimes early properties were laid out in a haphazard way with little concern about size, a situation later rectified in some towns. At Perth and Aberdeen there is evidence of a shift in boundaries in some

areas, evidently with the intention of making the widths of the
properties more uniform. In Perth there seems to have been some
experimentation, with lines being laid out and in some cases rejected. In Aberdeen reorganisation on two sites apparently took
place at about the same time, in the late thirteenth or early fourteenth
century.[29] If similar patterns are found on other sites, this may
indicate a degree of centrally-controlled town planning, something
for which no documentary evidence survives, although the analysis
of later maps may also suggest this.

Boundaries were marked in several ways, by gullies, wattle fences,
march stones and, occasionally, stone walls. In parts of Aberdeen,
boundary ditches were replaced by fences in the fourteenth century,
while in Elgin, fences were in use from the thirteenth century. At
Forfar, Glasgow and parts of Perth, gullies were common boundaries, probably providing drainage as well as property markers. In St
Andrews some boundaries were marked only by march stones,
perhaps a common practice as the burgh laws instruct a liner on what
to do if a boundary marker is moved. On the other hand, the garden
of one St Andrews property was enclosed by a stone wall in 1348.[8]
The type of boundary varied depending on a number of factors such
as whether animals were kept on the rig and needed to be enclosed
by fences, lack of trust in a neighbour leading to strict boundary
definition, the inability to afford a stone wall, or the need for a quick
and easy plot marker which could be redefined without difficulty.

Properties might also be separated by paths or closes which ran
between them to give access to buildings and yards behind the
frontages and sometimes replaced earlier boundary gullies or fences.
Closes were a common feature of medieval burghs and can still be
seen in many towns today. They were of gravel or cobbled, some
being provided with drains. The responsibility for their upkeep
varied – sometimes a path was completely on one property, at other
times it was on both.[31] More substantial divisions were provided by
the vennels or lanes which ran from the main street to streets running
parallel to it, to back lanes behind the burgages, or to particular sites
such as the parish church or a religious house. Sometimes the vennel
was included in the ownership of the adjoining property. The
Blackfriars of Elgin held a perticate of land with vennel in the burgh
in 1374. Other vennels were considered to be part of the street plan
and held in common by all.[32]

'Individually, the private house is a reflection of necessity or
status.... If we want to know how people lived in towns, we must
study their houses.'[33] Here many would spend the greatest propor-

tion of their lives and thus any information about these structures reflects the conditions of life for most of the burgh inhabitants. No fourteenth-century domestic buildings survive above ground in Scottish burghs. Provand's Lordship in Glasgow, which dates to the late fifteenth century, and a house of similar date in Inverkeithing are the earliest surviving urban dwellings. Nor are there any pictorial representations of the urban dwellings of this period, except for a sketch of the town of Stirling in a mid-fifteenth century manuscript of the *Scotichronicon*.[34] Scattered references in documents reveal little about the structure of the buildings beyond the fact that some had forestairs and upstairs rooms or 'solars', and that a few were built of stone, while most were constructed of wood. For construction methods and most housing materials, for size and shape, the evidence comes almost entirely from excavation.

In recent years archaeological work in several burghs, especially Perth, Aberdeen and Inverness has produced remains of enough structures to suggest some conclusions about the nature of medieval secular buildings. In 1980, Dr Hilary Murray presented the results of a study of nearly forty buildings excavated from the Perth High Street and various sites in Aberdeen.[35] The buildings ranged from the twelfth to the fourteenth century in date, but the development of building techniques was uneven and it is likely that all these types could be found in the burghs of the fourteenth and early-fifteenth centuries. Poorer inhabitants often lived alongside or behind wealthier townspeople, so that any one area might have a variety of structures. Nor can it be assumed that because one building is constructed in a more sophisticated way than another, the simpler one is necessarily earlier in date. Building techniques depended on wealth, available resources, or personal taste, while constant repairs might mean that one building could show a variety of types of construction.[36]

Documentary and archaeological evidence suggest that most urban buildings were made of wood; in 1236, for instance, Alexander II gave the burgesses of Ayr the right to take wood from the countryside to build their houses. The frequent conflagrations to which medieval burghs were prone – in 1244 alone seven of them were burned, while in the early fifteenth century at least one burgh every two years endured a similar fate – and also the speed with which they were rebuilt, implies mainly wooden houses. Writing in the late fourteenth century, Froissart reports that the Scots were not too worried about the destruction wrought to their homes by the English as rebuilding would only take them three days.[37]

According to Froissart, the Scots said they they needed only "'five or six poles and boughs to cover them'" to construct their buildings. This statement, although somewhat over-simplified, is supported to a large extent by excavations. The great majority of buildings uncovered have been of post-and-wattle construction, similar to the structures of Viking age Dublin and York. The predominance of this type of construction may be partially due to the fact that most sites excavated have been in the backlands of the burgages, and these buildings may therefore represent workshops or the homes of poorer inhabitants of the burgh, but similar structures have been found on frontage sites as well, and it seems reasonable to suppose that the poorer homes of the larger burghs may well represent the norm for many smaller burghs. Wattle materials were fairly quickly replenished, easy to cut and light to transport and were the most readily available materials. At Perth, they seem to have been cropped on a fairly *ad hoc* basis, rather than as the standard output of well-regulated woodland, suggesting that many burgh inhabitants were left to their own devices to build their houses in whatever way they could.[38]

Post-and-wattle walls consisted of a series of upright posts between which were woven flexible pieces of wood, such as hazel, ash, birch or willow. In the simplest construction methods the walls were set directly in the earth, sometimes in shallow gullies. Other homes had additional posts inside or outside the walls which helped support the roof. A more sophisticated technique, which was in use by the thirteenth century, was to set the walls in a horizontal sill beam which might itself be laid on a stone foundation. This helped prevent the rotting of the wood which affected the other wall-types with their posts set directly into the ground. The evidence of frequent rebuilding shows the shorter life of these buildings which seem on average to have stood for about twenty-five years or even less.[39]

Walls were often covered with daub which provided insulation and helped strengthen the structure. Clay was often used but other materials such as dung, mud and turf were also suitable, although these are more difficult to recognise in excavation. The use of daub depended to a certain degree on the function of the building. While insulation was welcome in a home, it was not crucial for an animal byre. In some homes where animals were kept in part of the building, the family end might have daubed walls while the other end did not.[40]

Plank walls have been found less often than wattle-and-daub, but may have conferred greater prestige. In Inverness some well-crafted frontage houses probably had plank walls, while a late-thirteenth century house from Perth suggests something about the value placed on such a feature. Here planking was confined to the west wall which fronted onto a path. Combined with the poor standard of carpentry in the rest of the house, this has led to the suggestion that it may have been built for effect rather than structural purposes. Indeed, the east wall was supported by buttresses which may have been needed to counteract the imbalance caused by the new west wall.[41] In this case, keeping up appearances risked knocking down the walls.

Other houses might have clay walls strengthened with heather or straw, while larger buildings were probably timber-framed, although this too is difficult to tell by excavation. Houses from the sixteenth century show that timber-framing was known in Scotland.[42] The stone houses associated with Scottish burghs today belonged only to the wealthiest families, and were sufficiently rare to merit being described as 'a stone house' in charters. Three in Ayr, one in Edinburgh and one in Aberdeen are documented in the fourteenth century. There were probably more but as the homes of the most prosperous members of the community they were unlikely to be sold, and thus documented. Excavation on the High Streets of Perth and Edinburgh has uncovered stone foundations which probably supported at least one floor of stone and perhaps a timber superstructure.[43]

Small wattle-and-daub buildings were only one storey but many of the houses of wealthier families were probably of two storeys or more. In thirteenth-century Perth a goldsmith owned a building which had two vaults on the ground floor and a living room, called a solar, above. When Perth was flooded in 1209, many of the burgesses took to their solars to escape the floodwaters. Solars are also recorded in other towns from the fourteenth century.[44] The second storey was often of wood. Advances in construction techniques allowed the building of jettied houses with upper floors jutting forward. Some of the houses in the *Scotichronicon* drawing appear to be of this type. Access to this second storey could be from within or by a forestair, an external stair which often protruded onto the street – some of more recent date can still be seen in towns such as St Andrews today. Permission of the town council or lord of the burgh was required to build these stairs, as they encroached on the land beyond the burgage plot, unless the house was set back from the street as seems to have been the case with some in Aberdeen.[45]

Two-storeyed buildings were probably the homes of the leading families of the town, at least in the early days of the burghs and thus tended to be concentrated near the market, the most prestigious area of the burgh. However, not all two-storey buildings were necessarily one-family dwellings. The tenement tradition has a long history in Scotland, going back longer than in many other countries to at least the late fifteenth century.[46] It is possible that highly-prized frontage accommodation was divided into flats even earlier than this, although no documentary evidence of such practice has yet been found.

Roofs were usually thatched, using straw, rushes, heather or whatever suitable material was nearby as the material was too bulky to transport far. Some people may have thatched their roofs themselves, others had professionals do it for them. There were at least two thatchers living in Aberdeen in the late fourteenth century. Thatched roofs had the advantage that when they were replaced, the old soot-encrusted thatch could be added to the byre manure and spread on the fields.[47] They had the disadvantage that they were highly inflammable. Legislation in the fifteenth century tried to prevent people from carrying uncovered candles too near the thatch. The hazard was made worse by the fact that the eaves often projected well beyond the walls, quite close to the ground, in order to give additional protection to the walls from the rain.[48]

Some larger houses with stronger walls had more elaborate roofs with wooden shingles or coloured pottery tiles, either combined with thatch at the apex of the roof or along the wall-line, or used on their own. Overlapping rows of tiles were nailed to boards and the roof was finished at the top with decorated ridge tiles. A pottery finial in the shape of an elongated face, found at Perth, probably came from the gable of such a roof, creating an impression not unlike that of the gargoyles carved on medieval churches. Such finds have suggested that the roof coverings of medieval urban buildings were much richer than earlier thought and indeed comparable to sophisticated English examples.[49]

For wattle houses a simple wattle hurdle or straw mat door across an entrance probably sufficed. Sometimes the wattle was carried on across the base of the doorway, both strengthening the walls and acting as a step to exclude dirt and rubbish. Other doors had a horizontal plank which fulfilled the same purpose. Some entrances also had a porch to help exclude the wind and rain. More substantial houses often had plank doors, hung on timber jambs.[50]

Little evidence has been uncovered about windows, as houses rarely survive much above ground level in excavations. Most window glass in Scotland has been found associated with ecclesiastical structures, but the presence of glaziers among the burgh craftsmen of

Elgin suggests that window glass may have been a feature of some urban houses, if these men did not spend all their time working on Elgin Cathedral after its destruction in 1390. For most inhabitants, however, windows would be little more than small openings with shutters or straw matting to cover them at night.[51] Lighting was provided by the glow of the fire, by rush candles, and by oil lamps, more than by the sun.

Floors were usually of sand, often strewn with rushes or straw to absorb food and cooking waste. Sand floors were easy to clean – when they became too filthy to endure, they could be swept out into the yard and a new layer of sand laid down, sealing any rubbish left behind. In Perth, it was the practice in some houses to cover the floor with vegetation to dry it before a new sand layer was laid.[52] Floors were also made of clay, cobbles, gravel and, especially for two-storeyed houses, timber. Some wealthy families floored their houses with tiles. Finds of tiles in urban houses have so far dated mainly from the fifteenth century, although they were used in ecclesiastical sites much earlier. A house on Edinburgh High Street had a colourful floor of yellow, green and black tiles, probably imported from the Low Countries. Some buildings had more than one type of floor surface, implying that the house was divided into areas with different functions.[53]

The conditions of excavation often prevent complete ground plans being uncovered, so it is difficult to judge the size of many of the buildings. In width, though, the structures would be restricted by the width of the burgages and the need to provide access from the street if they were in the backlands, and also by the length of timber for roof rafters. The smaller houses were generally no more than 3.5 to 4.3 metres wide, although their length, which varied considerably, was usually greater than this. It has been suggested that some exceptionally long buildings in the Perth backlands may have been terraced rows of cottages, similar to thirteenth- and fourteenth-century cottages found at Winchester.[54] Most backlands buildings lay at right angles to the street. Frontage buildings sometimes appeared smaller than the backlands structures in groundplan, but this was probably compensated for by an extra storey. Some frontage properties lay parallel to the street, others lay gable end on – variety, not uniformity, was the order of the day.

The smallest wattle-and-daub houses consisted of only one room where all the activities of the household, eating, working and sleeping, were carried out. More prosperous houses might be divided into two or more rooms. Two houses in fifteenth-century

Perth consisted of cellars, a hall and a chamber. Sometimes the
divisions were made by internal walls, at other times the partitions
might only be wattle hurdles. As in a modern house, different rooms
had different functions. In some houses, following a practice common in the countryside until the nineteenth century, the family's
livestock were sheltered at one end, keeping the animals safe and
providing extra warmth for the human inhabitants.[55] In wealthier
households, such as those whose occupants were responsible for
providing hospitality to the abbot of Arbroath when he came to town,
there was an eating hall, sleeping chambers, a kitchen and a larder.
Some houses had a central hall with chambers at each end, a
common arrangement in noble households of the period. Two
dwellings at Perth even had the rather odorous luxury of indoor
latrines.[56] Other buildings contained both homes and workshops,
while those on the frontages often had their living quarters above
their shops.

By modern standards, most medieval houses were fairly sparsely
furnished. The poorest houses might have no furniture at all, other
than beds made from blankets or canvas over a pile of straw, rushes,
wood chips, or bracken.   Cooking and eating were done around a
central hearth. Better-off families had benches and a trestle table
which could be put away against the wall when it was not in use.
Tables may not have been as commonly used as work-surfaces as
they are today. Many pottery containers recovered from excavations
have rounded or sagging bases suggesting that they were rarely
placed on hard surfaces as only a few were sufficiently stable to
remain upright.[57] Chairs were uncommon, seating being provided
by benches, stools, wall-seats or chests.

A list of goods which a burgess was expected by law to pass on to
his heir shows a slightly higher standard of living for some members
of the burgh. As well as tables and benches, a burgess was supposed
to have at least two beds, probably feather beds if he was wealthy.
Some possible parts of stick furniture have been found in Perth,
probably belonging to a burgess household.[58] Otherwise, little
evidence of furniture has been uncovered, partly because wood does
not survive well; moreover, the wood from discarded furniture may
have been used for other purposes. There were skilled woodworkers
in many burghs, who could probably provide for the apparently
modest needs of burgess families.

One of the most important household activities was the preparation of food. A great variety of implements connected with cooking
and eating have been found, revealing not only domestic activities

but also the work of local craftsmen. Food was usually cooked in pots suspended over a central hearth fire, although outdoor ovens were often used for baking. Frying pans were introduced from the Low Countries in the fifteenth century.[59] Cooking pots could be of metal, leather or pottery. Few traces of metal pots remain as broken ones were usually melted down and the metal re-used, although a mould which may have been used for casting cauldrons has been discovered in Aberdeen. Froissart, describing the habits of Scottish soldiers, mentions that they used cauldrons 'made of leather with the hair on the outside which were hung on the fires full of water and meat, ready for boiling'.[60] The most common cooking-vessels found are pottery pots and jugs, perhaps because pottery survives more easily than other materials. During the fourteenth century it may be that, as in England, metal cooking-pots were gradually replacing the pottery ones. There was no strict separation of function according to form. Cooking pots were used not only for cooking, but also as tableware and for storage, while jugs showing traces of fire-blackening may have been used to heat up liquids or re-used as cooking pots when their necks had broken. Pottery vessels were also used for butter and cheese-making, to preserve fruits, to wash clothes and as plantpots and watering jugs.[61]

As well as cooking pots the medieval cook had a variety of implements, mostly of wood or pottery, supplied by local craftsmen. Dripping trays, colanders, large ladles, spoons, strainers and what look like spatulas have been found. Many have cutting marks on the undersides, implying that they were used as chopping surfaces on occasion.[62]

Most people ate from wooden plates and drank from wooden or pottery cups, although wealthier families might have dishes and goblets of pewter or more precious metals. Pottery vessels could be quite delicate. At Aberdeen there were some unique well-made thin-walled beaker vessels which may have been drinking vessels. Local woodworkers produced both turned and staved vessels including bowls, mugs, tankards and porringers. Staved bowls especially seem to have been fairly inexpensive – the fact that staves of small bowls were discarded in good condition suggests that such bowls were cheap and readily replaced.[63]

The most important eating utensil was the knife, which often was used for general cutting purposes as well. Most had handles of wood or bone. A knife could also express its owner's status, by an intricately decorated leather sheath, or by the material of which it was made. A Perth craftsman began work on a knife of imported walrus ivory, although it was never finished. Spoons were also used; burgesses were to pass on at least twelve spoons to their heirs. Much eating was done with the hands. Aquamaniles, large vessels containing water, were provided for the diners to wash their hands between courses. As they were often in the shape of fantastic beasts, they also provided an element of decoration to the meal.[64]

Utensils, food, clothes and other possessions were stored in pottery containers, baskets, barrels, chests, and buckets, wrapped in coarse cloth sacking, or hung from the roof rafters. Baskets made from rushes or underwood were used to bring food home from the market and to keep it. Water barrels set outside the home were used to collect rainwater, while old barrels were often used to strengthen pits in the yards, as at Elgin, where a pit was lined with a barrel with the top part sawn off.[65]

Hearths, usually placed in the centre of the main room, provided both cooking fires and heat for the houses. Their presence in an excavated building helps to distinguish it as a dwelling and not a shed or stable, although sometimes their absence can be explained by the use of a brazier, which might not leave any trace.[66] Hearths were usually set directly on the floor, into clay-lined hollows, or on stone slabs, although some larger houses had stone-lined hearths. Peat seems to have been the most common fuel. Several royal grants to various burghs made provision for the burgh inhabitants to have a supply of peats, while others gave protection to those bringing fuel to the burgh. Many of the burghs had particular lands from which they obtained their fuel: Peebles the moss of Waltamshope; Stirling the peat moss of Skewok; Aberdeen the forest of Stocket; and Irvine the tenement of Hormissok.[67]

As well as hearths, the townspeople had ovens in which to bake bread, although in some towns the possession of these may have been restricted to burgesses. Some ovens appear to have been domestic, perhaps catering for the needs of a burgess family on the frontage and servants or workers living in the backlands. Others had a more commercial capacity and were probably used by bakers. Arbroath had a public bakehouse which was granted by the abbot of Arbroath, overlord of the burgh, to a local noble. Because of the fire risk, most ovens were situated outside in the backlands and as far away as possible from combustible wooden buildings. That this was a wise precaution is shown by the discovery of one oven which burnt down.[68]

Domestic sanitation was an important concern, but documentary references to sanitation measures in the fourteenth-century burghs are very rare. In Berwick the responsibility for cleansing the town appears to have lain with the burgh officials and was probably paid for out of the burgh fermes, as the king granted the burgh four merks for this purpose. Perhaps the responsibility was contracted out, as in the reign of Robert I the chamberlain was ordered to find out into what private hands the four merks had come. An earlier method of rubbish disposal in the town is revealed by a late thirteenth-century Berwick Guild statute forbidding inhabitants to put filth, dust or ashes in the common roads, in the market or on the banks of the Tweed.[69] Making dunghills in the streets of Aberdeen was a common offence in the late fourteenth century. In the late fifteenth century that burgh attacked the problem of cleanliness by charging a tax of 1d per house and booth to be used to clean the street, and to hire a person to clean the gates and vennels. The Inverness fosse, which by the fifteenth century was known as 'the Foul Pool', provided a convenient disposal site for the inhabitants of that town.[70]

A glimpse of what was probably a common practice in many burghs is given by a charter of the mid-fifteenth century in which an Edinburgh burgess is granted the forehouse of a tenement, to be held 'with the liberty of removing and depositing dust and ashes to the tail or rear of the said tenement'. The discovery of large pits filled with domestic refuse at most urban sites suggests that disposal of rubbish in the backlands was very common. Sometimes the finds from these pits were richer than would be expected considering the quality of the structures there, suggesting that they came from burgess houses on the frontlands. Backlands were sometimes used as communal middens, with little attention being paid to plot boundaries. A Perth backland seems to have been used in this way, with properties not being properly demarcated until the fourteenth century.[71]

Cess pits were usually found outside the houses, although a few houses did have inside latrines. A large Perth house had a private latrine leading off from one of the end rooms, while a fourteenth-century house in the same burgh had an indoor latrine complete with toilet seat. It may earlier have formed part of a more extensive latrine system, with the seat pegged in place. The Edinburgh High Street house had a garderobe, emptying down the hill towards the Cowgate. Such garderobes were found in the larger private houses of thirteenth-century England and usually consisted of stone-lined pits.[72]

The removal of rubbish from the inhabitants' properties could take place in a number of ways. Rubbish might be burned in the backlands. Middens were depleted by cats, dogs, rats, foxes and crows, or the refuse could be used to manure fields or to level a site for building.

Cleaning floors by laying down new ones had an advantage in that it raised the internal level of a structure above an adjacent path or midden, thus keeping out some of the outside filth and providing better drainage. Drainage facilities for entire plots also seemed to be quite common, with ditches performing the dual function of marking property boundaries and acting as drains. Drains could also be independent from boundary markers. Culverts sometimes carried surface water to the street. In Perth, a mid to late fourteenth-century gully was probably a drain for the gravel path beside it, the yard of one plot and the whole of the adjoining plot.[73]

The backlands of the burgage plots did not serve only as rubbish tips. Here servants or craftworkers had their dwelling houses and workshops, animals were stabled, and even small-scale cultivation might take place. If the burgh population was expanding, the backlands might even become largely residential and the familiar pattern of closes fronted by a whole row of buildings begin to appear. Many burghs, however, did not begin to build up their backlands until long after the medieval period.

There is evidence that much of the open space within the burghs was used as garden area. Seventeenth-century maps such as that of Aberdeen by James Gordon of Rothiemay show many of the backlands being used as gardens. The grounds of religious houses were also frequently put to agricultural use. In 1407 the Friars Preachers of Ayr granted a portion of their garden 80' x 20' (24 m x 16 m) to an Ayr burgess. In Perth the backland of a South Street property was apparently used as both midden and garden until the sixteenth century; other backlands on the same street also showed evidence of cultivation in most parts during the fourteenth century.[74] In Lanark, there were fifteenth-century agricultural lands in Broomgate. At Elgin a road ran behind the gardens of the burgh in 1363. References to arable land within the burghs also show that agriculture continued to play a part in the lives of the burgh inhabitants. The ploughing of a burgage in St Andrews, even if undertaken as part of a ritual, emphasises the agricultural nature of much burgh land-use. In another property in the same burgh, garden soil was apparently deliberately brought in for use on a site which had earlier been occupied.[75]

Many of the areas excavated show evidence of having supported animals at some time in their history. Organic layers and a series of wattle fences at Aberdeen sites in the late thirteenth/early fourteenth century suggest that animals were kept in the backlands. Some fragmentary buildings may have been sheds for the keeping of livestock, while some boundaries running across the properties were perhaps stock barriers to protect the domestic area from the incursion of animals. In Perth a number of buildings showed evidence of adjoining stockyards, while the existence of byres underlines the involvement of the burgh inhabitants in pastoral agriculture. A 1318 charter to Haddington confirmed the burgh's right to common pasturage in its moors.[76]

Animals other than cattle might be kept on a burgage. The burgh laws refer to the keeping of pigs, piglets, geese and hens. Horses were also kept by many burgesses if not by the poorer inhabitants of the burgh. The Berwick guild laws required all burgesses with goods worth £10 to have a 'seemly horse worth at least 40s' in their stables, while another law made in 1295 referred to the burgess's horse and his palfrey. Remains of horses have been found at Aberdeen, Edinburgh, Inverness and Perth.[77]

Townspeople's involvement in agriculture was illustrated by the often extensive arable and pastoral lands which belonged to the burgh. Someimes this became the site of suburban occupation, further blurring the distinction between town and countryside. By the fourteenth century, the extensive croft territories around Aberdeen which belonged to the burgesses, were being bought and sold independently of the burgh properties to which they probably originally belonged. But they continued to be farmed. Suburban occupation elsewhere, for example north of Perth near the former site of the castle, was characterised by an interest in cultivation.[78]

Burgage backlands also provided the main sites for local industry. Often workshops were situated in the rear of a craftsman's property while the finished products were sold in a shop on the frontage. Apprentices and assistants might also make their homes back here, beside or in the same buildings as the workshops. If space was limited in the burgh, a craftsman might rent part of a backland from a property-owner and set up shop there. Just as a merchant often lived above his shop, craftsmen might use part of their homes for their crafts. Several excavated buildings have shown evidence of both domestic and industrial use, underlining the fact that most industrial production in medieval towns was based around the household. Family members were expected to help in the business, if not in the actual manufacturing process, then in selling the finished product. Most burgh industry, with the possible exception of cloth-making, was carried out on a small, almost domestic, scale. Between them the crafts catered for a wide variety of needs, both for their fellow townspeople and for the surrounding countryside. There is no

evidence of single-industry towns in medieval Scotland. Craft surnames show the wide range of crafts which could be found in the
towns; there were fullers and dyers, tailors and turners, baxters and
brewers, goldsmiths and even the intriguing hangpudying – perhaps
a smoker of black puddings?[79]

In some towns there seems to have been an effort made to concentrate certain trades in particular areas, in some cases because of the
raw materials required by the craft – potters, for example, required
a nearby source of clay as well as water and suitable sites for their
kilns, preferably away from the risk of setting fire to crowded
buildings. The fire risk is also cited in the fifteenth century as the
reason for siting brothels on the outskirts of the town. Other trades
might be sited outside the town, in quasi-industrial suburbs, because
of the noxious nature of their work. At Perth, fourteenth and
fifteenth-century occupation of the areas to the north and west of the
burgh bounds was probably partly industrial in nature.[80] Dyers,
tanners who soaked their hides in vats of urine, smiths whose work
was noisy and smelly, were often to be found on the waterfront, away
from the market and the homes of the wealthier members of the
burgh. Sometimes street names reflect the concentration of crafts in
a particular area, for example Skinnergate and Barkerrow in Perth,
Smithyrow in Aberdeen, perhaps even Cambergate (woolcombers'
street) in Ayr.

Archaeology is beginning to reveal more about the nature of
burgh industry. In the deserted burgh of Rattray, in Aberdeenshire,
a whole industrial complex has been uncovered while elsewhere
tanneries, iron bloomeries, and possible brewing or milling sites have
been found.[81] Since the government records of the period are
concerned almost exclusively with the export trade in the raw
materials of wool, woolfells and hides, this new evidence helps
provide a more balanced picture of the burgh economy of the period
and also of the economy of the hinterland. For its raw materials and
often its labour, burgh industry was tied to the farming cycle of the
countryside. Industry also encouraged emigration from the countryside by offering opportunities for employment. The town was the
best place for craftwork – there was usually a plentiful supply of raw
materials because of the pressure to bring cash crops to market, the
waste product of one craft could supply the raw material of another,[82]
and there was the company and expertise of fellow craftsmen.

One of the most important functions of the burghs was to provide
revenues for the crown. As international trade developed, the bulk
of these revenues began to come from the customs charged on the

export of wool, woolfells and hides. As the centres of export for these commodities the burghs had access to a large supply of sheep and cattle, and a number of industries based on these animals could flourish. Once the wool, woolfells and hides had been removed, the other parts of the animal were available for use.

Analysis of animal remains from Aberdeen, Perth and Elgin has suggested that sheep and pigs kept by the townspeople were raised mainly for meat. Wool and hides for export came mainly from animals raised in the countryside specifically for that purpose, although the cattle may have been killed in the burgh itself. Perth, an important exporter of hides, had proportionately more cattle remains than Elgin or Aberdeen.[83]

Cuts of meat were prepared by the burgh fleshers; many bones show signs of the butchering process. Fleshers often prepared carcasses, perhaps belonging to those who had cattle of their own, for individual families. A burgh law stated that the fleshers should serve the burgesses from Martinmas to Yule, preparing and cutting flesh in their larders. The fact that while doing this the flesher was to eat at the burgess's board suggests that the process was carried out on the customer's property. Other sites suggest more permanent workplaces.[84] References to numerous fleshers in Aberdeen from 1398 imply that there was a considerable demand for meat in that burgh.

Animals were not used solely for food or export. A great many crafts and industries in the medieval burgh were animal-based. Wool and hair were used for textiles; grease and tallow for candles, tapers, soaps and lubricants: antler, hoof, horn and bone for ornaments, keepsakes, personal and useful goods; the toebones and hooves of cattle for 'neatsfoot oil', a lubricant for leather; dog's dung for treating leather before tanning; even goose feathers for flights for the bolts of crossbows.[85]

One of the most important of these industries, and the one most hedged around with restrictions and monopolies, was the production of cloth. This had been a significant industry in the twelfth and thirteenth centuries and the privileges of the cloth merchants were among the earliest to be confirmed in royal charters to the burghs. From about the mid-thirteenth century, the growth in the wool export trade meant that much of the raw material was leaving the country. Poorer-quality wool was not exported and a native cloth industry continued to meet the needs of the vast majority of the population who could not afford to buy high-quality imported cloth. From the late fourteenth century, with the decline in the wool trade, cheap cloth rather than wool was sent overseas and the cloth industry seems to have expanded once more.[86]

For twelfth- and thirteenth-century Perth, Professor A. A. M. Duncan has drawn a picture of cloth production controlled at every stage by the merchants who employed different workers to carry out the various processes involved.[87] Certainly there seems to have been a great desire to keep the production of finished cloth confined to the burghs, although the coarse unfinished cloth which probably furnished the bulk of the clothing of the rural people was apparently of less concern to the legislators. An old burgh law forbade wool-combers to leave the burgh if there was work for them there, while only burgesses were permitted to buy wool to dye or cloth to finish or shear. There was also discrimination against those who carried out such processes as dyeing with their own hands, as they were excluded from the merchant guild, while waulkers and weavers were forbidden by royal charter from entering the merchant guild of Perth or Stirling. In practice, however, the conditions of the fourteenth century and the financial obligations placed on the burghs by David II's ransom probably led to an easing of these restrictions, as, in Perth and Dunfermline at least, both waulkers and weavers were to be found in the guild in the fifteenth century.[88]

While archaeology can reveal little about the actual organisation of the industry, it can provide evidence of some of the processes which were carried on in the burgh and give some idea of the quality of the cloth being produced. On the whole, the textiles uncovered so far seem to support the picture of a less quality-conscious native industry, often dealing with poorer wool that was probably not thought suitable for export. It is difficult to be certain about the provenance of many of the textiles and it is possible that some of the better-quality cloths found may also have been made in Scotland, but generally the cloth uncovered is of moderate to poor standard.[89]

Many different crafts were involved in the various processes required to make cloth. The wool was first prepared by combing, which produced a hard worsted cloth or by carding, which resulted in softer woollens. Carding was a newer method, not recorded in Scotland before the fifteenth century. After this initial preparation the wool was then spun to produce yarn, usually on a spindle with a whorl to weight the thread. This might be carried on full-time, or between their household tasks, providing a way for women to supplement the household income. Spinning wheels were known in England by the fourteenth century and may have been introduced into Scotland by this period, but as yet no evidence of them has been found.[90]

After spinning, the yarn was sometimes dyed, although this process could also be carried out on the woven cloth. Pits which may have been used for dyeing have been found in Aberdeen, and also Perth where it is possible that heather tips were used as a dyeing agent.[91] Woad, madder, and brasil for blue, red and brown cloth were used from an early date and were fairly common imports. One property in Aberdeen was known as 'the Madder-yard'. Weld or dyer's rocket was a native dye plant, producing a yellow colour, and was widely cultivated as well as growing wild on wasteland. Yellow dye could also be extracted from the remains of useful crops, such as the skins of onions. Not all cloth was dyed, however. A large proportion of the cloth found retained its natural pigments. Such undyed cloth was probably the type referred to in a burgh law which stated that if a man was forced to alienate his heritage land because of need and it was bought by his kin, they were to provide him with meat, clothes and other necessities, the clothing to be of one colour, grey or white.[92]

The yarn was next woven to produce cloth. There seems to be some evidence that the vertical loom, which is believed to have been generally replaced by the horizontal loom in Europe about A.D.1000, continued to be used in Scotland until a much later date. Many of the artefacts associated with vertical looms such as weaving swords, pin beaters and loom weights have been found in excavations, while the cloth often has the type of starting edge produced by such looms. It is possible that the vertical loom survived as a domestic tool, the horizontal loom being used in more professional cloth production.[93]

Fulling of the cloth could be carried out by hand or at one of the fulling-mills which are recorded in Scotland from the 1260s. In England, the development of the fulling-mill encouraged the cloth industry to move from the restrictive atmosphere of the town to the countryside. In Scotland, there is little evidence of such a move, with fullers continuing to be numbered among burgh craftsmen. Moreover, there was less incentive to move the cloth industry close to such mills as fulling was by no means an integral part of the Scottish cloth industry. Even some of the finest pieces of cloth were unfulled.[94]

Cloth was sometimes finished by raising the nap with imported teasles, and then shearing it with iron shears. This treatment may have been reserved for higher-quality cloth provided for the nobility and wealthy burgess families. Many of the fabrics that have been found were neither napped nor sheared.[95]

Once the cloth was made it could then be sold to be sewn into clothes at home or by tailors. Tailor is one of the most common occupational surnames of the fourteenth century, suggesting that the burgh tailor was a common figure in the towns. His raw materials probably consisted of both imported and native cloth and he used bone, copper and iron needles.[96]

Local cloth was not used solely for clothing. Coarse tabbies were probably used for matting, although more closely-woven ones were suitable for sacking. Similar fabrics could be made into horse-blankets or used for sacking or packaging, although vegetable fibres such as linen were more commonly used for this purpose, as they were cheaper and more robust. Wool not suitable for clothing was sometimes used to sew up shoes. Better-quality cloths could be made into blankets and furnishings as well as clothes. Felt might supply the lining for a leather object or be made into a hat or the inner shoe of a boot.[97]

Linen was also used in the manufacture of clothes, but little evidence of linen has been found as it does not survive well. Its use as sewing yarn can usually only be conjectured from the evidence of empty stitch-holes and such indirect finds as flax seeds, a possible flax-breaking mallet,and linen smoothers.[98] Flax was also used to produce oil.

As important as wool to burgh industry was leather. 'Leather kept the rain off you, shod you, saddled your horse, made up your armour, held your drink and even cooked your food.'[99] Street-names, sur-names, occupational designations and archaeological finds all pro-vide evidence about this industry. Leather offcuts have been found in most burghs where excavations have taken place, while soutars, skinners, and tanners are found in many documents. Leatherwork-ing included several specialised crafts; surnames suggest the pres-ence of barkers who prepared bark for the tanning process, cordiners who made shoes of new leather, and cobblers who repaired old shoes.

While hides for export were usually dried and salted, the prepa-ration of hides for the burgh leatherworkers required that they be skinned and tanned, a much more time-consuming process. Re-cently a large tannery site was uncovered in Aberdeen, near the Loch which provided a source of water, complete with hearths or ovens and a range of tanning pits. It was pulled down about 1400, but records show that tanners continued to practise their craft in the burgh. Tanning was an industry common to most towns, even very small ones such as Inverurie and Newburgh, Aberdeenshire.[100]

Once the leather had been prepared it formed the raw material for various types of leatherworkers. Cordwainers were important to the community, providing the shoes of the burgh inhabitants. There were also cobblers to repair worn shoes as new ones tended to be expensive. One cobbler used part of his home as his workshop in the backlands of Perth. Many of the shoes found show signs of frequent patching and almost all of the soles were heavily worn, sometimes even entirely worn away.[101] Medieval townsfolk made sure they got their money's worth out of their shoes. Leatherworkers also provided their customers with belts, knife-sheaths, saddles and even armour.

Other burgh crafts based on animals included the working of horn, antler and bone. Waste from these industries has been found in many burghs. Sometimes the quality of the workmanship was very high – at least one talented antlerworker was in business in Perth.[102] Bone plates with lovely incised decoration found at Perth may be the work of one of the more artistic and skilful craftsmen of the burgh, while knife handles, bobbins, buttons and spindle whorls represent the more run-of-the-mill products of the horn, bone and antler workshops.[103]

As the centre of rural hinterlands and engaged in agricultural pursuits themselves to a certain extent, the burghs had access to a wide range of plants and vegetables, and many of these were used by the burgh craftsmen. Dye-producing plants and flax were used in cloth manufacture, with flax seeds also being used in the production of linseed oil. Heather and bracken were the raw materials for the thatchers, plants such as turnip and rape could be used for both food and oil, potentilla roots were sometimes used for dyeing and tanning and mosses could be formed into ropes or act as packing.[104]

Two of the most important industries based on the agricultural produce of the area were baking and brewing. References to those carrying out these activities abound in the burgh laws and Aberdeen council records, and Baker, Baxter and Brouster are among the surnames of the period. Wheat, oats and barley formed the main staples of everyday diets in Scotland, and therefore those involved in processing them occupied an important place in the burgh economy. Both brewing and baking could be carried out either domestically or commercially. Each burgess was allowed to have an oven on his land, while among the goods that were to pass to his heir were a 'leyd' (a brewing implement), a 'mask-fat' (a brewing vat), and a 'gylfat' (a vat for fermenting wort).[105]

Grain was often dried before it was milled, barley to stop it from germinating. Several drying furnaces have been found, often with remains of grain which carbonised in the drying process. In Perth evidence of a malt kiln with remains of the peat which heated it and a vat for steeping the barley have been uncovered. A large complex outside the burgh may have been used for brewing. Brewhouses were considered an important part of the burgh economy; the brewhouses of Newburgh, Fife were the focus of a dispute beteen the inhabitants and Lindores Abbey in the early fourteenth century.[106]

Baking was also of central concern to the burgh and those who earned their living by it were, like the brewers, carefully supervised by the burgh government. The many regulations governing brewing and baking afford some glimpse into these industries which seem to have been organised on an individual basis. Brewing ale was a common activity of townswomen. Women brewing ale were to sell it all year round, not just occasionally, but they were not to buy more than one chalder of oats per week to make malt. They were also to sell by the potsful and not by sealed measures. The ale was subject to testing by the official ale-tasters of the burgh; seven were chosen in Aberdeen in 1398. Bakers were to bake bread to a quality determined by the leaders of the community, and were not to have more than four servants working at their oven. The trade of each burgh's brewers and bakers was safeguarded by a law that no burgess might bring bread or ale from one burgh to another to sell.[107]

While much of the grain for baking was brought to the market by country-dwellers, many townspeople produced their own on arable holdings around the burgh and took it to the burgh's mills for grinding. The mills were not always owned by the town, although by the fourteenth century many burghs had gained possession of them. The mills generally lay on the outskirts of the town, (the mill lade of Perth helped define that burgh's boundary) although if there was a suitable stream they might also be situated within the burgh bounds. Aberdeen had mills both within and outwith the town. The miller could make a good living from the fees of the burgesses, who were required to bring their grain to the burgh's mills and were forbidden to try and evade the mill fees by using hand querns instead, although the fact that a number of querns have been found in excavations[108] suggests that some were willing to try.

Fish was an important food in medieval Europe where the Church decreed days of fast, on which meat was forbidden. Fish was also an important export, one for which Scotland was renowned. Fishermen sometimes lived in the burgh but often they and their families formed separate little communities, outside of but connected with the burgh. At Aberdeen there was a fishing community at Futy (Footdee).[109]

Fishermen may have built their own boats, coracles of hides over a wicker frame – the paddle of such a boat was found at Aberdeen.[110] Boats and ships were also built in the burghs. Ships were built at Inverness and Ayr in the thirteenth century and may have been built at Perth, as the components of nine separate boats have been found. Most of these craft appear to have been clinker-built boats, serving as river craft and ferries, but one artefact may have come from a more substantial sea-going sailing vessel. Boat timbers, possibly from foreign ships, were often re-used for structural purposes in burgh buildings.[111]

Shipbuilders were not the only workers in wood. Turners and woodcarvers made many of the implements in daily use in burgh households, as well as pins for tailors, shovels for construction work and gardening, and even pattens to keep people's feet dry. Carpenters found work building the better-quality homes of the burgh, and making furnishings for the burgh church and tolbooth.[112]

Underwood was often used for basket-making. The surname Leiper, meaning 'basket-maker', occurs in fourteenth-century Edinburgh and Aberdeen, while remains of baskets were found in Perth. There was a great demand as baskets were used throughout Europe for storing and carrying goods. Large, finely made baskets for bread were among the most expensive, while coarser-woven meat baskets were cheaper.[113]

For the more substantial buildings of the burgh, such as the parish church and perhaps the houses of the wealthier burgess families, the services of stone masons would be required. A late fourteenth- or early fifteenth-century effigy of a mason was found in St Andrews, surrounded by representations of his mallet, hammer and mason's square. In 1387, an agreement was made by the burgh of Edinburgh with three masons who were to build five chapels on the south side of the parish church. William Plumber of Tweeddale, burgess of St Andrews, seems to have been able to work in both stone and lead, as he was hired by the abbot of Arbroath to repair the choir of the abbey with both these materials. In 1399 Henry Slater was probably slating some of the roofs of Aberdeen. Stone workers also made other useful objects such as sandstone sharpening wheels, spindle whorls and whetstones.[114]

Metalworkers were found in most burghs and because their products, or at least the waste from their work, are of durable material, evidence has been found at many urban sites, including towns such as Lanark, Elgin, Dumfries and Hawick, as well as the larger burghs. Scotland had a tradition of fine metalwork, as can be seen in the collection of fourteenth-century silver brooches in the

Royal Museum and the beautiful Bute Mazer with its skilfully carved lion and brightly enamelled crests.[115] Patronage by the court and nobles probably brought many talented metalworkers to the burghs.

Metalworking included the fashioning of objects in gold, silver, bronze (copper mixed with lead, tin or zinc),lead and iron. John the Goldsmith, burgess of Edinburgh, gilded plate and made ornaments for David II after his return from England. At Aberdeen, a small balance arm may represent the activity of a goldsmith or worker in another precious metal as it was found in association with a number of metal objects. There was a goldsmith in Aberdeen in 1364.[116] Several copper alloy sheets and objects such as buckles, pins, and brooches suggest the existence of metalworking in the burgh, as do copper alloy objects at Inverness. There was also evidence of bronze-working at Dundee and Lanark, while one site at Perth had finds indicating the casting of non-ferrous metals there in the fourteenth century. Probably most burgh craftsmen worked with the metal itself, the smelting of the ore being carried out outside the burgh, or even abroad.[117]

Considerable evidence of iron-working was found at Inverness, disproving Froissart's statement that all manufactured iron goods had to be imported from the continent. The iron itself was often imported, however, as there was little high-quality ore in Britain. There was Spanish iron at Ayr in the later thirteenth century. Sweden was another major supplier.[118] Iron was used for a wide range of objects, from agricultural implements and horseshoes to nails and military equipment. Iron barrel padlocks from Aberdeen and Perth were probably made locally, as the record of a Robert 'lokessmyth' in Scotland in 1214 suggests the existence of such a craft from at least the thirteenth century.[119]

Workers in lead were in demand to make window kames (the lead surrounding the panes) and roofs for ecclesiastical buildings and other large structures. Pewter was a widely-used metal, not only for plates and goblets but also for such objects as trade tokens, used instead of coins. A late thirteenth-century token at Perth shows the quality of workmanship which craftsmen could bring even to humbler materials.[120]

A more specialised type of metalworking, and one which was under strict royal control, was the minting of the Scottish coinage. The records of the Exchequer and the coins themselves, usually carrying mint names, provide evidence about the industry. Although in most finds, Scottish coins are greatly outnumbered by foreign, especially English, coins, there was a regular production of Scottish coinage.In 1250-1, to issue a new coinage, Alexander III put into operation mints in sixteen burghs.[121] During the fourteenth century mints were to be found at various times in Edinburgh, Aberdeen, Perth, Dundee, Dumbarton, and possibly Glasgow. Adam Tore, burgess of Edinburgh, was made master of the mint in Edinburgh in 1357, his duties probably including the buying of bullion and the issuing of new coins. The design of the coinage seems to have been entrusted largely to foreign craftsmen, perhaps because they had experience with the production of the English mints which served as a model for the Scottish coinage. Local craftsmen did have some part to play in the workings of the mint, however, as John the Goldsmith was paid for work in connection with the Edinburgh mint in 1364.[122] The operation of the mints was very strictly controlled; when a false coiner was discovered in Edinburgh in 1398, he was boiled to death.[123]

One other industry produced a great number of the objects used in everyday life. Pottery survives in large quantities at most sites, and can suggest patterns of development and change, as well as allowing comparison between various burghs. A native pottery industry existed from at least the early thirteenth century, apparently much influenced by wares from Carlisle in the west and by Yorkshire pottery, especially Scarborough ware, in the east. White Gritty ware, produced at such kilns as Coulston near Haddington and possibly Balchrystie in Fife, was a common ware in the east, and was also found in northeast England and at least some parts of west Scotland. English and Continental wares were also very popular.[124]

In the late thirteenth/early fourteenth century a change took place as local pottery became increasingly predominant. The development of this industry may have been partly in response to the demand created by the sale of such imports as Scarborough ware, although it did not necessarily involve slavish copying. Another factor may have been the disruption to English imports caused by the Wars of Independence, which would also disrupt the distribution of White Gritty ware as many of the kilns were in areas subject to frequent English occupation.[125] If this was the case with pottery, could it be true of other industry as well? A recent study of Scottish trade has suggested that the wars with England caused a decline in native industry,[126] but the archaeological record may suggest otherwise. If English blockades made it more difficult to import goods, there was an incentive for native craftsmen to fill the gap in the market. The high quality of many goods found at fourteenth and early fifteenth-century sites shows that Scottish craftsmen did not lack in skill.

Further excavation may show similar patterns to pottery for other crafts, although their survival rate is rarely comparable.

Local pottery became increasingly popular during the fourteenth century. Elgin, Inverness, Aberdeen, Perth and Linlithgow all produced their own wares. As yet, no urban kiln site has been definitely identified. Usually potteries were located on the outskirts of the town, near sources of water and clay, and with plenty of room for kilns and storage. Fire risks also dictated their location at a distance from the burgh. The potters themselves might live in the burgh, away from their workplace. In Aberdeen there were probably potteries at Clayhills, south west of the town. Clay may also have been quarried from a site near the centre of the burgh and transported to the potters' kilns.[127]

White Gritty ware continued to be made until at least the fifteenth century, and was marketed along with local ware, perhaps for different purposes or customers. Local potters sometimes imitated it and foreign wares in colour and decorative motifs – some common Scottish forms such as three-handled jugs and two-handled cooking pots were probably originally developed in response to foreign influences.[128]

The pottery industry illustrates another feature of burgh industry. Although on one hand the manufacturing process could be broken up into a number of specialised tasks each carried out by different people, at the same time individuals might carry on more than one craft. Potters were probably located near tilers producing roof and floor-tiles, and perhaps iron-workers, and it has been suggested that the same people might carry out these different activities.[129] The replacement of wooden roof shingles by cheaper pottery tiles, which seems to have happened at a site in Perth, may indicate the growth of the pottery industry after the mid-thirteenth century. Itinerant tilers were known to have set up temporary kilns near religious sites.[130] If the work was intermittent, it may have been an excellent part-time occupation for potters as well.

There is some evidence from the objects of how people clothed and fed themselves and even how they entertained themselves. Most clothing was of wool, made into gowns, tunics, shawls, plaids and hose. When they reached the end of their life as clothes, they were used as rags. Waterproof clothing was made of hides and skins. Dress fastenings also give some idea of garments. Brooches, pins, buttons, toggles and buckles were often both useful and ornamental, for some are highly decorated.[131]

Those who could afford it were as fond of fashionable clothes as people today. Living in centres of trade, burgesses had access to imports of fine cloth and furs (which might also be brought from other parts of Scotland). Silk, net, and tablet-woven braid found in Perth and Aberdeen show that there was a demand for high-quality textiles to adorn clothes and hair. Some people dressed in striped cloth, a fashionable import from the cloth towns of Flanders. By the fifteenth century, the clothes of some burgesses and their wives had become so luxurious that sumptuary legislation was passed by Parliament, restricting the wearing of certain furs and fabrics to those of the highest social status.[132] It is doubtful if the legislation had much effect.

Most people wore boots and shoes of leather, usually made from local hides, although richer individuals might be able to afford soft cordovan leather from Spain. Shoes are among the most common finds in excavations. Most were of the common medieval turnshoe construction, in which the flesh side was outwards when the shoe was made and then turned inside out so that the grain was on the outside and the sole/upper seam inside. Fashionable pointed shoes were popular in fourteenth-century Perth. For wet weather or work in marshy fields, pattens were sometimes worn. In 1399 a woman in Aberdeen suffered the theft of one pair of 'galochis' or shoes with wooden soles, while in St Andrews the presence of Arnold Patynmaker in 1404 suggests that pattens could be obtained locally.[133]

The quantity of hides available for local leatherworkers and the evidence of cattle in the backlands of the burgage plots suggest that townspeople may have eaten more meat than country people, although this probably varied according to wealth, the urban poor differing little from their country fellows in diet. Aenius Sylvius in the fifteenth century commented on how much meat and fish was eaten by the common people – it seems likely that it was townspeople with whom he came in most common contact. There may also have been variations between the burghs. More meat may have been eaten at Perth than Aberdeen and Elgin as a result of the importance of its hide export trade. In Aberdeen younger animals were eaten at one site, suggesting a higher standard of living. There were also changes over time, with pig becoming a more common source of meat at another Aberdeen site in the fourteenth century. Venison was available in some burghs, although this was an uncommon dish, restricted mainly to the nobility. A cheaper source of meat was goat which could be raised quickly, was easy to tend, and could be nourished on rough pasture[134] – an ideal animal for town-dwellers.

While meat was quite common in urban diets the real staples were bread and ale, their importance being reflected in the concerns of the burgh government to ensure their availability at a reasonable price and quality. Supplementing this diet were dairy products such as cheese, butter and eggs. Vegetables, including kale, beans and mushrooms were grown in the gardens in the backlands while wild fruit and nuts could be gathered from the countryside surrounding the burgh. Imported spices could be bought at the burgh market to help flavour meat, while occasionally wine and exotic fruits might also grace the table.[135]

On the whole, the Scottish diet was quite healthy by medieval standards but this did not necessarily prevent townspeople from becoming ill. Evidence from cess pits and from skeletal remains, including those from a number of Carmelite friaries which have been excavated in several towns, reveals some of the aches and pains from which medieval people suffered.[136] Children were especially susceptible to disease and make up a large proportion of the burials. Those who survived childhood had often faced at least one illness serious enough to halt their growth for a period. Partly as a result of this, medieval townspeople were on the whole somewhat shorter than today. In Aberdeen the men averaged 5'5", (1.7 m) the women 5'2" (1.6 m).

Skeletal evidence reveals that townsfolk suffered from tuberculosis, leukaemia, and cancer, while records tell of plague and other epidemics which periodically swept the towns. Less fatal diseases such as arthritis inflicted many while others had to cope with severe back pain. Gum disease and abscesses were common; dental care was limited to the removal of teeth. Shoes show traces of foot deformities, corns and bunions.

Dirty water, lack of proper heating, and the constant risk of potentially fatal infection all contributed to disease. Many people also suffered from parasites which lowered their resistance to illness.[137] But attempts were also made to fight back. After the experience of the Black Death in 1349, in time of plague efforts were made to exclude strangers from the town to prevent the disease coming within the burgh bounds. Strict rules were enforced against anyone unfortunate enough to contract leprosy which was regarded as infectious. Leper hospitals were situated away from the town and lepers were excluded from the community, except for certain hours when they were allowed to beg at the entrances to the burgh.[138] For more minor illnesses there were herbal remedies available, often from the herb gardens of the religious houses. Purgatives were used to alleviate some problems, while seeds of opium poppy imply that sedatives might be available to alleviate the most excruciating pain.[139] With the help of these and traditional remedies, medieval townspeople managed to survive and even to enjoy life.

One of the advantages of town life was that it generally offered more varied opportunities for leisure and recreation than the countryside. Both individually and together, townspeople could enjoy relaxation from their daily work. Dice have been found in several excavations. They may have been used alone or with board games with playing pieces of bone, wood, pebbles or other common objects. Although no gaming boards have yet been found at urban sites, two thirteenth-century merelles boards were carved on the stones of Dryburgh and Arbroath Abbeys, probably during construction work. The desire to win was as strong as it has always been – one of the dice was loaded.[140]

Another common pastime was drinking in the taverns of the town. Indeed, sometimes measures had to be taken to control drunkenness. Healthier activities included sport, especially ball games such as football, although the crown tried to ban it in the fifteenth century in order to encourage archery practice instead. In the winter if the river or loch froze, townsfolk could go skating on smooth skates of bone, propelling themselves along with a pole.[141]

Towns also provided many occasions for public celebrations and entertainment. A visit by the royal court provided the excuse for pageants, music and speeches of welcome, and perhaps a tournament to watch. A somewhat different spectacle was staged at Perth in 1396, when Robert III ordered two troublesome clans to settle their differences by fighting it out in his presence just outside the town. On a more peaceful note there were religious festivals with pageants and processions in which the whole town became involved. Important events were also marked with communal celebrations. When St Andrews received the papal bull establishing its university, the citizens of the town rejoiced in the streets.[142] Townlife was not always easy but on occasions such as this hardships could be forgotten as people took pride in being part of a community.

2 The Governance of the Burgh

One characteristic which distinguished late medieval European towns from the surrounding countryside was separate legal jurisdiction and the accompanying apparatus of government and administration. Whether holding their lands from the crown, the church, or a lay lord, the townspeople of Scotland enjoyed a measure of self-government, centred on the burgh court. Only a few burgh court records survive from before the mid-fifteenth century but combining this material with the information contained in the *Burgh Laws*, a collection of 'laws' dating from the twelfth to the fourteenth centuries,[1] reveals something about the structure of local administration and the duties of the people involved.

Like most European towns in their early days, the Scottish burghs had little independence at first. In the twelfth century they were under the control of the burgh lord's officers. While the burgh was a new institution, established to foster trade, some measure of supervision over its development was essential, as it was unlikely that newly-arrived settlers would set up a local administration immediately, unless they were sent specifically for that purpose. Mainard the Fleming, burgess of Berwick, was sent by the king to help the bishop of St Andrews establish his burgh c.1150,[2] but this was not usual practice for royal burghs. The sheriff, living in the royal castle beside which most early burghs were established, was a natural choice for supervisor.[3] Where a burgh was created on the site of an already-existing settlement, the original inhabitants were accustomed to control of their affairs by the sheriff or other officials.

For the burgh overlord, one of the most important aspects of his new trading centre was financial. Not only did the burghs provide protected places for commerce, benefiting the economy of the country as a whole, but – and this was probably of greater interest to their superiors – they also contributed directly to the revenue of their overlords through rents, market tolls and other such payments. To an abbot, a bishop or a noble, the grant of a burgh was far more valuable than mere grants of land, for burghal privilege included the right to defend any commercial privileges against encroachment by others.[4] The king's burghs, as centres of overseas trade, became the collection points for the customs dues imposed from the late thirteenth century. It is significant that it was the chamberlain, the chief financial officer of the crown, who conducted the yearly inquiry, or ayre, into the affairs of the burghs. Nobles might also appoint their chamberlain to supervise their burgh, as Robert Stewart did for Irvine before he became king in 1371.[5] Other officials appointed by the king to work in the burgh had duties which were mainly concerned with the financial administration of the towns.

By the late Middle Ages the local government of many burghs had developed into a fairly complex administrative structure, as trade prospered and the population grew. New burgh offices developed as specific responsibilities were delegated to different individuals. This process was well underway by 1300; almost all the offices found in the fourteenth-century records are referred to in the *Leges Burgorum* (*Burgh Laws*) or the *Statuta Gilde*, (*Statutes of the Guild*) which were both in existence by the late thirteenth century. In those burghs such as Edinburgh and Aberdeen with a well-developed administration, the officers of the town included the alderman or provost, the bailies, the sergeands, the liners, the tasters of wine, the tasters of ale and the apprisers of flesh. The structure of municipal government could vary widely, individual burghs using or ignoring whichever customs they saw fit: 'If a system worked, however illogical or unlegalised, it stood.'[6] For example,at the other end of the scale from the larger burghs were those which may have accounted to the king through the sheriff, a method which implies a less developed local administration.[7] Surviving evidence reveals something both of the more complex administration and of the variations between burghs.

The sheriff or other presiding officer was originally assisted by officials known as *prepositi* or *ballivi*, bailies, who helped collect the burgh revenues. By the late twelfth century,if not earlier, it became the practice in at least some burghs to choose these officials from among the burgesses. There were burgess *prepositi* in Perth before 1162 and in Inverkeithing by 1170.[8] From here it was only a short step to having the burgesses themselves choose the officials. As long as the revenues were rendered regularly it was unlikely that the king or burgh superior would have much objection. Moreover, the *prepositi* and bailies were still the lord's officers and as such were ultimately responsible to him rather than to the burgh. This was demonstrated at the chamberlain ayres when the bailies answered to the crown for their administration, acted as executive officers for the chamberlain, and were held responsible for the issues of the ayre.[9]

During the fourteenth century the role of the *prepositi* changed.

Until 1359, they rendered the burgh fermes to the Exchequer, although bailies also performed the same functions for some burghs. After 1359, only bailies appeared at the Exchequer. In several burghs, the *prepositus*, the provost or alderman had become the head of the community and, as such, left the crown's financial concerns to the bailies. Dickinson points out that the time of the change was significant, as it occurred shortly after arrangements were made to pay David II's ransom and therefore at a time when the burgesses were taking on increased financial responsibility in the nation.[10] This required a more extensive administration on the part of the burgesses and led to a division of responsibilities between the *prepositus* and the bailies. It did not mean, however, that the provost was now independent of royal control. It remained common practice for the king's pre-cepts to be addressed to 'the provost [or alderman] and his bailies'.

In a few burghs such as Lanark and Linlithgow, the administration was entrusted solely to the bailies, but in most towns the chief magistrate was the alderman or provost, or, in the case of Berwick where the alderman was head of the guild, the mayor.[11] He was appointed with the bailies at the first head court after Michaelmas 'thruch the consaile of the gud men of the toune, the whilk aw to be lele and of gud fame'. This description suggests that the electorate was restricted to those who were burgesses of the town. Alderman and bailies then swore fealty to the king and to the burgesses, emphasising their responsibility to both crown and burgh community, promised to uphold the customs of the town, and swore that 'thai sal nocht halde lauch on any man or woman for wroth na for haterent na for drede or for lufe of ony man, bot thruch ordinans consaile and dome of gude men of the toune'.[12]

Although the alderman was the official head of the community, his official powers and responsibilities were rather limited. Two fourteenth-century tracts on burgh administration virtually ignore his existence. There is no oath for the alderman among the oaths to be sworn by various burgh officials, nor was he called to stand challenge at the chamberlain ayre, as other officials were. In many burghs he may have been more a figurehead than an officer with true executive powers. The men who became aldermen were often among the most prominent merchants in the kingdom, men such as John Mercer of Perth who was heavily involved in national affairs. Perhaps the position was regarded as one of honour and prestige rather than of onerous responsibility, although the lack of town records for the period makes it difficult to assess the extent to which

these men involved themselves in burgh affairs. In smaller communities with less developed administrations the alderman, if there was
one, probably had more duties to perform.

Early laws are mainly concerned with defining the limits of his
power, perhaps to prevent any one member of the community from
becoming too powerful. The alderman's consent was required if a
burgess wished to poind (that is, take a pledge for a debt) another
burgess, but a burgess could poind anyone dwelling outside the
burgh, or a tenant who owed rent, without the alderman's permission. If the alderman accused anyone he could not bring witnesses
to testify against the accused, presumably because he might use the
power of his position to convince people to be false witnesses. He
could not make bread or brew ale for sale while he was in office. Not
only were such activities seen as beneath the dignity of his office, but
– and perhaps of greater importance to his fellow burgesses – he
might also enjoy an unfair advantage over the competition. To
actually maintain the laws he was to choose twelve of the wisest men
of the community. In Berwick he was not even given this much
responsibility as the council was to be chosen by the community.[13]
This became general practice by the end of the fourteenth century.

Nevertheless, the prestige of the alderman's office was high, an
important consideration in a society very concerned with status.
Despite the apparently limited nature of his executive powers, the
alderman was no inconsiderable figure. The records show him
carrying out a variety of functions and the prestige of his office was
an important factor in several of these.

The alderman often witnessed grants and sales of land both within
and outwith the burgh. He was sometimes responsible for taking
intoll and outtoll pennies from those receiving and selling property.[14]
His presence at land grants was not a legal requirement, but it added
authority to the transaction. This is even more apparent in those
cases where the land concerned was outwith the burgh and the
parties were not burgesses, as the grant did not involve burgh
jurisdiction.[15] The prestige of the office extended beyond the boundaries of the burgh.

The alderman appears as a witness or a party in affairs concerning
the burgh as a whole, although it is difficult to tell how active a part
he took in negotiations. An indenture between Forfar and Montrose
in 1372, giving each other reciprocal trading rights, was witnessed by
the two aldermen but was made by 'the burgesses, guild brethren,
and inhabitants' of the two burghs. Sometimes the alderman was
actively involved. In 1330 the provost and bailies of Elgin, in the

name of the community, made an agreement with Pluscarden Abbey about payments due from the mills of Elgin. The alderman of Cupar led the guild brethren in a trading dispute with St Andrews in 1370, although it might have been better for the guild if he had not, as they lost the case.[16]

The burgh lord reinforced the prestige of the alderman by directing most of his charters and precepts to the alderman and bailies. Feu-ferme charters were often addressed to the alderman and community of the burgh. The alderman was obviously expected to play some part in burgh affairs; indeed, attendance at the burgh court was one of his responsibilities. He often witnessed the decisions of the burgh court,[17] but his actual role in the court proceedings is unclear, although on one occasion he acted as a procurator.[18] Practice varied between burghs. In Aberdeen the burgh courts were held by the bailies but a 1392 head court in Elgin was held by the provost, two bailies and the community.[19]

The alderman did have responsibility in connection with the religious concerns of the townspeople, being involved in several aspects of church administration, both in conjunction with other officials and as leader of the community. Some aldermen were instrumental in extending the burgh church, a focus of community life and spirit. In Aberdeen, William de Leith extended the church of St Nicholas to the altar of St Leonard in 1355, 'with the assistance of the community'. He contributed £40 of his own money to the work and collected the rest of the expenses from the burgh. In 1356 he extended the choir to the south by sixteen feet and there established the altar of Saints Laurence and Ninian with the money granted for this purpose by William de Meldrum in the 1340s. In Edinburgh the provost, with the community, made an indenture in 1387 with three masons for the construction of five chapels in the parish church of St Giles.[20]

The administration of lands and rents granted to the church was largely the responsibility of the alderman. Aberdeen had 'kirk masters' who dealt with the financial affairs of the church, but the alderman still played a role in the administration of church lands granted by the burgesses. William de Meldrum's grant gave the care of the revenues he had assigned to an altar in the parish church to the alderman, four bailies, and the conservators of the fabric of the church.[21] It was the alderman alone who put these moneys to use in 1356. In Edinburgh, the alderman Wiliam Gupild and the community decided in 1368 to have the grants made to St Giles recorded in a book, in order to safeguard the revenues owed to the altars of the church.

Any additions had to be licensed by the alderman and community.[22] Such grants by townspeople were common throughout medieval Europe. In Scotland the usual way of administering them was for the administrators of the grant to lease the land to an individual and his heirs, who then paid an annual sum to the altar or chaplain specified in the original charter. John de Allincrum, burgess of Edinburgh, granted the lands of Craigcrook to the chaplain of the altar of the Virgin Mary in St Giles. In 1376 the alderman, bailies and community leased the lands in perpetuity to the burgesses Patrick and Andrew Leiper who were to pay £6 6s 8d annually to the altar and chaplain. Most such grants gave the main responsibility to the alderman and community.[23]

When a grant was made to found an altar or chantry, the founder usually reserved the patronage of it for life. It was often specified that after the granter's death the patronage was to pass to the alderman and the community. John de Allincrum wished the alderman and community to choose a priest for the altar within two months of his death. In Roxburgh, a grant by Roger de Auldton provided that if Kelso Abbey was negligent in instituting a chaplain, the alderman and community were to take over the task.[24] He did not say what was to happen if the alderman was negligent in his duty – perhaps the idea never crossed his mind.

In considering the importance of the alderman's role individual personalities must also be taken into account. As with governments of any period, some officials were more conscientious than others. William de Leith took an active interest in promoting the welfare of the burgh church, a focus of community pride. Adam Forrester continued to display an interest in the affairs of Edinburgh, even when he was not in office.[25] As the explicitly stated powers of the office were few, it was up to the individual to make as much or as little of it as he chose.

In the late fourteenth century a royal grant to Perth resulted in the expansion of the role of the chief magistrate of that burgh. In 1394 Robert III granted to the provost, burgesses and community the sheriffship of the burgh. This extended the jurisdiction of the burgh to include major criminal cases, in addition to petty crimes and offences against the burgh laws. The grant was put into effect by conferring the office of sheriff on the provost, so that a number of grants made in the burgh in the years after 1394 were witnessed by an individual who was styled 'provost and sheriff'. Similar grants were made to other burghs in the fifteenth century.[26]

Second in status to the alderman stood the bailies. They, far more than the alderman, were the officers of the king, responsible to him for rendering the rents and revenues which pertained to the crown, and thus they had close contacts with the central government. Royal precepts ordered them to make various payments from the burgh revenues, and dealt with other affairs as well. In 1363 David II ordered the bailies of Peebles to assign a space in the common of the burgh to John of Peebles, master of the hospital there, on which he might build a chapel. The chamberlain was to enquire whether the bailies 'execut nocht lauchfully the commandment of the king or the chaumerlane to thaim direkit'. Another article also stressed the responsibility of the bailies to the crown: 'wha sa chalangis ony bailye of the burgh of ony thing as tuichand his office, he au nocht to ansuere bot befor the chalmerlane.'[27] Complaints against the bailies went to one of the king's highest officers.

According to the *Statuta Gilde*, four bailies were to be chosen by the community at the same time as the mayor and a council of twenty-four.[28] In fact, the number of bailies varied between towns – in Aberdeen there were four, but in Edinburgh there were only three. The size or importance of a burgh was not the only factor determining the organisation and size of its administration.[29]

According to the *Leges Burgorum* the bailies were to swear the same oath as the alderman, although by the fourteenth century this oath was ascribed to the bailies only. To be a bailie an individual had to be a burgess with habitable land in the burgh, which could be distrained for abuse or non-fulfilment of duties.[30]

The administration of justice was one of the primary concerns of the bailies. In Aberdeen, courts of the bailies were held very frequently and dealt with all types of business. The bailies presided over the head courts, the fortnightly *curiae legales*, and the ordinary courts which sat between them. According to a fourteenth-century 'law', all the bailies were required to be present at the courts. A record was kept of all courts and assizes held by the bailies and a separate roll was made of pleas pertaining to the king which occurred between ayres. Officially, the courts could be held every day except holy days, although they were often held then as well. The bailies could also hold special courts for merchants, as cases between merchants and burgesses were to be decided by the third tide.[31]

The administration of lands was another responsibility accruing to the bailie's office. They often acted as witnesses to land grants. As officers of the burgh lord the bailies gave sasine, legal title, of burgh lands to individuals, thus putting land grants into effect and giving a person the necessary qualification for burgess status. Resignation of land and the offering of an inherited property to the nearest heirs in cases of necessity took place before the bailies. Lands belonging to the community were largely under the bailies' control. They were usually involved in actions in which the community set land at ferme to an individual, and they also received the rents on such lands. They had the power to distrain lands administered by the community in order to ensure the payment of rents. As officers of the king, they administered those burgh lands which escheated to the crown through forfeiture, lack of heirs or bastardy. In the 1380s the bailies of Perth sold the land of a burgess who owed export customs to the king. In 1398 an Aberdeen bailie gave sasine to the Blackfriars of the lands of the late William de Dunbar, whose property had returned to the king because of William's bastardy.[32] They were also responsible for maintaining the boundaries of the burgh. In Banff in 1401 they complained to the king about the incursions of a neighbouring lord on the community's lands and fishings.[33]

The bailies' interests included matters connected with burgh trade. In Aberdeen the prices of bread and ale were usually proclaimed at a burgh court, once a month. The bailies also collected the market tolls charged on goods, and for setting up stalls, the toll for a covered booth being twice as much as for an uncovered one. Sometimes the bailies showed excessive zeal in their collecting duties; in 1347 a Dundee bailie wrongfully demanded 1d stallage toll from a servant of Arbroath Abbey, despite the fact that the abbey had been exempted by the crown from all market tolls.[34] The Abbey was quick to point out the mistake. The bailies were also ultimately responsible for the quality of the staples of bread, ale and meat sold at the market, as it was their duty to ensure that the burgh tasters examined these goods at least every fifteen days.[35]

Sometimes the bailies acted as representatives of community interests, as when the bailies of Banff complained about the incursions on the burgh's fishings. In 1380 an agreement was made with Pluscarden Abbey by the bailies of Elgin 'in the name of the community'.[36] A case in Ayr suggests that the bailies' financial liability for the debts of those whom they represented was limited. In 1386 the papal legate asked that the bailies and all burgesses involved in a dispute with the Friars Preachers of Ayr over a £20 pension claimed by the Friars compear before him by 26 July to hear the case decided. Judgment was given in favour of the Friars and the provost and bailies were ordered to pay the pension. It was the goods of the burgesses, however, which were to be distrained if the officials did not pay the required sum,[37] suggesting that the provost and bailies were not expected to make up any shortfall themselves.

What happened to the normal jurisdiction of the burgh officers during the time of the burgh's annual fair? In the *Leges Burgurum* there is a reference to the *ballivos nundinarum*, the bailies of the fairs, but whether these were the same men who filled the office of bailie during the rest of the year is not clear. The ordinary laws and courts of the burgh were suspended during the time of the fair, in order to expedite justice and so adapt it to the needs of a largely transient population. Possibly the bailies supervised the Pie-poudre (literally, 'dusty feet') courts which dispensed justice at the fair.[38] Unfortunately, no early evidence survives to show fair-time laws in operation.

Next in status in the urban administrative hierarchy came the sergeands. On taking office they swore loyalty to the king, the burgh magistrates and the men of the town, and promised to distrain and present distraints as required by law, and to perform all other duties pertaining to the office.[39] A sergeand's duties related mainly to the execution of justice by the burgh court. The Aberdeen court rolls of 1317 and 1398 show him at work. If a townsperson wished to bring a charge concerning property against another, he presented a brieve of right, acquired from the king, to the bailies. The bailies passed this on to the sergeand, who then went to the accused's house and, before witnesses, summoned him to the next court. The defender gave a pledge to compear, and if he failed to do so, the sergeand took a distraint of 8s. The same procedure could be carried out four times, but if the defendant failed to compear a fourth time, the case was heard in his absence and he also lost a total of 32s in fines.[40]

A person who could find no pledge for his compearance was kept in his house for fifteen days by his fellows. If after this time he was still unable to find a pledge and the burgh had no prison, he was taken to the house of the sergeand who was supposed to bind him with 'fastening good and stalwart'. The burgh prison tended to be used as a place of confinement for those awaiting trial, rather than as a form of punishment for the guilty. Often a burgess was ordered to ward himself and did so voluntarily. The system did not always work so smoothly, however. In 1398 Maurice Swerdsleper was ordered to enter himself into prison, but six days later he was amerced for attacking one of the sergeands.[41]

The sergeand was also involved in the settling of debts. Both sergeands and bailies went to the house of a debtor to carry off sufficient poind for his debts and to give it to the creditor. The creditor and the sergeands then offered the goods for sale at three market days, and sold them to the highest bidder on the fourth. In some burghs the sergeand may have been involved in other financial affairs as well. In 1369 a man appeared on behalf of the sergeand as a witness to the payment of tithes by the bailies of Elgin to the bishop of Moray.[42]

The sergeands were responsible for aiding the examination of bread and ale, helping to choose which pot of ale should be sampled by the taster of ale. Along with apprisers of flesh and tasters of wine, tasters of ale were chosen annually, swore to carry out their duties faithfully, and were examined at the chamberlain ayre. The apprisers of flesh were expected to be always ready to apprise flesh and to be present on each market day to watch over the quality and price of the meat sold. Similarly the tasters of ale were to be ready to do their duty whenever required – perhaps an attraction of the office to some. Sometimes the problem of collusion between the ale-taster and the brewer arose, resulting in a stipulation that tasters were to drink the ale outside and not inside the house of the brewer.[43]

The burgh administration alloted a significant role to 'liners'. With burgess-ship dependent on the possession of a burgage rood, property boundaries were very important. The survival of many property lines through to the present day suggests how carefully they were safeguarded. The *Leges Burgorum* state that at least four liners were to be chosen to line the land according to the traditional boundaries. Another chapter gives the responsibility to the bailies and 'loyal men of the town', perhaps liners chosen for the occasion, while the formula for a royal brieve orders the provost and bailies to have 'the best and most trustworthy burgesses' line a particular land. It seems likely that the liners were chosen on an *ad hoc* basis rather than yearly.[44] Both liners and bailies were responsible if a complaint was made. If the boundary marks were laid and used for a year and a day, the land did not need to be lined again. If a mark was moved, the bailie was responsible for seeing that justice was done.[45] The existence of the liners also suggests that responsibility for town planning as the burgh expanded lay with the burgesses. Possibly the king or burgh superior gave permission for the burgh to expand its boundaries, and the actual lay-out of the new area was determined by the burgess administrators.[46]

Some burghs also had officials responsible for specific revenues. From at least 1394 Aberdeen had *depositores* or treasurers, responsible for the 'common good', the money pertaining to the community. These revenues came from burgess and guild admiss-ions, petty tolls and customs from the market, and court amercements which belonged to the burgh after the annual ferme was paid to the king. There is no reference to such officers before the fourteenth century, so the office may have developed after the burghs began to receive feu-ferme charters, which had the effect of increasing their responsibility for their own financial affairs. Moneys owed to the church were the responsibility of the *magistri ecclesie*, the masters of the kirk. Four of these were appointed in Aberdeen in 1399.[47]

As elsewhere in Europe, written records became increasingly important in government administration from the thirteenth century onwards. In the Scottish burghs this led to the development of the office of clerk of the community. In Inverness and Lanark, the clerk of the community appears as witness to charters, while in 1368, the common clerk of Edinburgh, John Rollo, was ordered by the alderman and bailies to enter all the grants of lands to St Giles in a register. Only the clerk of the community was to make any new entries. A land grant in Perth was witnessed by the notary Nicholas de Mar, who was also the clerk of the community. It seems likely that in burghs without an official town clerk, local notaries might take on his duties on occasion.[48]

The charters written up by the town clerk had to be sealed, and in Ayr this resulted in yet another office. On 16 May 1348, a grant of lands both within and outwith the burgh by John Kilmarnock to the Blackfriars was witnessed by the alderman, two bailies and William Halfemarck, 'custodian of the seal of the community'.[49] The existence of such an office exemplifies the development of more complex government as responsibility for the different parts of the administration was delegated.

Effective government usually requires an advisory body. Early records refer to a group of burgesses who probably made up a form of town council. It is possible that at first groups were called on to witness certain transactions or advise on specific cases, the size and membership of the group varying with the occasion. For example, the burgh laws stated that for a man to recover land he had given to his heir he had to prove his need by oath of twelve neighbours, four from each side of his home and four from opposite. The giving of sasine was supposed to be done in the presence of 'twelve burgesses and neighbours of the burgh specially called' as a late-thirteenth century charter to Paisley Abbey expressed it.[50]

The need for a more permanent council developed as the burgh grew larger and the administration more complex. The size of councils varied. The *Statuta Gilde* specified twenty-four members for Berwick, while the *Leges Burgorum* were content with twelve.

Berwick's council, as befitted the leading town of Scotland in the thirteenth century, was probably unusually large.[51] A 1469 statute stated that the new council of each burgh throughout Scotland was to be chosen 'in sic noumyr as acordis to the toune'. The variations in size could take place even within one burgh: in 1399 twenty men were on the common council of Aberdeen, while in 1400 there were twenty-one.[52]

Councils usually appear in the records in conjunction with the alderman. In Dundee the founder of an altar entrusted its patronage to his heirs, or failing them, to 'the alderman of the burgh and twelve honest men of his council annually elected'. In Aberdeen in 1399 the alderman and common council held a *prima* or court. In late fourteenth-century Perth the burgh seal was in the custody of the provost and council.[53] The function of the council seems to have advisory and legislative. According to the *Leges Burgorum*, it was 'to treat concerning the common business' of the burgh and to give ordinance and counsel to the burgh officers.[54] In some burghs there is no evidence of a council until the fifteenth or sixteenth centuries, so the community as a whole may have sometimes acted in an advisory or decision-making capacity. In 1360, for example, the burgesses and community of Inverness all met in the churchyard to resign land to the king.[55]

In theory, the burgh administration described above represented the community. The physical symbol of this connection was the burgh seal, usually called 'the common seal' or 'the seal of the community'. It first appears in the records in the early thirteenth century; by the fourteenth century its use was well-established. By 1400 at least thirty-two burghs had their own seals, and it seems likely that wherever a burgh had local government officials, a burgh seal existed, although strictly speaking it could operate without a seal.[56]

The seal was used in a variety of ways. Almost any transaction involving the 'community' carried the common seal, often accompanied by the seals of the burgh officials. Individual burgesses, when granting land both within and outwith the burgh, often requested that the burgh seal be affixed to their charters, especially if they had no seal of their own or if their seal was not well-known. In 1286 a burgess of Glasgow, selling his land to Paisley Abbey, requested that the common seal of Glasgow be attached to the charter for this reason.[57] Indeed the attestation of such grants was one of the most common uses of the seal, as the burgh administration had not yet distanced itself from the individual concerns of those it governed.

Occasionally the burgh seal is found on charters which have no apparent connection with the burgh. The seal of the burgh of Ayr was attached to a sale by Marjory de Montgomery to John Kennedy of lands in the sheriffdom of Ayr. The same seal is found on a 1379 resignation of lands to John de Caldecotys by his daughter Elena, which was witnessed by the alderman of Ayr.[58] It seems likely that the seal had the same function as the presence of the alderman, giving added authority to the charter. The office of custodian of the seal, which existed in Ayr by 1348, did not confine the use of the seal to actions involving the burgh.

Indentures between the burgh and neighbouring landowners were made under the common seal. A 1375 indenture between Montrose and Sir David Fleming about the boundary between the burgh territory and the lands of Hedderwick bore the seal of the community on Sir David's half. A contract made with the burgh superior was sealed with the common seal, as in the 1394 harbour agreement made between the abbot and the burgesses of Arbroath. Contracts between burghs were authorised by the use of each other's seals, as in the 1372 grant of reciprocal trading rights between Forfar and Montrose.[59]

Within the burgh, the seal was used on agreements concerning municipal affairs of the town, such as a 1344 indenture between the burgh of Perth and William de Spens for maintenance of the bridge over the Tay, and the 1387 agreement between Edinburgh and the masons who were to extend St Giles. It also appears in connection with the appointment of various officials. The statutes appointing two treasurers in Aberdeen in 1394 were sealed with the common seal. The commissioners of Ayr chosen to represent the burgh in its dispute with the Friars were 'appointed under the common seal', and the bailies of Dundee were constituted burgh representatives in a 1347 dispute with Arbroath by letters patent of the community of the burgh under the common seal.[60] The seal was also used when the burgesses were involved in affairs of national importance. The seals of all the burghs which sent burgesses to discuss the ransom of David II were affixed to the document they agreed to and the Franco-Scottish treaty of 1296 bore the seals of six burghs.[61]

As administration became more complex, the need for written records increased. Although the population of medieval Scotland was largely illiterate, the burghs with their religious communities and merchants had a high proportion of literate inhabitants. As in other European towns, documents played an increasingly important role in the government of the burgh, at first supplementing the oral and symbolic proceedings and later largely replacing them. For example, the method prescribed for an inhabitant to demonstrate possession of property to the court was to bring earth and stone from the land, but in the later Middle Ages many began to bring charters as well as, or even instead of, these symbols. The fifteenth-century increase in the number of notaries who recorded these deeds reflects the growing respect for the written word.[62] Symbolism was still an integral part of many transactions, but records were becoming increasingly important.[63]

The existence of the written compilations of burgh laws themselves indicates that the value of written records was recognised at an early date. It is probable that copies of the laws were to be found in many of the burghs and were consulted regularly; certainly the proceedings of the burgh courts indicate familiarity with the 'laws of the burghs'. Moreover, the burgh laws required a number of lists to be kept by the burgh officials, implying a fairly widespread use of written records. The bailies were to record all courts and assizes and to enroll all pleas pertaining to the king for the time of the ayre. There they presented the names of all officials, suitors, guild brethren, and owners of merchant booths 'in sufficient rolment distinctly writtyn'. A list of forestallers was also drawn up by the bailies and given to the sheriff.[64] Dickinson, in his description of the sheriff court, suggests that notes were taken during the court and a more detailed account written up later; the same was probably true of the burgh court.[65]

Robert I ordered all justiciars, sheriffs, aldermen and bailies to have parliamentary statutes openly read in courts and public places, and copies given to those in charge of the administration of the law. Edinburgh acknowledged the importance of written record in its decision to enter the grants to St Giles in a register to safeguard the church's property as 'from the ravages of war, the mortality of man, and the ignorance of youth, many bequests to St Giles and the altars endowed therein by the burgesses, have been abstracted or misapplied, to the diminution of divine worship.' The belief that the keeping of the register would prevent such losses implies a strong belief in the efficacy of written record. In 1416 the Ayr burgh governrnment tried to safeguard its property by having a number of notarial instruments drawn up recording fourteenth-century grants to the burgh.[66]

Individual burgesses were also aware of the authority of written record. A claimant in a court case about a disputed land grant in Edinburgh asked that the verdict be recorded in the register of the burgh, thus seeking to guarantee the preservation of his rights. A description of the case was entered in the *St Giles Register*, although it did not involve church possessions. Perhaps the burgh had as yet no property register of its own – most burghs did not until the appearance of notarial protocol books in the late fifteenth and sixteenth centuries – although it is also possible that such a request was an unusual one, with which the officals hastened to comply by entering the verdict in the record closest to hand. Record-keeping in the fifteenth century was a haphazard procedure in many burghs with entries from guild and burgh courts intermingled in no real order,[67] and there is no reason to suppose that the situation would have been much different in the earlier period.

In the end it is the written record which proves central to a thorough understanding of the municipal organisation of the burghs. From 1398 the first surviving continuous records appear in Aberdeen. From this time on, information about the workings of local administration becomes increasingly detailed. Some council records and guild books survive from the fifteenth century, in which we can see some of the day-to-day functioning of municipal government in burghs such as Perth, Edinburgh, Aberdeen and Dunfermline. The research which has recently started on these records may help throw some light on earlier town government as well.[68]

The privileges of the burghs were granted to them by the king but, as was common in communities throughout medieval Europe, it was the townspeople themselves who upheld them.[69] Through the burgh court, they safeguarded their rights and punished transgressors; for example, in 1323 the abbot of Kelso agreed that any new burgesses he made would be presented to the burgesses in their court to be deemed satisfactory.[70] But the burgh court did more than this, dealing with all aspects of town life, dispensing justice in disputes, electing officials to govern and declaring and approving laws and statutes. As it was the duty of all burgesses to compear at the three head courts each year, the burgh court represented the voice of the community.

The origins of the burgh court are unclear,[71] but it seems likely that a similar organisation existed from an early date in order to deal with disputes within the burgh and to assist officials in local administration. The seal of Berwick was appended to a plea made *in plena curia placitorum*, in the full court of pleas, in 1212, suggesting that some type of court existed in Berwick by this date. There are also references to the *tota curia burgensium*, the whole court of the burgesses, in St Andrews in the early thirteenth century, and a *curia burgensium* in Perth in 1245. Possibly the main purpose of these early courts was to witness important acts, as the public validation of private transactions was an important element in medieval European society. In England after 1066 many private charters refer to the witness of the courts.[72] In Scotland burgh courts became a recognised feature of the burgh, with the 'issues of the court' being included in burgh revenues in most feu-ferme charters.

The burgh court provided a valuable privilege to the towndweller as it allowed him to be tried by his peers, and under the burgh law with which he was familiar, although, as has recently been pointed out, in most points this did not differ so greatly from the law of the rest of the land.[73] The court had jurisdiction over all cases arising in the burgh except the four pleas of the crown: murder, rape, arson and robbery. These were heard by the justiciar with the burgesses as suitors. A burgess who was charged with wrongdoing outwith the burgh could be freed from the jurisdiction of a sheriff or baronial court by being 'repledged' to the burgh court. In 1330 the burgesses of Ayr were allowed by the crown to extend this privilege to their servants as well.[74]

The head courts of the burgh were held three times a year. At the first one, held on the Monday after Michaelmas (29 September), the burgh magistrates were chosen. The other head courts were normally held the Monday after Epiphany (6 January) and the Monday after Easter.[75] The burgesses were bound to attend these courts, thus performing the urban equivalent of the three suits of court demanded of feudal tenants outwith the burghs. Those who did not attend were fined, unless they had a lawful reason for their absence. Acts and statutes affecting the whole community were read out here, and approved by all the burgesses, although it is not clear to what extent they had power to amend or reject the acts.[76]

The head courts were important for land transactions. A townsperson wishing to recover a property for which rent was in arrears brought his case before the court by presenting earth and stone from the land before four head courts. The resignation of such lands could also take place in the head court. It was here that an impoverished burgess, wishing to sell his heritage land, had to offer it to his relatives on three separate occasions before alienating it to anyone else. The records of such transactions show that they were common to many burghs, as they state that the process was carried out *secundum leges burgorum*, according to the laws of the burghs.[77]

The head court also carried on the business of an ordinary court. In the Yule head court at Aberdeen in 1399, two men were amerced for disturbing the town and two other cases were continued until the following week. At the head court of 26 April 1400, a man was amerced for not prosecuting a case for which he had found a pledge, while another case was continued to the next court day because of the 'weakness of the court',[78] a phrase which suggests that the duty of the burgesses to attend the head courts was not always strictly observed.

The head courts were supplemented by fortnightly courts, known in Aberdeen as _curiae legales_, and the more frequent _curiae tentae per ballivos_, courts held by the bailies. The _curiae legales_ were held on Tuesdays in Glasgow, on Mondays in Aberdeen and at intervals of a fortnight or a multiple thereof. The _curia legalis_ was apparently more formal than the _curia tenta per ballivos_, the distinction perhaps lying in the type of business which the courts were allowed to transact. As Dickinson points out, all cases begun by the king's brieve or letters were heard at either head courts or _curiae legales_. It was also at the _curia legales_ that the assize, the legal price, of bread and ale was announced, usually at every second session. As well as these more specialised tasks, these courts carried out ordinary business. The _curiae tentae per ballivos_ were held frequently, on any day of the week, and sometimes for several consecutive days. Such extra courts were probably necessary because of 'the growth of the burgh, the complexity of its affairs, and therewith the increase in the work of the court'.[79]

The procedure of the burgh court in Aberdeen, a royal burgh, has been fully described by Dickinson so that only a summary need be given here. The court was formally opened in the name of the king, then the suitors brought their cases before it. Prosecuting a case was a serious business, and in an attempt to discourage frivolous litigation, the court demanded pledges from the plaintiff that he would continue a case once he had begun it. Both plaintiff and defendant were required to give pledges at every step of the case. Non-compearance at court was a serious problem and the use of pledges was a method of controlling it. Moreover, mercantile activity involved frequent use of pledges for future payment or delivery of goods, so that what may seem excessive to modern eyes would have been regarded as commonplace by medieval towndwellers.

Court cases usually dragged on over several weeks or even months, as each stage took place on a different day. After the plaintiff had informed the court of his complaint, the defendant was summoned by the sergeand. If he failed to appear after summons to four separate courts, the case was judged in his absence. If he did appear, the plaintiff then made his charge, the defendant refuted it if possible, and both gave pledges to continue the action. A day was then assigned for hearing the plaintiff's case. On that day he brought witnesses to court to support his charge, although whether they gave evidence or merely swore to the truth of the charge is not clear. If the defendant still maintained his innocence, he was then assigned a day to bring witnesses in his defence. The burgesses constituting the court were then supposed to reach a verdict, but often were unable or reluctant to do so. Cases were frequently continued from one court to the next almost interminably. Sometimes the court relieved itself of the responsibility of making a decision by submitting the case to 'compositors' or arbitrators to determine the question. The speed of this process was especially welcomed by merchants and strangers, who would then be delayed in the burgh for as short a time as possible.

Cases of theft and assault were usually dealt with by amercements, although abusing the burgh magistrates could lead to the use of the cuckstool as punishment. In Aberdeen it was situated beside a site known as the 'Pudlepace'. An ordinance of 1405 laid down that the perpetrator of such an offence was to kiss the cuckstool, but if he repeated the offence he was to be 'placed on the cuckstool and befouled with eggs, dung, mud and suchlike'. Pledges were often taken in an attempt to prevent assault, both with reference to particular individuals and as general pledges for future good conduct. Banishment could be the punishment for repeated offences. If a person was not a good member of the community, then, as one court said of an offender, 'scho was nocht worthy to remayn in the town'.[80] The importance placed on preserving the peace of the burgh was reflected in the severe penalties for breaking pledges of good conduct, penalties which even extended to life and limb.

Most of the work of the court was concerned with civil actions relating to property, either moveables or land. This predominance of land disputes is partly due to the nature of the surviving evidence, most of which is in the form of land charters or registers giving details of landed possessions, but it also reflects the importance of land-ownership to burghal society, both as a qualification for burgess-ship and increasingly as a source of income for the wealthier burgh land-owners.

Those not satisfied with the outcome of their case could appeal to the next chamberlain ayre held in the burgh. In one instance, an Aberdeen man finally lost patience with the slow, cumbersome burgh court procedure and brought his case before the chamberlain on the grounds that the court had deferred judgment through three successive sittings. The ayre also provided yet another way for the court to avoid giving judgment as it could defer difficult or important cases to the ayre.[81]

Did the feu-ferme charters make any difference to the role of the burgh court? It seems unlikely that the new privilege, which mainly affected the financial administration of the burgh, would greatly affect the court's day-to-day functioning. Towns were used to farming their revenues – the charters only made the arrangement more permanent. The main effect of the charters was to allow the building up of a 'common good' fund, the administration of which would perhaps be supervised by the burgh court. But the court's powers could be expanded in other ways. By making the burgh of Perth into a sheriffdom, Robert III increased the court's competence to deal with criminal matters. In 1384 Sir James Scrymgeour, the constable of Dundee, resigned various rights pertaining to his office, including 'correction of blood', and all pleas pertaining to the burgh's liberties, to the burgh court of Dundee. He also granted the bailies the right to sit in the constable's court if any townsperson was arrested by the constable or his deputy, to ensure that justice was done.[82]

Some burghs had other government institutions as well as the burgh court. The Aberdeen records refer to sittings of the *prima prepositi*, the *prima* of the provost. Who made up the membership of this body is not clear, although it probably included members of the town council and other prominent townspeople.[83] The *prima* dealt with extraordinary business, outside the usual transactions of the courts of the bailies. It was here that ordinances were made and measures taken for the protection of the burgh, actions which suggest the work of the town council. On 2 December 1401 measures were taken to stop the spread of pestilence from the southern parts of the kingdom, while on 1 October 1400, William Walker was charged with procuring lordship against his neighbours. At other *primae*, several ordinances for the good of the town were made with the assent of the major part of the community. The *prima* also punished the infraction of trade laws – among its actions was a prohibition on townsfolk from baking cakes for sale.[84]

Many burghs also had guilds – there were at least thirteen towns with them by 1400.[85] The function and composition of the guild have been the objects of much controversy among Scottish historians. Knowledge of the workings of the early guilds is hampered by the fact that no guild records, other than the Berwick statutes, survive from before the fifteenth century. Influenced by the idea of merchant-craftsman conflict which has permeated most writing about the later medieval town, urban historians have tended to assume that the roots for this conflict must lie in the early exclusiveness of the guild merchant. Recently, the picture of such conflict has been called into question,[86] and it follows that the idea of the exclusiveness of the early guild should also be questioned. Perhaps any exclusiveness was rather against non-burgesses than burgesses of certain occupational status.

The study of early guilds has also been influenced by the concept of uniformity of the burghs, leading historians to suggest that the situation described in the thirteenth-century *Statuta Gilde*, where the guild apparently dominated the burgh government, applied in other burghs as well. It is probably misleading to take Berwick, described by one enthusiastic chronicler as 'the Alexandria of the north', as typical of most Scottish burghs. Many burghs had guilds of their own by the time of the *Statuta Gilde* and there was no particular reason for them to imitate the organisation of the Berwick guild. Moreover, Berwick at this time was a town dominated by the manufacture of cloth. By the fourteenth century, the economic interests of the towns had changed to a concentration on the export of wool, and early statutes dealing with the cloth industry were often of little relevance.[87]

There is small evidence of a distinction between merchant and craft guilds until the fifteenth century, about a century later than in England and much later than on the continent. The distinction between craftsman and merchant was only just starting to be made in the fourteenth century; craftsmen who bought their own materials and sold their own products were as likely to see themselves as merchants as those who bought and sold the work of others. In smaller burghs, especially, the size of the population would have precluded the formation of several separate guilds. In larger burghs such as Aberdeen, the lack of craft guild bequests to altars in the burgh church before the fifteenth century suggests that the crafts did not formally organise themselves into guilds until then, despite the tradition of the Perth Glovers and Hammermen that their origins go back to the time of William I.[88]

When craft guilds began to form, however, they may have had some precedent. Charters granting guilds to Perth, Aberdeen and Stirling exclude waulkers and weavers from membership. These cloth workers may have been part of the Flemish population of the towns, and may have combined in their own groups as they did in other European countries, leading to their exclusion from the guild. By the fifteenth century, they were well-integrated with the rest of the community in many burghs. The guilds of Dunfermline and

Perth both included waulkers and weavers.[89]

Hints of the development of separate craft guilds begin towards the end of the fourteenth century. The chamberlain was to inquire during his ayre if there was any confederacy among the burgh inhabitants which might injure neighbours. Were these confederacies being made by those excluded from the guild, or by members of particular crafts within the guild who wished to break away? In either case it suggests anxiety about the forming of rival groups to the guild. In the Aberdeen bailie court of 29 October 1398, the weavers of the town were charged with making a conspiracy among themselves in prejudice of the community.[90] Although this was probably a combined effort to raise prices rather than an attempt to form a formal organisation, it was in such joint efforts that craft guilds could find their beginnings. They began to be incorporated in the later fifteenth century.

Until 1400, however, the *gilda mercatoria*, the mercantile guild, was the main burghal institution concerned with trade. One of its major concerns, as its name suggests, was the merchandising of goods by the burgh and its inhabitants. Because the burgh existed primarily for trade, such a function could lead to a certain degree of overlap between the activities of the guild and the burgh government, but there is little evidence to suggest that the guild actually took over the administration of the burgh.[91] Rather, the guild should be seen as part of the burgh government, concerned primarily with the regulation of trade. It need not even have constituted a formal part of the administration, as its representatives, the guild brethren, would probably hold a large number, if not all, of the burgh offices. The relationship between the guild and the burgh government was therefore a close one, but they seem to have remained as two separate bodies in most burghs.

The presence of guilds in most burghs involved in overseas trade suggests one of their characteristics, a monopoly over the trade in certain goods. In charters of the twelfth and thirteenth centuries when the production of cloth was seen as one of the most important burgh privileges, it was the cloth trade which was put under guild control. In Perth and Aberdeen only members of the merchant guild were allowed to make or have made fully-finished cloth in their respective sheriffdoms. As the export trade in wool, woolfells, and hides increased in importance in the thirteenth century, the members of the guild became more concerned with establishing a monopoly over the trade in these staple goods. For example in a 1370 dispute the guild brethren of Cupar complained that the men of St

Andrews were infringing the rights of the guild of Cupar by buying fleeces, skins, hides and other things which pertained to the guild and that the guild brethren of Cupar had the sole right to buy such articles. In fifteenth-century Dunfermline, the guild claimed a monopoly over the trade in staple goods, furs and skins and the right to control the related trades of dyeing and tanning.[92]

Sometimes the interests of guild brethren led to inter-burghal co-operation. On 4 April 1370, David II granted freedom of entry to the waters of the Tay and Northesk to the merchants of Brechin, notwithstanding grants to the burgesses of Dundee and Montrose, and forbade the burgesses and guild brethren of those two burghs to disturb the men of Brechin. This must have irritated the merchants of Forfar as well, as five years previously David had ordered the removal of Brechin's market privileges and the protection of the rights of the guild of Forfar. In 1372 the Montrose and Forfar guilds retaliated with an agreement which allowed reciprocal trading rights to the members of the guild of each burgh in all things pertaining to the guild, and explicitly excluded the men of Brechin from such privileges.[93] The fact that the agreement was between guilds shows their responsibility for maintaining the burgh's trading monopoly in certain goods, and shows the power of the guilds within their own sphere of influence as they were granting trading privileges to burgesses, an action normally reserved to the crown.

In Perth, the powers of the guild increased in the late fourteenth century. A royal charter in 1397 confirmed to the burgesses and guild brethren the licence to arrest forestallers within the sheriffdom of Perth, and emphasised that the grant pertained to both the burgesses and the guild brethren. Perhaps the forestalling of staple goods came under the jurisdiction of the guild, while other merchandise was the concern of the burgh government. In 1406 a charter refers to separate courts of the bailies and the guild, suggesting that there was some distinction in the jurisdiction of the two. The inclusion of the dean of guild among those magistrates who were allowed to make statutes for the governance of the burgh, and the fact that the statutes were to be made with the consent of the guild brethren, suggests that by the early fifteenth century the guild had come to play an integral part in the legislative powers of the Perth burgh government.[94] In practice, the statutes made by the guild were probably mainly concerned with trade matters, but it was a recognition of the guild's prominent position in Perth that its assent to all statutes was required.

On the whole there is little evidence for the primacy of the guild in most burgh governments before the fifteenth century, although the membership of many burgesses in both guild and burgh administration could result in the strong influence of guild interests on the policies of the burgh. The guild's main concerns, however, were with trading matters; it would be a mistake to argue that the use of the term alderman for the head of the burgh government necessarily implied the dominance of the guild, as in many burghs both *prepositus* and *aldirmannus* are used to refer to the head of the burgh government. From 1400, if not earlier, the dean of guild was head of the guild.[95]

The guild did, however, supplement the government of the burgh in several important ways. The recent publication of the guild of Dunfermline's records, which begin in 1433, underlines the importance of the social functions of the institution, among which was the connection of the guild to the church. Guild funds often went to support specific altars. In fifteenth-century Edinburgh and Perth the guilds, probably influenced by continental fashions, were patrons of the altar of the Holy Blood. On holy days guild brethren marched in religious processions carrying the banner of their altar aloft. In Dunfermline the guild was responsible for collecting 'light money' for the church candles. Guild funds might also be used to help pay for repairs to the burgh church.[96]

The brethren of the guild formed a community within a community, looking after its own. In the absence of extensive social legislation, the guild provided for its members by caring for the elderly, impoverished and infirm, and the widows and orphans of members. A guild brother had his spiritual needs seen to as well. When he died, it was the duty of all his fellows to attend his burial and to arrange masses to be said for his soul. Moreover, the guild contributed to the community at large, giving charity to the less fortunate of the townspeople and encouraging individual generosity by granting guild membership as a reward for deeds done for the benefit of the town.[97]

The guild also offered another attraction to its members – conviviality. The frequent imposition of a wine penalty rather than a fine suggests that not all guild meetings were given over entirely to serious discussions. Indeed the Dunfermline guild accounts of 1443 reveal that almost two-thirds of that year's expenses went to liquid refreshment of an alcoholic kind.[98] The feasts of the guild allowed the privileged members of the burgh to gather together in an atmoshere less formal than the burgh court, less holy than the burgh church and less commercial than the marketplace. For those who could afford to join, the guild complemented not only the government of the burgh, but burgh life itself.

3 Trade and Traders

At the heart of the medieval Scottish burgh stood the mercat cross, symbol of the king's peace which protected the trade of the town. The market-place was the centre of the commercial activity crucial to the burgh's existence. Indeed, a burgess's heir was considered to be of age when he could number silver or measure cloth with an ell-wand.[1] Nor was the market's importance confined to those living within the burgh. The market linked the burgh to the surrounding countryside, and gave many townsfolk a role in the international trade of the kingdom.

Because the surviving records are concerned mainly with royal revenues rather than with the details of burgh life, more evidence exists for the international trade which provided customs revenues for the king. By the time burgh accounts appear in the Exchequer records in the early fourteenth century, several of the burghs had leased their fermes from the chamberlain and recorded only the amount of the lease. Even those burghs which accounted for a different amount each year usually recorded only the total from the burgage rents, court fees, petty customs, and all other sources of revenue, so that the amount contributed by market tolls cannot be determined.[2] The lack of evidence, however, does not necessarily imply a lack of local trade. For the inland burghs especially, as for their English counterparts, 'what provided the basis of most towns' livelihood was not the cake of overseas commerce but the bread and butter of distribution and marketing for the surrounding region.'[3]

The charters granted to various burghs reveal something of the nature of this local trade. Most of the early charters are largely concerned with commercial matters, granting privileges to stimulate the growth of trade in the burgh. From the time of David I, it was royal policy to make the burghs the commercial centres of the country and this was done by restricting the establishment of markets to the burghs. The importance attached to the market by the burgesses was shown in the years 1303–07, when the royal burghs petitioned Edward I, who ruled much of the country at that time, not to allow markets to be held anywhere except in the burghs.[4] In England it was common to have markets outside the boroughs as well, and the burgesses were probably protesting against attempts to introduce the English practice into Scotland.

Several royal charters gave the burgh a monopoly on trade and cloth manufacture in a certain area, known as the burgh's 'liberty'. Unlike their counterparts in England and the Continent, the Scottish burghs continued to enjoy these monopolies throughout the later Middle Ages. The liberties could be very large, sometimes corresponding to the sheriffdom of which the burgh was the head.[5]Foreign merchants could only buy the produce of these areas from the burgesses in the appropriate burgh, and those with goods to sell who lived in the liberty had first to present them at the burgh market. In 1363 David II gave the burgesses of Inverkeithing the power to enforce their trading monopoly by granting them the right to arrest anyone trading in the burgh liberty to their prejudice, and in 1397 a similar right was confirmed to the burgesses of Perth by Robert III. The records of Aberdeen show the vigilance of the burgesses there in protecting their trading monopoly.[6] The system of burgh liberties was reinforced in 1364 by a charter of David II to the burgesses of Scotland, which confirmed their right to freely buy and sell in their own liberties, but stipulated that they must obtain licences to trade in the liberties of other burghs.[7] In some cases, such as that of Forfar and Montrose in 1372 this led to two burghs granting each other reciprocal trading rights, but occasionally disputes erupted as different burghs attempted to assert conflicting privileges over the same area.

The concentration of trade in the burghs had several advantages for the townspeople. It helped make trade more secure by forcing the sellers to bring their goods to what was usually the most important settlement in the area. It ensured the supply of food and fuel for the townspeople, at prices which were under the burgesses' control. The country folk coming to the burgh provided a market for urban manufactures and goods imported by the merchants. The petty customs charged on goods bought and sold and other market fees contributed to the burgh revenues which increasingly came under the control of the burgesses with the granting of feu-ferme charters. The provision in many charters that all those living and trading in the burgh should pay aids – special royal taxes – along with the burgesses meant that the financial burdens imposed on the burgesses were lessened.[8]

Within the burgh itself, the market was supervised by the burgesses, although in some towns a certain amount of control was also exercised by the burgh superior – for instance, the abbot of Kelso claimed the right to appoint stall-holders and grant licences for brewing.[9] In most burghs, however, the burgesses were in control, proclaiming the regulations, enforcing them and punishing those who infringed them. The picture of the local market presented in the burgh laws is largely reinforced by the late fourteenth-century records of Aberdeen and the fifteenth-century records of other burghs.

As the market was the primary source of many supplies for the burgh inhabitants, it was important that all goods be brought there and displayed openly so that all might have the chance to buy what they needed. Forestallers, who bought goods before they reached the market, and regraters, who purchased goods before the burgesses had been served solely in order to resell them, were punished as acting against the interests of the community. Such restrictions were irksome to many and the Aberdeen records are full of references to those guilty of these practices. Rural tanners were particularly prone to buying hides before they had been brought to the Aberdeen market. Fish was also often bought outside the burgh.[10]

Private sales were discouraged by regulations meant to ensure that all might have an equal opportunity to buy the goods brought for sale. All goods brought by ship, except salt and herring, were to be sold on land. In 1399 the master of a ship at Aberdeen was accused of selling apples and pears in his ship. Goods were to be displayed openly on market stalls or, if in shops, at the windows. These rules were broken frequently by Aberdeen residents who sold both flour and malt in their homes.[11] As many of those convicted did not enjoy burgess status, they were probably attempting to avoid the payment of market tolls and stallage fees from which the burgesses were exempt.

On market day, the street was lined with stalls and booths; strangers paid ¼d toll to the bailies for an uncovered booth and ½d for a covered booth. In Aberdeen the stallage fees went to pay the sergeands for their services in 1399.[12] There is no record of any burgh having more than one market-place within its bounds before 1400, although the development of streets in Aberdeen suggests that there may have been an early market in Broadgate as well as Castlegate. Multiple markets were common in many burghs from the fifteenth century, with Edinburgh having fifteen by 1477.[12a]

In keeping with the policy of promoting the interests of the community, the burgh magistrates controlled the price and quality of basic foodstuffs. In Aberdeen, from 1398 and probably much earlier, the price of a boll of corn and a boll of malt was announced periodically - usually every fortnight - in the *curia legalis*. In the late fourteenth century the price of corn ranged from 3s to 4s, that of malt from 2s 8d to 4s. Fleshers and bakers were both fined for selling their goods at other than the stipulated price. Ale-tasters checked the quality of the brewsters' ale, while bakers were to bake bread according to the dictates of the ruling burgesses. Strict control was also kept over weights and measures, a woman being fined in 1399 for selling flour in unsealed measures, and five men later the same year for selling wine in insufficient pints.[13]

Goods which were brought to the Aberdeen market from the hinterland included corn, barley, fish, cows, malt and flour, as well as the staple goods of wool, woolfells and hides. Some idea of the products sold in other burghs can be gained from the records of purchases for the royal household: among the commonest items were herrings and haddock from Ayr, eels from Forfar, herrings and Isle of May rabbits from Crail, and salmon from Perth. For David II's coronation the burgesses of Perth supplied swine, a boar and five dozen lampreys, while in 1342 large supplies of fish were sent from Crail to the king. In 1379 salmon were bought for Robert II at Inverness and Banff.[14]

Supplementing the weekly trade of the burghs were annual fairs, usually lasting one or two weeks and attracting traders from throughout Scotland and abroad. Unlike English fairs, Scottish fairs were largely confined to the burghs and steps were taken to suppress any competing ones. In 1352 fairs were prohibited anywhere within the bounds of Montrose and also at Coupar Angus or anywhere else prejudicial to Dundee, while in 1368 the holding of a fair at Newbattle was forbidden as being damaging to the burgesses of Edinburgh.[15] For inland and western burghs, the fairs probably represented the main occasion on which foreign traders would bring their wares to the local market. At these times the normal trading restrictions of the burgh were suspended and special courts were set up to dispense speedy justice. Local rural produce could be sold to anyone, the exclusive rights of the burgesses being relaxed. Burghs which had fairs by the fifteenth century included Dundee, Perth, Whithorn, Aberdeen, Edinburgh, Roxburgh, Haddington, Auchterarder, Dumbarton, Glasgow and Renfrew.[16]

Among the visitors to these fairs were inhabitants of other burghs. Aberdeen fair was very important to the people of the north-east burghs from at least the late thirteenth century. Many burgesses were exempted by charter from tolls throughout the kingdom – for example, the burgesses of Arbroath[17] – and were thus encouraged to travel freely either overland or along the coast in their ships. Professor G.W.S.Barrow has demonstrated the existence of a wide-ranging network of roads between burghs, along which traders could bring their wagons and packhorses, but also points out that these land routes were not necessarily easy ones and that sea-borne communication was common. Perhaps the small boats, *batella*, mentioned in the custumars' accounts, traded along the coast rather than overseas.[18] At the different burghs the traders would find both a market for their own goods and a further source of supply of products for the export trade.

Burghs may have been established to encourage inland trade, but their influence soon expanded beyond Scotland's borders, through the activities of the burgh merchants. Trade with England had probably always existed to a certain extent, but the development of the weaving towns of the Low Countries opened up a new market for wool which, along with woolfells and hides, became Scotland's major export. Scotland does not possess the detailed records which make possible a proper study of the full scope of her overseas trade, although fairly full accounts of the export of wool, woolfells and hides exist from the middle of the fourteenth century. Other sources such as diplomatic records, however, reveal something of the country's trading patterns.

The most important market for Scottish wool was Flanders. Flemish interest in Scotland is first recorded in the twelfth century, when contacts were established between Flanders and the Cistercian monastery of Melrose. The Cistercians were renowned in Europe for their interest in agriculture and sheep-raising and, not surprisingly, Melrose became one of Scotland's first large-scale wool-producers. As Flanders prospered through its manufacture of cloth and other products, the city of Bruges became a major entrepot for trade between Northern Europe and the Mediterranean and a favourite destination for Scottish merchants who had their own quarter there in the later thirteenth century. By this time, Scottish wool was a familiar enough product on the Continent to be differentiated according to port of origin. That from Perth was valued the most highly, followed by the wool of Aberdeen, Berwick and Montrose.[19]

What appears to have been a fairly flourishing international commerce was seriously hurt by the outbreak of war with England in 1296. Indeed, recent studies of Scotland's economy in the late Middle Ages have argued that the country's overseas trade never really recovered from this blow, and that, other than a brief flourishing in the 1370s, the picture for the fourteenth and fifteenth centuries is one of decline.[19a] Trading links were not cut off completely, although the type of trade underwent some interesting transformations. Ignoring both English complaints and the shifting alliances of their political leaders, Continental merchants gave aid to the Scots throughout the Wars of Independence, attacking English ships and running English blockades to bring supplies to the hard-pressed people. Not that this was completely altruistic. Large profits could be made by seizing English ships and then selling them and their contents, most likely at inflated prices, in Scotland. Any remaining goods could then be taken back to the merchants' own countries to be sold there. In 1313 some enterprising Flemings seized three ships laden by English merchants on their way to Brabant and took them to Aberdeen where they left the merchants in the custody of the Scots and then took the stolen goods to Flanders. German, Norwegian and Dutch traders were also active in this commerce.[20] Even Genoese merchants were accused by Edward II of supplying ships and arms to the Scots.[21] In 1317 the Dutch were able to make use of an Anglo-Dutch trade agreement to take their ships into English ports and load them with supplies to take to Scotland. German merchants did the same. They probably had the collusion of English merchants in this traffic. The English king expressed his suspicions in the safe-conducts he granted to English merchants which stipulated that they were not to take corn and victuals to the Scots.[22]

With Scottish independence secured and Robert I in firm control, the 1320s saw the reestablishment of formal commercial relations with Continental countries. Scottish merchants played a part in negotiating treaties, reflecting royal recognition of the importance of commerce to the Scottish economy. Relations with England, meanwhile, were marked by a series of broken truces and an attempt to come to a final peace. Here also the importance of merchant interests was realised. In 1323 Robert I promised to restore goods cast ashore from English ships while Edward II allowed English merchants to go to Scotland to trade as long as they did not include military supplies among their wares. Scottish merchants were also allowed to trade in Ireland.[23] Anglo-Scottish trade looked set to undergo a revival until the overthrow of Edward II plunged the relations between the two countries into confusion once more.

An invasion of Scotland in 1328 was met by determined Scottish resistance, with Flemish help. The failure of the expedition led to English attempts to establish peace on all sides and after the treaty of Edinburgh-Northampton between Scotland and England, the

Scots were able to resume peaceful commercial relations with Continental merchants unhindered by the English. Flemish merchants played a major role in securing supplies for the state wedding between David Bruce and the English princess Joan of the Tower. The Scots felt secure enough about Scottish trade to impose a countervailing duty on English goods when the English imposed a duty on Scottish goods in 1329.[24] But the outbreak of war in 1332 once again disrupted Scottish commerce.

As in the earlier war, the English tried to cut off all Scottish trade, but in vain. In 1333 Edward had to write to the count of Flanders requesting him to prevent his subjects from aiding the Scots.[25] Later, when Flemish help declined, due to civil war in Flanders and an alliance with England against France at the outbreak of the Hundred Years War, the Scots benefited from illegal trade with English merchants. Edward continually had to issue proclamations against the sending of arms and victuals to Scotland,[26] which continued even after David II's return in 1341.

With the capture of the Scottish king on a raid against England to help the French in 1346 and the victory of Crecy over the French in the same year, Edward no longer regarded Scotland as a threat and left the country free to reestablish commercial relations with the Low Countries. The early years of David's captivity saw a strengthening of Scottish commercial ties with Holland at the expense of Flanders. Some trade had continued to be carried on with Flanders, but in 1347 Scottish merchants and their goods in that country were arrested, leading to retaliatory measures by the Scots on 12 November 1347. On the same day, probably due to merchant pressure on the governing council, an agreement was made to establish a Scottish staple port at Middelburg in Zealand.[27]

Despite this, the Scots were still anxious to retain the Flemish trade links and in 1348 two Scottish merchants were sent to Bruges as representatives of the *quatres grandes villes de Escosse* to resolve disputes and restore good relations. By the 1350s Flanders was once again an important trading partner of the Scots, as is shown by the number of Flemish ships carrying Scottish goods wrecked on the English coast.[28] Civil war in Flanders resulted in the banishment of pro-English Flemings, and probably brought about an increased interest in Scottish trade.

Meanwhile, moves were being made to establish a final peace with England. The defeat of the French at Poitiers left Scotland isolated, and in 1357 a ransom for David was negotiated with the English. In preparation for this, Edward allowed many Scottish prisoners to go home in December 1356 to find their ransoms. Several were merchants, who may have been sent back to Scotland to help negotiate the ransom payments for David II as well as to secure payment for their own release. From his own experience of financing his Scottish and French wars, Edward knew that it would be through the wool trade that much of the money for the ransom would be raised.[29]

The years after David's return saw a gradual growth in Anglo-Scottish trade. From 1357 an increasing number of safe-conducts were issued to Scottish merchants, allowing them to trade in England and Edward's other domains. In the early 1360s, when Edward tried to negotiate with David for the succession of an English heir to the Scottish throne if David died childless, the number of safe-conducts multiplied rapidly. The encouragement of Scottish trade may have been part of Edward's plan to make the idea of an English heir more palatable to at least one part of Scottish society.[30] Edward granted several privileges to Scottish merchants, including freeing them from having to observe the English staple at Calais. David II's general grant of privileges to the Scottish merchants in 1364 also encouraged commercial activity.[31]

These years formed the most favourable period for Anglo-Scottish trade during the fourteenth century. Fish and hides went to England in return for manufactured goods and food. Grain was in high demand and the amount allowed to be exported to Scotland from England during these years totalled over 20,000 quarters. In fact, the export of grain seems to have been used as a political bargaining lever. In 1365 exports of grain were not licensed until a new ransom agreement was made on 20 May, and about half the licences granted in that year were issued on that date.[32]

The cessation of hostilities with England left the Scots free to re-establish more formal diplomatic and commercial links with Continental trading partners. The next twenty years saw a recovery in Scotland's export trade: from 1357 to 1377 about 5000 sacks of wool were exported annually. Flanders actively sought commercial links with Scotland. The Calais wool staple had drawn English merchants away from Bruges, and from the mid-fourteenth century the Scots became the most important traders there after the Germans. As the Flemish cloth industry moved to the rural areas and into the production of cheaper cloth, there was more demand for the cheaper Scottish wool, along with native and Spanish wool.[33] By the early 1360s Bruges had once again become an important commercial centre for the Scots.[34] Scottish merchants were also welcomed in Holland.

After Edward III's death, tensions with England mounted again, but a truce of 1388 once more recognised the importance of trade to both countries. The merchants of the two realms were the only subjects permitted to communicate with each other. To protect them, vessels wrecked on the coast of either country were to be rescued with their cargoes and crews and delivered as in peacetime.[35] The truce was periodically renewed during the 1390s and a time of relative peace followed until the end of the century. Safe-conducts were again issued to Scottish merchants, although in nowhere near the numbers granted in the 1360s.

The resulting decrease in Anglo-Scottish trade was compensated for by expanding trade with other countries. Prussian and Flemish merchants were active in Scotland. Scottish knights had established contacts with the Teutonic Knights who founded Prussia in their crusade against Lithuania. According to an English complaint in 1388, the Prussians were aiding the Scots against the English by giving them arms, victuals and other supplies.[36] By the early fifteenth century Prussian merchants had agents in both Edinburgh and Linlithgow. A list of Scottish debtors to the Teutonic Order was drawn up between 1396 and 1417, and included several of the leading Scottish merchants of the time as well as a number of apparently less significant ones, suggesting the far-reaching involvement of Scottish townspeople in international trade. Commerce with the German merchants of the Hanseatic League also grew, although there seems to have been a shift in Scottish trade away from the ports of the North Sea towards the Baltic ports.[37]

The Flemish trade was not forgotten. In June 1387 the count of Flanders granted specific privileges to the Scottish merchants, with the additional security of their being given 120 days to settle their affairs if international troubles arose.[38] In 1394 a mission including merchants set out for Bruges to negotiate new trading privileges, the grant satisfying many of their demands. Two even more generous grants were made in 1407, one by the count and one by Bruges. The city took advantage of the count's grant of trading privileges to try to secure the bulk of the Scottish trade for itself.[39]

Despite these grants, the Scottish wool trade, like the English, was beginning to decline. Possibly due to climatic deterioration, the quality of the wool seems to have worsened and demand for it fell off. By the early 1400s, wool exports were less than half what they were in the mid-1390s. Scotland's deficit trade balance grew worse and her currency declined drastically in value, especially against English money. An import duty imposed on English cloth in the late 1390s suggests that, as in England, wool was now being increasingly used for domestic cloth production. Imports of items related to the production of cloth in the 1390s also support this picture. New export duties in 1398 on salmon, salt meat, suet, butter and horses imply that Scotland was looking to new resources to pay for its imports. The great days of the wool trade were over by 1500 when wool exports were less than 25% of what they were in the heyday of the 1370s. Such wool trade as remained was increasingly dominated by Edinburgh which, after the loss of Berwick to the English, began the rise which was to make it by far the most prominent Scottish burgh for the rest of the Middle Ages.[40] The other Scottish towns were faced with a period of economic reorganisation to take account of changed conditions.

Diplomatic records give a general picture of Scottish trade, but provide little information about the life of the individual trader. What were the conditions faced by a Scottish merchant following his career? How did he buy and sell his products, organise his business? Unfortunately, there is no merchant of Prato with his thousands of business records in medieval Scotland, but scraps of evidence scattered through medieval documents allow us to reconstruct some of the conditions of mercantile life in this period.

The wool trade illustrates one way in which merchants obtained their goods. Wealthy merchants often carried on an extensive business with the monasteries, the largest producers of wool. The dealings of a Berwick merchant, Thomas of Coldingham, with Durham Priory from 1310 to 1315 show a merchant at work.[41] Thomas dealt in futures, advancing a certain sum of money to the Priory in return for the wool from the annual clip of one or more years. This ensured that he had wool to export and probably enabled him to pay a lower price, while the lump sum gave the monks extra money for any immediate projects. It seems likely that the English custom was followed whereby the monasteries made up any shortfall in the contracted amount by buying the produce of smaller wool-growers,[42] although the 1364 grant of privileges stating that wool could only be sold to merchants might have affected this practice.

Not all wool was of the same quality and some fetched higher prices than others. Francesco Pegolotti, an Italian merchant who drew up a merchant's handbook probably sometime in the first half of the fourteenth century, gave a list of wool-producing monasteries in Scotland, and for several of them noted three separate prices for different qualities of wool. As the charges for packing, transport, customs and foreign tolls depended on quantity rather than quality, it was in the merchant's interest to purchase the best-quality wool in order to realise the largest profit.[43] Thus the overseas merchant's skill rested on his ability to acquire the best wool possible at the lowest price possible. For those supplying the home industry and not faced with heavy customs duties and the cost of transport overseas, poorer quality wool would probably suffice. Certainly the quality of what was probably locally-made cloth at Perth does not suggest the use of the best wool.[44] Sometimes the purchaser might be given a variety of qualities of wool, in which case he might follow the English example of employing a packer to sort the wool as he packed. The best would then be available for export and the rest could be used by the craftsmen involved in the native cloth-making industry.[45]

Not all exporters dealt directly with the producers of their goods. There were many opportunities for middlemen, who were employed by exporters to purchase a certain quantity of goods, or who bought goods themselves and then brought them to the burgh market to sell to the merchants. The restrictions on foreign merchants proved advantageous to such middlemen. In many burghs foreigners were allowed to buy goods only from the burgesses; in some English boroughs there were official brokers who acted for foreign merchants by securing wool for them. In Leicester in the early fourteenth century the brokers had to be sworn in by the town authorities, and it seems possible that the brokers mentioned in the *Statuta Gilde* were part of a similar system in Berwick in the late thirteenth century.[46]

Having secured his goods the merchant had then to export them. One of the reasons for the Scottish king's concern for his merchants was that the export of the staple goods of wool, woolfells and hides provided him with a major source of revenue in the form of the great customs. It is not clear when these export duties were first imposed, although there is a reference to such customs in Berwick in 1282, and they were in operation by 1316 when a grant of Robert I refers to 'the new customs called maltot'.[47] The first custumars' accounts appeared in 1327. The rate on wool was 6s 8d per sack or per 360 woolfells, while that on hides was 13s 4d per last (about 200 hides). The duty on woolfells was later amended to 6s 8d per 240. It has been suggested that prices for Scottish wool were probably similar to those calculated by historians for Northumberland wool and that therefore the customs rate represented about 7% of the purchase price.[48] The customs rate increased when more money was required by the king. The Scottish payment to the English for the peace of 1328 was probably a major reason for the increased rates charged on staple goods exported by foreign merchants in 1331–3. In order to raise the money for David's ransom, the customs rates for all merchants were first doubled and then trebled after 1357. In 1368, Parliament ordered a quadruple customs to meet both the ransom demands and the king's increased expenses.[49]

The collection of these revenues was controlled by restricting the export of staples to those burghs which were granted a cocket, a seal which was required before staple goods could be sent overseas. Grants of the cocket were made mainly to the king's burghs, although certain ecclesiastical and baronial burghs such as St Andrews and Dunbar also received them. Royal officials in the burghs were responsible for enforcing the customs system. Foremost among these was the custumar, who received the customs and paid them to the Exchequer. He was often, although not invariably, a prominent local burgess. At first the custumars of the burgh, usually two in number, were probably responsible for all the operations carried out in connection with the customing of exports, but in time responsibility came to be delegated. In January 1364 Parliament ordered that a competent person representing the crown should be in attendance at the weighing-house of each burgh in order to prevent fraud, and in December of that year it was ordained that a tron for weighing wool should be set up in every burgh of export, the tronar being paid a fee of 1d per sack. The cost of maintaining the tron was paid from the customs receipts. Some burghs also had a clerk of the cocket who acted in conjunction with the custumars and the tronar and prepared the letters of cocket which certified that a particular merchant had paid the customs on his goods.[50] This document was sealed with the cocket seal, of which each custumar held half so that both were required to be present when goods were exported. In Dundee in 1381 enumerators of skins and hides were appointed. This became a national office in 1396.[51] Rental of a customs house was an additional expense, although in Stirling in 1370 an attempt was made to decrease this cost by using the house of one of the custumars. This proved to be a short-term saving as one night the customs money was stolen from the house.[52]

The merchants did not always export goods from their own burgh. From about 1362 it became increasingly common for merchants to have their goods customed and cocketted in their own burghs, and then taken to another burgh to be exported. The merchants presented their cockets to the custumars of the second port, who entered the exports in their cocket book without collecting the duty. This practice was most common among the merchants of west coast burghs, especially Ayr, whose access to continental ports

was restricted by geography. Blackness at Linlithgow was the favoured alternative for the traders of Ayr.[53]

How much of the foreign trade was carried on by Scottish merchants going overseas as distinct from foreign merchants coming to
Scotland is not clear.[54] Scotland was capable of building her own
ships; the count of St Pol placed an order for a vessel to be
constructed in Inverness in 1249. Scottish merchants made use of
these ships; the chronicler Bower reports that Alexander III was
worried enough about the loss of ships through piracy, wreck and
detention to forbid Scottish merchants from exporting goods.[55]
Such an act, if effectively enforced, must have limited the scope for
native overseas enterprise, while at the same time forcing foreign
merchants to come to Scotland to obtain Scottish products. The
Redhall, a Flemish factory, was established in Berwick before 1296,
as was the Whitehall, possibly a factory for merchants from Cologne.
A story of an attempt by a group of Lombards to set up a trading post
at Cramond or Queensferry, whether true or not, suggests that
Scotland was recognised as a fruitful place for the trading activities
of foreign merchants. By the fourteenth century, however, Scottish
merchants were once again active in transporting their goods overseas. By 1333–5, five-sixths of the export trade was in Scottish
hands.[56]

Having paid the necessary customs and laded the ship, the
merchant or his agent – who was also often the master of the ship –
set off. If the journey was to Flanders the route hugged the English
coast most of the way south, thus accounting for the predominance
of Flemish or Flanders-bound ships among those wrecked on the
English coast in this period. A trip overland to Dover and thence to
the Continent was an alternative, although it did not allow the export
of a great quantity of bulky goods and increased the cost of the goods
as transport overland was more expensive than transport by water.[57]

In the absence of detailed customs records such as the English
particular accounts, most of the evidence about the merchant ships
sailing to and from Scotland during the 1300s comes from records
of disputes, wrecks, captures and arrests. Such evidence only reveals
information about a very small percentage of the ships involved in
the Scottish trade, and is further biased by the fact that most of the
documents are to be found in English sources and thus deal only with
ships involved in English and southern North Sea trade. Nevertheless, they give some information about the organisation and activities
of the traders.

Scottish merchants did not restrict themselves to using Scottish ships, but sailed in whatever ships were available. Of the ships carrying the goods of Scottish merchants and wrecked on the English coast during the century, almost two-thirds were Flemish. Zealand ships sailed from Sluis carrying the goods of Scottish merchants, while other ships had on board men of Scotland, Flanders and Germany. Cargo space was shared between merchants of different nationalities, each merchant paying a freight charge for his own goods.[58]

It is sometimes maintained that the Scots were short of ships and heavily reliant on the shipping of other countries for their maritime activities,[59] but the evidence is not sufficient to support this statement. Certainly at two periods during the fourteenth century the Scots were being heavily supplied with ships from other countries, but this was during war with England, when extra shipping would be required to make up for war losses suffered, to protect merchant shipping, and to pursue the conflict at sea. Robert I was supplied with ships by the Flemings and Germans and even looked to the Genoese for vessels. The second occasion on which Scotland received foreign ships was in 1336, again in the midst of a struggle against the English. On 3 November, Edward III wrote to the king of Norway and the counts of Hainault and Gueldres requesting them to forbid their subjects letting ships to the Scots.[60]

In more peaceful times, Scotland does not seem to have been particularly dependent on foreign shipping, although the ships of other countries were used in a number of trading enterprises. References in the *Exchequer Rolls* show the ships of individual merchants being used to carry out duties for the crown. The ship of John Scot of Inverness was used to take building materials to St Monans for the erection of a royal chapel there. About one-third of the ships captured or wrecked in England were Scottish and some could be identified with specific burghs. Thus Inverness, Aberdeen, Dundee, St Andrews, Edinburgh, North Berwick and Linlithgow merchants all had access to Scottish ships in their home ports. A 1428 Act of Parliament which refers to earlier acts restricting Scottish merchants to using Scottish ships,[61] also implies that Scottish ships were available in this period.

Foreign ships sometimes carried the goods of both Scots and the merchants of their own country, but at other times they were chartered by the merchants of a particular burgh. When two Continental ships were wrecked on the English coast in 1370, the goods of one were claimed by merchants of Aberdeen, and the goods of the other by merchants of Edinburgh. The ships might also carry the goods of individual merchants. William Johnson of Aberdeen laded a ship of Sluis in 1368 and his goods apparently made up the entire cargo.[62] Merchants of different burghs sometimes shared cargo space in one ship, international trade encouraging co-operation between burghs. In 1372 Edward III ordered the restoration of goods from two Scottish vessels, wrecked on the Northumbrian coast on a voyage from Bruges to Scotland, to merchants from Edinburgh, Perth and Dundee. Probably the merchants of Perth and Dundee shared one of the ships as a later Perth custumars' account for 1380–1 refers to goods being laded at both Perth and Dundee.[63]

The routes followed by merchants could also be triangular. In 1380 Finlay Usher shipped sixteen lasts and two barrels of herring and two chests of cloth from Schoewen in a Zealand vessel for Flanders.[64] The cloth suggests that this was the second part of a voyage in which he had exchanged some of his Scottish goods for Zealand ones which he would then use to acquire goods in Flanders to take back to Scotland.

In the earlier years of Scottish foreign trade, the only restrictions placed on the destinations of Scottish traders were those dictated by market demands and foreign relations. Certain towns, however, were favoured above others. Bruges was one of these. As an important centre of international trade, Bruges provided the Scots with contact with foreign merchants and new commercial ideas were brought back to Scotland, such as the concept of a staple port, an institution with which the English were to experiment throughout the 1300s. The worsening of relations with Flanders led to the first recorded staple being established in Middelburg in Zealand in 1347, although it is possible that Bruges may have been recognised as the staple previous to this.[65] The actual terms of the agreement which established the staple at Middelburg have not survived, but the general idea was to concentrate the Scottish trade in staple goods in one particular town, in return for various privileges such as lower tolls or a mayor or conservator to safeguard the interests of the merchants. Unlike the English staple it was not regarded as compulsory, although the advantages which accrued to those doing business there would encourage most Scottish merchants to use the town. In practice, it resembled the foreign factories of the Germans. The Scottish merchants brought their goods to the staple port and traded them either personally or through agents or factors. Probably many of the Scots who lived in Bruges earned their living as factors or brokers for their countrymen. There is no indication that the staple became fixed at any one town during the fourteenth century, although the various privileges granted by Bruges to the Scots suggest that this was the usual staple port. During the fifteenth century the staple moved back and forth between Bruges and Middelburg.[66]

The grants of the counts of Flanders and those of the count of Holland give some idea of the conditions under which the Scots traded on the continent, as well as showing the abuses to which they were subject. Unlike English merchants who gained exemptions from various payments, Scottish merchants remained liable for payment of customs and tolls at Continental ports throughout the century. In Holland in 1323, this amounted to 1% of the value of their goods. At Sluis, customs officers inspected the goods brought by the merchants, then a toll was charged for their unloading and transit to Bruges, where there were petty customs to be paid. The Scots complained about the opening of their parcels by the customs officers and asked that the word of the merchants' hosts be accepted for their contents. This was refused but it was agreed that if baggage was opened and everything was in order, the officials would pay for the expense of repacking.[67]

The Scots were also subject to the laws of the country in which they were trading, again unlike the English in Holland who were allowed to choose their own governor to settle disputes among themselves. Not until 1407 were the Scots granted permission to have a conservator to look after their privileges.[68] Immunity from arrest for another's debts, however, was won during the century, and supposedly guaranteed the merchant protection from arbitrary arrest. In fact continued piracy and the retaliatory measures taken against countrymen of the pirates as well as the expiry of grants and privileges meant that this continued to be one of the hazards of overseas trade.

Scottish merchants suffered from overcharging by the brokers who handled the sale of their goods in Bruges. The broker was a useful servant to the merchant as, through residence in the town, he was able to establish contacts with prospective buyers and dispose of the goods quickly. He probably also arranged storage for the merchandise, most of which was sold directly from storage cellars, although wool and woolfells had to be sold in the woolhouse. The employment of brokers may have been compulsory, for in the fifteenth century the Scots gained the right to trade without them.[69]

The weighing of goods was also subject to abuse, with delays of up to two or three months before wool was weighed. The Scots in Bruges requested the right to have their own weigh-house and weigher. This was refused, but in 1394 Bruges promised to correct the abuses in weighing and allowed the Scots to have priority at the English weigh-house. A glimpse of the abuses which the Scots had suffered earlier was revealed in the stipulation that the weigher was to keep his hands off the balance or he would be punished.[70]

In common with their counterparts from other countries, the Scots made increasing use of credit throughout the medieval period, a date and place for payment being specified at the time of the sale. Not surprisingly, the making of such contracts often resulted in problems of recovering debts. In 1359, the Scots complained of delays of up to four months before they received payment for their goods, and in 1394 they asked that if a Bruges burgess defaulted, his goods should be forfeited to pay the debt. One of the privileges granted in this year was that buyers would be compelled to pay at the agreed time.[71]

One of the chapters in the count of Flanders' grant of 1407 states that when loading and unloading the Scots could place their ships side by side or in rows abreast of one another up to the number of four. This suggests that it was common for Scottish merchant ships to travel together, as does the wreck of the two ships of Edinburgh and Aberdeen in 1370. During wartime, especially, it seems likely that Scottish merchants would follow the English practice, and travel in convoys. Convoys to the Baltic were common in the fifteenth century.[72] Largely due to the political situation, co-operation in commercial ventures was not only desirable, but necessary.

On a more individual basis, co-operation was also a major feature in the activities of Scotland's merchants. Trading partnerships were the order of the day. Unfortunately, the evidence is too sketchy to determine the nature of most of these partnerships, but if they followed the pattern of other countries, they could assume a variety of forms, ranging from a true joint venture in which all members contributed both goods and services, to a sleeping partnership where one or more merchants contributed goods and another carried out the actual overseas enterprise.

For all but the very wealthiest merchants, partnerships were necessary in order to raise the capital required for a trading venture. It was common to grant the English safe-conducts issued to Scottish merchants in the 1360s and 1370s to an individual and a certain number of *socii*. This almost certainly indicated a partnership – the fact that not all the partners were named could be due to the temporary nature of the partnership which meant that it had not yet been formed when the named merchant applied for a safe-conduct.

Protection was thus assured for prospective members. Presumably, if the safe-conduct was valid long enough to allow more than one journey, the partners could even be changed. Such temporary partnerships were a common feature of the wool trade in England and Italy.[73]

In some cases more than one merchant is named in a single safe-conduct, implying that a formal, even if temporary, partnership had been established. One of the earliest recorded grants was issued on 6 May 1348 to three Aberdeen merchants, Adam de Frendraught, Robert de la Bothe, and John Taillour. It was repeated on 12 November of the same year and allowed them to bring twelve other persons, probably mariners, with them. In October 1357 four more Aberdeen men were granted permission to trade in England and Ireland in a single ship. In a list of safe-conducts issued to various Scottish merchants in 1358, one on 11 July was granted to three men, Robert de Nesbit, Robert de Paxton and Adam de Paxton.[74] The placing of their names together in what is otherwise a list of individual names with *socii*, and the probable family connection of the two Paxtons, suggests an established partnership.

Two safe-conducts of January 1359 were granted to John Wigmer, burgess of Edinburgh, and Alexander his brother, and to Robert Hogg of Edinburgh and John de Peebles, merchant of the same town. The Wigmer partnership lasted for a number of years, with the brothers being granted safe-conducts in 1360 and 1361. The Hogg-Peebles relationship also remained close, on a social level at least, as after her husband's death, Margaret Hogg married John de Peebles.[75] Other family relationships included those of William and Walter Guppild of Edinburgh, Andrew and Walter son of Augustine of Edinburgh, Hugh de la Leys and his brother Thomas of Dundee, and Henry and Walter de Edinham of Aberdeen. Nor were trading enterprises restricted to the male members of the family. As in other countries, women often took an active part in commerce. In 1362 a joint safe-conduct was issued to Roger and Margaret Hogg, and in 1365 Margaret herself is styled a Scottish merchant, suggesting that in 1362 she was taking an active part in her husband's trading activities. In 1379 Annabella Guppild was given permission to accompany her husband on a trading journey to Flanders.[76] Some trading ventures involved moving the entire family. In 1373 a safe-conduct was granted to the merchant William Prudhomme to come to England for one year with his wife, children and servants.[77]

It was common for merchants' sons in this period to gain practi-

cal experience of commercial enterprise through working for their
fathers as factors and servants. A probable example of this is found
in two safe-conducts issued to Alan de Ballon, a prominent Edinburgh merchant, in 1394 and 1396. In both cases, Alan's servants
included Thomas de Ballon, who was probably his son. The fact that
Alan's ship was called *la Thomas* may support this conclusion. The
three other servants listed in 1396 all bear the surname Fersith, and
could quite possibly be the sons or grandsons of the wealthy
Edinburgh merchant William Fersith, who was an active trader in
the 1360s and 1370s.[78] In the absence of more positive evidence,
some of these connections are fairly speculative but given the
strength of family ties in medieval Scotland they are not at all
unlikely.

During the medieval period it was becoming increasingly common for European merchants to employ factors to deal with the
merchandising of their goods in other countries. Royal clerks were
often called upon to write letters of protection for merchants' servants going abroad.[79] Many Scottish merchants, however, continued to accompany their goods overseas. The passengers in the
Scottish ships captured by the English, often included merchants,
most of whom probably had a share in the cargo. John Mercer, one
of the wealthiest men in Scotland, was captured in 1376 when
returning home with his ship, and the reprisals carried out by his son
Andrew, who gathered together a fleet and attacked Scarborough,
show that the younger Mercer was no stranger to seamanship. Men
such as William Feth and Adam Tore who were sent on diplomatic
missions to the Continent probably had some familiarity with the
countries with which they were dealing.[80]

Except in the cases of wealthy merchants such as John and
Andrew Mercer and Alan de Ballon, who had their own ships, most
merchants crossed the seas in other men's ships and in the company
of others – not only merchants, but also scholars, pilgrims and other
passengers. This did not always protect them from attack, as a 1327
massacre of the thirteen pilgrims and nine merchants on the Flemish
ship *La Pelarym* shows. In 1337 a Flemish ship carrying the bishop
of Glasgow and 'other Scottish enemies' with goods and armour was
arrested, and in 1327 a ship of Flanders which had among its
passengers two Scottish friars and five Scottish merchants was
wrecked in a storm while at Scarborough. The Scottish merchants
managed to escape from the town, but the unfortunate friars were
forced to seek asylum in a church.[81]

Almost all English safe-conducts included provision for escorts to accompany merchants on trading journeys. The number of such escorts, servants and boys varied from two to thirty and does not seem to have been related necessarily to the wealth and status of the merchant. The usual number was two to four per merchant, although in 1359 John Scot of Inverness was granted a safe-conduct for himself and twenty escorts[82] – perhaps a comment on the perils of journeying through the north of Scotland. There are no complaints in the English records of assaults on Scottish merchants travelling overland through England, suggesting perhaps that they were sufficiently well-protected against attack – or that they were not carrying enough goods to merit a protest to the government.

The references to these escorts serve as a reminder that it was not only those of merchant status who were involved in Scotland's commerce. If the number of associates and servants mentioned in the safe-conducts is added to the number of named merchants, the total of potential trade-related visitors to England in the period 1357–1400 increases considerably. Over 900 safe-conducts were issued, allowing over 3500 entries to England, and involving over 500 different merchants. If even half these safe-conducts were used, then the mercantile traffic between England and Scotland, especially in the peak years of the 1360s when 733 were issued, was by no means inconsiderable. Moreover, the above numbers refer only to royal safe-conducts. Many more licences may have been granted but not recorded as Edward III sometimes delegated the responsibility for issuing such protections to others. On 24 November 1366, for example, Henry del Strother, sheriff of Northumberland, was given power for one year to grant safe-conducts to Scots wishing to trade in Northumberland.[83]

As well as those who served the merchants, Scottish commerce involved those whom the merchants served. From the thirteenth century onwards there are records of merchants carrying on trade on behalf of members of the aristocracy, and a great many merchants must have found their major employment in this type of service. Whether the merchant simply performed the duties of a hired servant or whether he also invested capital in the enterprises is not clear, but probably both types of association were to be found.

From the earliest days of Scottish trade, merchants had served the crown by importing luxuries and household requirements. Sometimes the merchant supplied goods on commission, as for the wedding of David Bruce in 1328. This particular commission was given to a Fleming, but later ones were given to Scottish merchants.[84] Many other royal household supplies also came from Scottish

traders, but in most of these cases it is unclear whether the purchases
were commissioned specifically or were simply chosen from what the
merchant had brought back to Scotland.

The fact that a merchant did not always act only for himself is
shown in a request by the Scots to the count of Flanders, asking that
if a merchant was sentenced to death in that country, not all his goods
be confiscated as Scottish merchants coming to Flanders were the
servants of others and not all their goods were their own.[85] Probably
this referred mainly to those involved in merchant partnerships, but
it could also apply to those who carried out commissions for
members of other classes.

Among the earliest examples of Scottish merchants supplying
goods for specific markets are those given licence by Edward I to
purchase supplies for the garrison at Berwick and other strongholds
under English control. In 1321 Edward II allowed Scottish merchants to come to England on more personal trading missions, to
buy cloths, jewels and other supplies for the chamber of the countess
of Fife. This was the first of many such English licences in which the
merchants were given permission to purchase supplies, especially
food, for the household of their employer. In 1331 David II was
allowed to buy 400 quarters of wheat and malt from Lincoln and this
transaction would most likely have been carried out by merchants in
his service. Merchants also secured supplies for the Scottish queen
in the late 1350s.[86] Most of the safe-conducts, however, involved the
purchase of food for influential figures outside the royal family, men
such as John of the Isles, Sir Archibald Douglas, the earl of March,
the earl of Fife and the bishop of Glasgow.[87] In some cases, safe-
conducts were granted at the request of a prominent Scottish figure,
and it seems likely that the merchants named would be involved in
securing supplies for their patron. Such requests were made by Sir
Archibald Douglas in 1359, the earl of Sutherland in 1361, and the
Scottish chancellor and the earl of Fife in 1384.[88] The timing of the
last two shows that conflict with England did not always result in a
complete cessation of trade.

Certain individuals were referred to as the merchants of a particular lord. For example, the earl of Fife and Menteith refers to John de
Bondington as 'his merchant' in 1385.[88] Other merchants served
more than one master, sometimes simultaneously. In 1369 Thomas
Clydesdale was given one safe-conduct to purchase food in England
at the request of Sir Robert Erskine, and another one at the request
of the bishop of Glasgow. Some merchants occasionally fulfilled
special commissions, but generally acted independently. In 1360

John Wigmer, a prominent Edinburgh merchant and burgess, was granted a licence to purchase falcons in Scotland and take them to England for Edward Balliol.[89]

The aristocracy did not only participate in commerce as consumers. The custumars' accounts contain several references to the remission of customs on wool to people such as the earl of March, the countess of Douglas, and the earl of Douglas. The right to export a certain amount of goods duty-free was sometimes granted to individuals by the crown; the abbot of Melrose had licence to export fifty sacks of wool without paying customs. In the case of ecclesiastical or baronial burghs, the overlord might be given a 'grant of cocket' which gave him the great customs of the burgh, thus allowing him to export his own goods duty-free and to charge customs on other goods exported from the burgh. The abbot of Arbroath was granted this privilege in 1357. Thus non-merchants were enabled to participate in the export trade, although it is likely that most of the responsibility for the disposal of the goods was delegated to the merchants.[90]

In one aspect of trade, some members of the upper classes played a more active part. This was the piracy which was a common feature of maritime life of the time. Conflict between two countries was frequently used as an excuse for uncontrolled privateering, and in this the fourteenth-century merchant was often deeply involved. The companion of the earl of Mar on many of his piratical ventures was Robert Davidson, the famous provost of Aberdeen who led the burgesses at the Battle of Harlaw in 1411. Scots were also to be found among the followers of some of the most notorious pirates of the century, including the Fleming John Crabbe in the first War of Independence and John de Sancta Agatha in the Second War, both of whom made life miserable for the English.[91]

Much of the piracy engaged in by the merchants during the early part of the century was largely attributable to the wars with England. If trade with the continent was not to be entirely cut off, the English blockade had to be run and this often involved attacks on English shipping. The effectiveness of the Scottish and continental piracy is shown by the English efforts to counteract it. In 1313, some merchants of Barton asked for royal permission to equip two ships to set out against the Scots who had taken goods from five of their ships. Such private efforts seem to have been of little use, however, and in 1315 Edward II appointed two men as captains of seven ships which he was sending to 'bridle the malice of the Scots'. The king's efforts met with little more success than those of his merchants, and the Scottish and foreign merchants and pirates continued to prey on English shipping and bring supplies to Scotland, thus contributing in no small measure to the successful Scottish resistance.[92]

Piracy was a two-sided coin, however, and the successful efforts of one Scottish merchant could have a detrimental effect on the enterprises of his fellows. During this period a doctrine of collective responsibility prevailed, by which all merchants of a certain nationality were held responsible for the actions of each merchant from their country. Thus the goods of Scottish merchants might be seized in England in retaliation for an attack upon an English ship by Scottish pirates, or letters of marque might be issued which enabled a merchant who had been attacked to prey on ships from the same country as his attackers in order to make good his loss.[93]

The pirates and merchants of the Continent were not the only suppliers to the Scots during the Wars of Independence. English smuggling also played a major role. Before the war, England had been an important trading partner and many English merchants saw no reason to end the commercial connection, especially during the years that the war was being prosecuted by the unpopular Edward II. Smuggling brought large profits, both because the Scots paid high prices for much-needed supplies and because usually the forbidden goods were taken out of the country uncustomed.[94] Smuggling by English merchants to Scotland continued throughout the century, despite royal efforts to stop it. Smuggling was relatively easy, especially when the customs officials were involved. Inquiries into the illegal trade were ordered repeatedly, but had little effect. The widespread nature of the smuggling – inquiries were ordered in nearly all the counties of England – suggests that it was a common activity among the merchants.[95] Undoubtedly, Scotland's merchants also partook in such activities, quite apart from their co-operation with the English smugglers.[96] Smuggling methods could include an individual with the privilege of exporting goods duty-free exporting other merchant's goods in his name, sailing from a remote part of the coast or even from a port and hoping that it would not be reported, bribing the custumars,[97] or whatever other method ingenuity could devise.

Even during times of truce or peace, when trade with Scotland was permitted by the English kings, certain articles were prohibited from export to the Scots. These included arms, victuals[98] and often wool. In peacetime, when there was less demand for military supplies, wool seems to have been one of the most frequently-smuggled commodities. This was due less to Scottish demand for

English wool than to the opportunity to take advantage of the lower
Scottish customs rates. English subsidies imposed in the fourteenth
century had raised the customs on wool exported from English ports
to £2 per sack, whereas in English-held Berwick, which had been
granted a low customs rate in order to encourage English settlement
there, it was 6s 8d, and in the Scottish ports even after 1368 it was
26s 8d. The merchants of Newcastle had a particularly strong motive
to ship their wool from Berwick and the Scottish ports as the lower
quality, and therefore the lower market price, of northern wool
meant that they paid proportionately more in customs than did their
fellow-merchants further south.[99] The trade in English wool appears
in the Scottish customs records from 1361. It is interesting to note
that the Scots seem to have given additional encouragement to the
shipment of English wool by permitting it to be exported at a lower
rate than Scottish wool and the increases in the Scottish wool
customs rate were not imposed on English wool. The English smuggling was in Scottish interests, as it enhanced the customs revenue,
partly compensating for the money diverted to the ransom payments.[100]

One other irregular form of trade grew out of the Anglo-Scottish
wars. Ransoms were often paid in kind rather than in cash. One of
the earliest examples of this occurred in 1320, when Edward II
permitted 1000 chalders of coal to be sent from Newcastle for the
redemption of an English prisoner. It is possible that many of the
Scottish merchants released from English captivity in 1356 paid
their ransoms in wool or other such goods. Malt was a common
commodity used for ransoms in the 1380s, but sometimes a great
variety of goods was involved. In 1388 John Hull of Liverpool was
given licence to take beans, peas, oats, malt, flour, cloth, muslin,
knives and belts to Scotland to redeem himself and other captives.[101]

This licence of 1388 gives some idea of the variety of goods which
was imported into Scotland during the fourteenth century. The
chamberlain's accounts list articles purchased for the king from
merchants active in international trade. Exotic foodstuffs which
could not be grown in Scotland's northern climate, including spices
and wine, were brought from overseas in merchants' ships or
sometimes purchased in England and carried to Scotland by land or
sea. The royal demand for luxury foods was accompanied by a
demand for luxury manufactured goods. Jousting equipment, suits
of armour, velvet, cloth of silk, pewter vases, brass pots and articles
of silver were among the objects purchased for the use of the king.[102]
The most common entry in the accounts of goods purchased by the

royal household was wine, which, to judge from the amounts imported, was the main drink of the upper classes. (We might, however, question the quality of the product when we read in an English account of wine imported by an English merchant which was considered unfit for consumption and was therefore shipped on to Scotland.) Payments for wine were often made as part of a sum for other victuals or goods as well, suggesting the diversity of goods in which the merchants supplying the royal household dealt. Unfortunately, the chamberlains' accounts share in the taciturn nature of the custumars' accounts to a certain extent, and the most frequent entry is 'for divers goods', which leaves open to speculation the nature of many of the king's luxury imports.

It was not just luxuries which were imported, however. Manufactured goods of every description, as well as raw materials, were brought into the country. Indeed, Scottish demand for all sorts of manufactures was probably a prime concern of both the merchants and craftsmen of Bruges in their efforts to keep the Scottish staple there.[103] A description of the contents of a Scottish ship arrested and plundered at Lynn in 1394 illustrates the diversity of goods which could be shipped in one voyage: two pieces of canvas running to 100 ells, seven new and three old swords, twenty-five gold nobles of English money, woollen and linen cloth, wax, pepper, brass pots and plates, ewers, basins, linen thread, woad, madder, white and black dyed wool, iron, combs for carding wool, hose, caps, hoods, saddles, bridles, spurs, boots, gloves, shuttles for weavers, paper, parchment, candelabra, a basinet, red leather and keys and locks. These goods were shipped by four merchants. In 1368 a single Aberdeen merchant shipped the following from Flanders: a pipe of red wine, thirty silver groats, silver ore and specie, three gold rings, a pipe of woad, three casks of 'waddase', twenty-eight wey of coarse salt and seven quarters of peas.[104]

Food shortages and the devastation of fertile crop-growing areas by war meant that food supplies were a major import. Licences were granted by the English kings to both Scottish and English merchants to take grain, malt and oats to Scotland. During the Wars of Independence, the supply of foodstuffs to the English armies also proved a profitable business to those Scottish merchants who had sworn allegiance to the English crown. Sometimes, these provisions ended up in the wrong hands. In 1316 the ship of a burgess of Berwick who had secured supplies in England for the town was seized by men of Lübeck, Stralsund, Rostock and elsewhere, and carried off to Scotland where the goods were sold to the Scots. Some

English merchants risked the king's displeasure and smuggled large quantities of foodstuffs to Scotland. Victuals were also imported from other countries. In 1369 John Gill of Perth shipped a cargo of barley from Normandy, and by the late fourteenth and early fifteenth centuries, Scottish merchants were going to the Baltic ports for grain.[105]

One commodity which was brought to Scotland seems to have been used rather to permit the export of a Scottish product than for domestic consumption. In 1367, Edward III gave permission to two men of London to take 100 quarters of salt to Scotland in order to salt fish there to bring back to England. Another shipment from London of cloth, wine and salt in 1393 suggests a similar use for the salt as the shippers were fishmongers. Apparently the salt found in Scotland was not well-suited to preserving fish, but salt brought from the Bay of Borgneuf by merchants from England and Flanders helped make up the lack.[106]

More bulky commodities included coal, which was becoming an increasingly important English export. In 1381–2 five ships of Dundee and one of Perth took coal from Newcastle, and in 1390 Scottish ships carried coal from the English port to Edinburgh.[107] The references to Scottish trade found in the surviving Newcastle customs accounts suggest that a search of other English accounts might throw further light on the nature of Anglo-Scottish trade. Timber was included among the items smuggled from England in 1343, but in general most of the supplies seem to have come from Norway and the Baltic. Baltic timber was being used in the 1330s, and a purchase of timber was made by the chamberlain from Baltic merchants in 1382. Iron, a major import, generally originated in Spain, but was bought in Bruges or Middelburg.[108]

One import of which there is almost no documentary evidence but which looms large in the archaeological record is pottery. Pottery evidence must be treated with care, as it was often brought into the country as containers for goods rather than as an actual import for sale. Nor can it be taken as evidence of direct trade links with its country of origin, as it may have reached Scotland through an entrepôt. Some of the Continental pottery was used domestically, and it seems almost certain that the wares from Yorkshire and Scarborough which are found in large numbers at almost every excavation enjoyed popular Scottish use. Local imitations suggest their widespread use. Pottery also came from France, the Low Countries, Spain and Germany, and it is possible that there were short periods of occasional trade in ceramics with these countries.[109]

Textiles were a common import. Several varieties were imported from England, worsted being among the goods for which the earls of Fife and Douglas sent two merchants to England in 1378, but the major source of this commodity was probably Flanders. In many cases, the imports of woollen cloth represented the return of Scottish wool to its place of origin, but in a different form. Sometimes luxury fabrics such as silk from Italy, Spain or the East were imported, but in general it was the Flemish cloth which was in the largest demand. Coloured and striped woollen cloth, canvas, napery and towelling were all brought to the markets of Scotland.[110]

As well as supplying finished cloth for the Scottish market, Flanders played a part in the Scottish domestic cloth industry. Dyes, mordaunts, soaps and teasles were imported by the early fourteenth century, and the cargo lists mentioned above show that many of the articles used in cloth production came from Flanders. The Flemings also participated in other stages. In 1366 wool was exported from Montrose to be dyed, and better quality Scottish cloth was sometimes sent to Flanders for finishing before being re-imported. Indeed, Flanders even provided a market for the cheap Scottish cloth which helped supply clothes for the poorer inhabitants of the country, although it refused to accept good quality Scotttish cloth for sale.[111]

To pay for her imports, Scotland exported a variety of goods. Because wool, woolfells and hides were the only items on which customs was paid for most of the century, it is difficult to determine what proportion of the country's exports these goods represented, but the impression gained from other sources is that they were indeed Scotland's most important exports. Most of the ships recorded sailing to Flanders were laden mainly with Scottish staple goods.[112] It is possible that Scottish staples were not so prominent in ships sailing to other destinations less concerned with cloth manufacture, such as the Baltic ports, but unfortunately there are few records of such vessels before the later fifteenth century.

Scotland exported other goods; the trade in livestock seems to have been a flourishing one. Horses were carried overseas to Flanders in 1368, but the main market was apparently in England. Horses, oxen, cows and other animals were sold there to help pay for the ransom of a Scottish prisoner in 1316, and in later years English safe-conducts were granted to both Scottish and English merchants to participate in this trade.[113] It seems likely that the export of livestock to England usually involved driving the animals overland rather than bringing them by sea.

Another common export was fish, of which salmon was especially in demand. Several of the English safe-conducts licensed English merchants to go to Scotland to buy salmon and other goods, implying that salmon was the most important purchase. It was probably in order to salt salmon that most of the salt was brought from England, although herring and cod were also sent abroad. By 1398, salmon was seen as an important enough export to be one of the commodities on which new export duties were levied. The other goods, reflecting Scotland's agricultural base, were horses, suet, salt meat and butter. In the fifteenth century with the drop in demand for Scotland's traditional exports, many burgh merchants diversified their business to include the sale of these and other products.[114]

Throughout the fourteenth century, Scottish trade had a role to play in the commerce of Northern Europe,[115] and increasingly international commercial enterprises became a central activity for many burgesses, contributing greatly to their prosperity. In turn their links were strengthened with the landed classes, whom they supplied with goods, and many of whom they began to equal in wealth. As suppliers of the royal household, their connections with the crown also increased. Most important of all, as promoters of trade, both through their diplomatic activities on behalf of the king, and through their commercial enterprises on their own behalf, they played a major role in the development of Scotland's nationhood from the fourteenth century.

4 Possession of Property

Although trade may have been the *raison d'être* of the burgh, it was the possession of property which made up its very essence. A burgess's privileges were dependent on his holding a specified amount of burghal property; the king, church and nobility were involved in burgh affairs through their possession of land in the burgh; the burgh itself was defined by the extent of land under its direct control; and the burgesses extended their interests beyond the burgh itself through their purchase of property in the surrounding countryside. The burgesses helped to bring a new commercialism to landholding in later medieval Scotland, reflected both in the active landmarket in the burghs and the beginnings of an urban rentier class, and in the increasing purchase of country properties bought with the profits of trade instead of being granted in return for feudal service.

This emphasis on property-holding resulted from a number of factors. As the burgh was a new institution, borrowed in large part from countries such as England and France where feudal ideas held sway, it reflected the central place of landholding within those societies. Moreover, there was a practical consideration. If trade was to be concentrated in certain centres instead of being in the hands of scattered or itinerant native and foreign merchants, the possession of land would serve as an excellent inducement to traders to settle themselves and their families in one place and carry out their business from there. The opportunity to purchase land would also encourage the settlement of numbers of craftsmen in one place and further aid the new trading centre through providing both goods to sell and the necessities of life for those who spent much of their time engaged in commerce.

When a new burgh was established, a potential settler was offered a piece of land rent-free for a certain period, during which time he was to build a house for himself. The length of this rent-free period, or kirset, was usually one year, but in more isolated burghs such as Dingwall it could be as long as ten years,[1] presumably to attract settlers to a remote area. The importance attached to actual residence, not just ownership, is shown in the requirement to build on the land, which continued to be specified in some late medieval charters.In 1318 the recipient of a land in Arbroath was required to build a house 'according to the custom of the burgh' within three years.[2] Having completed this condition, the individual was then eligible to receive the trading privileges which were the essence of burgess-ship, subject to his paying an annual rent, usually 5d or 6d, to the burgh overlord. Thus the right to trade was directly connected to property-holding. The appointment of liners to ensure the integrity of the burgage plots, emphasises the importance of this relationship for the burgesses.

After the initial grants of burgage lands by the burgh superior, the acquisition of burghal property was no longer entirely dependent on such grants. For those born into burgess families the gaining of burgh lands and the rights that went with them was mainly a matter of inheritance. Several of the burgh laws deal with the heritability of property and the protection of the rights of the burgess's wife and children. The son of a burgess enjoyed the rights of burgess-ship while he lived in his father's house, but once he left the family home he needed to acquire a burgage of his own in order to be entitled to the burgh trading privileges. This was not generally very difficult. If a burgess was wealthy and had acquired more than one burgage during his lifetime, he could grant the extra properties to his sons as they attained their majority or married and moved away from home. Others might be able to purchase properties with the profits made in partnership with their fathers. Eldest sons inherited their fathers' burgage, although it was not uncommon for them to take up residence on properties of their own long before their fathers' death. Documents in which both father and son are identified as burgesses probably indicate such a situation.[3]

Inheritance was not restricted to the eldest son. If a burgess's only child was a daughter she had the same rights of inheritance as an eldest son. (She could also pass on the rights of burgess-ship and membership of the guild to her husband.) The burgh laws made provision for the welfare of the widow and children of a burgess. Moreover, where there was no direct heir, it was possible to ensure that the land went to a certain individual, usually a near relative, rather than reverting to the burgh overlord. This was accomplished in the same way as with feudal estates, by a regrant of the burgess's lands with a clause added to ensure a specific succession. For example, in 1400 Andrew Leiper, burgess of Edinburgh, resigned his burgh lands to Robert II, who regranted them to Andrew and his wife Mary Forrester. If they had no heirs, the lands were to pass to Adam Forrester, Mary's father.[4]

Because the possession of a burgage was the qualification for burgess-ship, certain laws were framed to prevent the alienation of the family inheritance to the detriment of the burgess's heirs. Inherited land, as against land which had been purchased during the burgess's lifetime, was not to be alienated except in cases of urgent necessity such as the relief of poverty. Even in such a situation there was an attempt to keep the lands within the family, as the owner had to offer the lands to his relatives at three head courts before he was free to sell it to anyone else – a procedure mentioned in a number of later medieval charters.[5] No such restrictions, however, were placed on lands acquired by purchase or grant and gradually an active land market developed as wealthy burgesses came into possession of more and more land. By the fourteenth century there are numerous examples of the active transfer of properties by their burgess holders. But burgesses were not the only people who held land in the burghs and before examining the dealings of the urban land market, it is necessary to see who else was involved in burgh property-holding.

When burghs were first established, landholding was primarily the concern of the merchants and craftsmen who worked there. As the new settlements grew and flourished, burgh land was seen as a valuable asset and its possession was no longer limited merely to the towndwellers although they remained the majority of urban landholders. Crown, church and nobility were all involved in burgh land transactions and thus exerted an influence on the lives of the townspeople.

The crown of course had had an interest in burgh landholding from the first days of the burghs. It was the king who gave the settlements the special status of burghs and in the royal burghs it was of him that all lands were held. Even in the case of ecclesiastical and baronial burghs, it was the king who ultimately sanctioned their existence. Despite the increasing independence of many royal burghs, the royal overlord could still be a potent force in the later medieval town, actively involved in the disposition of certain burgh lands, especially those which had been forfeited or resigned, and open spaces which had not been granted earlier. Moreover, it was the king's lordship over the burgh which enabled him to grant feu-ferme charters to the townspeople from the fourteenth century.

Most of the royal grants of burgages were from lands which had been held previously by another individual but had returned to the king's hands: failure to pay rent, lack of heirs, bastardy and forfeiture could all lead to the escheat of burgh lands. The law of bastardy forbade a bastard to pass on his land to anyone but the lawful heir of his body, although the king could grant dispensations as he did to Patrick de Innerpeffer, burgess of Dundee, and William de Dunbar, burgess of Aberdeen. For some reason, the dispensation to William did not prove effective, as his lands returned to the king after his death 'by reason of bastardy'. Alexander de Fairley of Edinburgh saw the opportunity to retain his lands in his family slip away when his son predeceased him.[6]

Treason could result in the forfeiture of lands to the crown, and such situations arose fairly frequently in the war-troubled years of the late thirteenth and early fourteenth centuries. Those who swapped sides between the English and the Scots were sometimes caught on the losing side. Thomas Harper had been granted lands by Robert I both within and outwith the burgh of Haddington, but he later forfeited a land in Edinburgh when he joined the English during the reign of David II. This Edinburgh land, the Quarrypits, was destined to undergo several changes of ownership for the burgess to whom it was granted was himself forfeited a few years later.[7]

Expansion of the royal burghs provided new opportunities for the king who controlled the disposition of any new burgages laid out, although he might entrust this to the burgh administration. He thus had available a supply of burgages which he could grant to those who served him well or who could pay for them. But there was also other land available in the form of the open spaces of the burgh and it was perhaps here that the royal influence on the pattern of landholding in the burgh was most marked, as only the crown had the authority to allow building in such areas. When the burgesses of Ayr wished to narrow the Sandgate to protect the town against drifting sand in the early fifteenth century, they had to apply to the crown for permission to do so.[8] The royal charters giving various burghs permission to build townhouses on land owned by the king are evidence of this royal control.

In making such grants the king could also promote the interests of individuals. In most grants of open space, the extra property was given to someone who held adjacent land so that he could enlarge his tenement or add new buildings to his property. Robert II granted a burgess of Inverness, Robert de Appleton, the former vennel beside his burgage, while Patrick de Innerpeffer of Dundee received a grant of land from the king's highway which bordered on his tenement. Institutions might also benefit – David II granted land in the common of Peebles to John of Peebles, master of the hospital there, to construct a chapel.[9]

Many kings followed the example of David I, that 'sair sanct for the croun', and gave extensive lands to the great religious houses of the kingdom, including properties in many burghs. As a result the church became a prominent landholder in several burghs, quite apart from being the overlord of ecclesiastical burghs such as Glasgow, St Andrews and Arbroath. The religious houses derived a number of advantages from their burgh holdings. First the possession of a burgage gave the monastery a base in the town from which it could buy supplies and sell its produce, especially the wool from the large monastic sheep flocks. Arbroath Abbey, for example, was specifically granted the right to trade in burghs in which it held burgages. As Wendy Stevenson points out, such grants also brought benefits to the burghs by helping to promote their economic growth. Second, in the case of religious houses outside the burgh, the burgage provided accommodation for the members when they travelled to the burgh on commercial business, to attend the itinerant king, or to hold an ecclesiastical court. Finally, the leasing of the property to residents of the burgh provided an extra source of income. From the thirteenth century this became a prime consideration and abbeys began to acquire additional urban lands largely for their value as rent-producing properties.[10]

The second and third functions were often combined, as in the case of Arbroath Abbey. Keeping property only for occasional use was wasteful so a number of grants of burgages were made with the proviso that the tenant provide hospitality whenever the abbot visited the burgh. The services to be rendered were set forth in great detail:

> providing good lodging for the abbot of Arbroath ... and for his monks, lay brethren, and clerks, their bailies, and attorneys, coming for the business and causes of the monastery, as often as they visit,   each according to his station, with their attendants; a hall in which they may properly eat, with tables and trestles and other furniture, a larder with buttery, a chamber or chambers where they may sleep comfortably, a decent kitchen, and a stable for at most thirty horses. They shall provide also ... sufficient fuel, in the hall and chamber as well as in the kitchen, white tallow candles ... bedding and straw in the hall and chamber and salt for the table.[11]

The tenants were not responsible for fuel and candles if the visitors stayed more than three nights. The abbot's messengers were to be admitted but were responsible for the cost of their own food.

By such leases the abbot assured himself of accommodation in the burgh, but also gained a valuable return from the property between visits. The arrangement was also profitable for the tenant, as a grant by William the Lion to Arbroath made tenants of the abbey's burgh holdings free from toll throughout the kingdom.[12]

It was only the great abbeys which held properties in many different burghs. Burgh properties enabled them to dispose of their agricultural surpluses, while the leading members of these houses tended to play an important role in royal government and therefore required accommodation in whichever burgh the king's court happened to be held. The members of religious houses within the burgh, on the other hand, were less concerned with national affairs and therefore less likely to visit other burghs. The main function of these institutions' lands was the provision of an income to sustain the members and it was thus most convenient for them to have all their lands in one burgh. This pattern was reinforced by the pronounced tendency of the burgh inhabitants to confer lands or grants of annual rents on local religious houses rather than on distant abbeys.

By the fourteenth century most abbeys had stopped acquiring new urban properties. Most documents of this period dealing with the abbeys' burgh lands are concerned with the leasing of burgages rather than the receiving of grants. By the 1300s it had become the turn of the friars to benefit from such charity. This may reflect the growing prosperity of certain towndwellers who had amassed enough property to give some of it to the religious houses, thus helping to ensure the salvation of their souls. Lands and rents were also held by the various altars of the parish church and used to sustain the chaplains serving them. Most of the grants were made by local burgesses who thus not only gained religious merit but did so in a conspicuous way. The fourteenth and fifteenth centuries witnessed a great increase in the number of chantries founded all over Europe; the Scottish church benefited from the townspeople's participation in this trend.

The religious houses affected the pattern of burgh landholding in another way. Their buildings and grounds took up a considerable amount of room, so they were often established on the outskirts of the burgh and might mark the limits of the burgage plots proper. Their gardens helped preserve open space within the burgh. They might also make productive use of burgh lands which were not well-suited for habitation. For example, in Aberdeen, the grounds of the Carmelite friary occupy the Green, an area prone to flooding and therefore more suited to cultivation than housing.[13]

The holdings of the nobility in the burgh appear to have been much less extensive than those of the church. This impression may be due to the pattern of survival of documents, as religious cartularies have better stood the test of time than the records of noble families. There are fewer incidental references to such lands in other charters, however, than to church-held lands. It was expected that some burgh lands would be held by nobles; a burgh law states that all tenants of lands of barony within a burgh should be subject to the laws of the burgh and be corrected by the bailies for breaking assize prices and all other civil causes and actions. Furthermore in the twelfth century, for reasons similar to those pertaining to the leaders of the great abbeys, the Constable and Steward of Scotland were granted properties in all the burghs by the king. These possessions were recognised as under their jurisdiction in the later medieval towns. In 1389 Robert II, former Steward of Scotland, granted to an altar in the parish church of Stirling, three pieces of land in the barony of the Steward of Scotland in the burgh.[14]

Some landholders were local lairds who had acquired lands through purchase or pledge, or, perhaps more likely, through marriage to a burgess's daughter. James Melville, lord of Gilcomston, outside Aberdeen, probably held his lands in the burgh by right of his wife, as her consent was required to a transaction concerning the properties in 1397. William Reid of Pitfoddels acquired a rent from a burgage in Aberdeen in return for a certain sum of money paid to the holders.[15] Land might also be held by a laird as the result of inheritance if a burgess married into a local landholding family and his son inherited both urban and rural property.

Usually, however, it was the burgesses who acquired lands from the nobility. There is little evidence of extensive holdings of the nobility in the burghs in the fourteenth and fifteenth centuries. In Scottish towns, unlike the towns of Italy and some other countries, there was not much interest among the nobility in acquiring urban properties. Indeed, in the fourteenth century the nobility do not seem to have been much interested in the burghs at all, unless they were the overlords. The problem of domination by a neighbouring lord, which was to arise in the later fifteenth century, finds little echo in the fourteenth. The only hint of such fears is found in a charter of 1385 involving the burgh of Ayr, and refers to lands outwith the burgh boundaries, which the holder of the lands promises not to let to any lord more powerful than himself.[16] Moreover, in this case the landholder was not a burgess and there was therefore perhaps a greater chance of the lands being passed on to a greater lord.

Generally speaking, in the fourteenth century it was the burgesses who were the dominant force in the burgh.

It was they who participated most in the increasingly active market in urban property. Inheritance restrictions did not apply to lands acquired by purchase or grant, and as wealthy burgesses came into possession of more and more land so the market grew. Later medieval town documents are full of references to the transfer of properties between burgh inhabitants. There were several ways in which burgh lands could be used to bring money to their owners, the most obvious of which was the direct sale, where land was exchanged for a certain sum of money. In a society where ready cash tended to be in short supply, but where a large amount might suddenly be required due to the exigencies of trade, the advantages to a burgess of a direct sale over a feu-ferme grant with its annual render could be considerable. Unfortunately, the purchase price of land is rarely stated in the documents of sale. All that is said is that the purchaser gave the seller 'a certain sum of money'. Presumably it was not felt necessary to include the price as it had no effect on the security of tenure, and the medieval clerk did not foresee future historians trying to work out urban land values. There are a few receipts for sales of land to the church which mention prices, but it is probably unwise to take these as representative of burgh land prices as, given the medieval concern with the salvation of the soul, it is quite possible that the lands were sold for a sum advantageous to the church. In 1305 Melrose Abbey purchased a burgage in Peebles for 14 merks sterling, while in 1331 it bought a tenement in Berwick from the widow and son of a burgess of Berwick for 10 merks sterling.[17] To make matters even less conclusive, both these sales took place at a time of unsettled political conditions.

An example of a straightforward sale between two burgesses occurred in Edinburgh in 1397, when Robert Rolland sold a burgh land to his co-burgess, Patrick de Hill. Patrick was to hold the land *a me*, that is, directly of the king without the intermediate lordship of Robert. The rents owed from the property to the king, to the altar of St Mary in the burgh church, and to Sir Roger Wigmer, were now Patrick's responsibility. Sales might also take place under the auspices of the burgh community because the landholder was in debt and unable to pay. Such a case occurred in Perth around the turn of the century. John Malcolmson, a merchant who had apparently fallen on hard times, owed the king £4 Scots in royal customs. In order to raise the money two of the burgh bailies offered a land belonging to John for sale to his friends. As the friends did not buy the land, the bailies sold it to one of the leading burgesses of the town, John de Spens, and gave him sasine.[18]

The pledge or wadset of land also brought a lump sum to the granter. Land was often pledged for a number of years after which, if the debt was not paid, the creditor could take possession. In the absence of large banking institutions, townspeople often acted as bankers for each other, providing loans and taking property as collateral. By allowing the creditor to enjoy the revenues of a land while he held it, the debtor was able to pay interest on the loan, thus getting around the medieval church's prohibition on usury or taking interest. The burgh laws regulating pledging show that it was a common practice.[19] The pledging of goods for all sorts of transactions was a characteristic of urban life throughout medieval Europe.

Pledges often involved quite large sums of money. Sums could range from £12 to £100. The parties involved were generally the wealthier burgesses whose business transactions (or losses) might require a large capital outlay, or who could provide the cash required by the debtor. Pledges involved land both within and outwith the burgh and thus brought the burgess into contact with local lairds. It was usually the burgess who received the pledge, as he had readier access to cash than did the lord whose rents were paid largely in kind. When a burgess figures as debtor, it is usually another burgess who is the creditor. Pledges could involve annual rents as well as actual lands. In 1370 Walter Martin, burgess of Edinburgh, pledged to his co-burgess William de Lauder a twenty shilling rent from a burgh land in return for twenty merks sterling paid to him by William.[20] The rent was to remain with William until the twenty merks was repaid.

The most common form of alienation was the grant. The reason for the grant is rarely stated but many of the charters refer to a sum of money given to the granter 'in his grave necessity' and it may be that these grants were disguised sales. Such grants could benefit the original landholder in a number of ways. If he himself was a tenant of another burgess or lord he could both gain money by alienating the land, as long as his superior permitted him to do so, and free himself from the payment of the rent. If he granted a land to be held *de me*, that is, of him, he received a steady yearly income from it. Moreover, a grant of land or an annual rent would be an easier method of paying off a debt than attempting to find ready cash to reimburse a creditor. There were some restrictions placed on such grants. As well as the laws against alienating heritage land, some grants of burgh lands by the church, especially the Abbey of Arbroath, forbade the tenant to dispose of the property withhout licence from the superior.[21] In general, however, burgesses enjoyed almost exceptional freedom in their ability to dispose of their lands and rents.

Grants were also made to provide for younger sons, as marriage portions for daughters, and to support wives in the event of their becoming widows. They were also used to ensure spiritual rewards, as is shown by the great number of grants to the church in this period. Although the high survival rate of records of such grants as compared to more secular transactions means that the proportion of religious to secular grants cannot be accurately determined, nevertheless the number of grants to the church by towndwellers shows that they were a common feature of urban society. Their value varied considerably. Due allowance must be made for the pattern of the survival of the sources and the piety of the granter, but generally the largest grants came as would be expected, from the most prominent members of the burgh community. It has been noted in studies of medieval European merchants that they were sometimes uneasy about the preoccupation with profit as against more spiritual concerns and that this uneasiness often led them to make large grants to the church in order to expiate this sin. Certainly, Scottish merchants were generous benefactors to their local churches. John Crab, a wealthy trader and property-holder in Aberdeen, made grants of several of his lands and annual rents to the religious houses of Aberdeen. But less prominent townspeople also made their contribution. William Braid of Arbroath granted a 12d annual rent from a land in Arbroath.[22] The grants were usually made in free alms, requiring no service to be rendered.

The practice of granting annual rents to the church could lead to some complexity in the payment of rents by the tenant. It was quite common to grant only part of the rent of a land to the church. In 1329, for example, James Adamson was granted a land in Aberdeen for which he had to pay annually 2s to the granter, 3s to another man, and 3d to the abbot of Kinloss.[23]. As well as being confusing for the tenant, this situation is unfortunate for the historian as it means that the amounts stated in grants of annual rents cannot be taken as the entire rental value of the property, although they may give a general indication of the worth of the land when compared with other properties.

Lands were granted to religious houses to provide maintenance for the friars and to the parish churches to establish or assist in the upkeep of a particular altar and the priests serving there. In 1401, Robert Brown, burgess of Perth, granted 10 merks annual rent from his lands in Perth to augment divine service at the altar of St Ninian in the burgh church. The community of the burgh was called upon to give advice on the choice of the chaplain. In other cases, it might be involved in the actual administration of the lands which had been granted. Most grants by the community to individuals specify payments to altars, suggesting that this process must have been a fairly common one.[24]

As we have seen, the rental income as well as the land itself could be granted. By the later Middle Ages, and possibly quite early on in prosperous burghs, many lands were rented to sub-tenants for sums much higher than the rent due to the burgh overlord. Grants and pledges of annual rents became as common as grants of land. The rents paid by James Adamson in Aberdeen show that the rent could be divided up among several recipients, perhaps one going to a business associate, another to a relative and a third to a church altar. As with land, rents could be inherited; there are frequent references to an individual's possessions including 'lands, tenements and annual rents'.

It would be interesting to know what rights were conferred on the recipient of the entire annual rent of the burgage. Presumably such a grant would not qualify the holder for burgess-ship as it was the land itself and not its income that was the qualification, but the lack of detailed town records prevents certainty on this point. Practice may have varied between the burghs. Perhaps if the holder paid the rent due to the burgh superior, he might be able to enjoy the privileges of burgess-ship as well. Most holders of annual rents were unconcerned about this right, as either they were burgesses already or they were chaplains or friars, who appreciated the income but were little concerned with membership of the burgess community. In practical terms, grants of annual rents probably had little effect on the pattern of landholding in the burgh. The tenant might pay part of his rent to someone else but the ownership of the property remained vested in the granter.

The practice of granting annual rents shows the importance of money in urban society, and represents a step away from feudal society where land was the main medium of exchange among property-holders. While land remained an important commodity, direct grants of money revenues were becoming more and more popular. But this did not represent a complete break from the feudal forms of the countryside, as the payments were based on the possession of land. Furthermore, the alienation of annual rents was almost identical in its features to the alienation of land, with rents being treated simply as another form of property.

Having acquired burgh lands, on what terms did the recipient hold them? Could the tenure be described as feudal or was it something quite different? David Murray, in his concern to emphasise the unique nature of the burgh, distinguished sharply between tenure in the countryside and that in the towns.[25] Yet it may be argued that while tenure in the burghs did differ in many respects from that in the country, notably in the greater freedom of burgesses to alienate their lands, it still had certain elements which owed not a little to feudalism. For example, the holder of a rural property might be expected to render military service or its equivalent to his lord; the burgess had to contribute his share of time to the duty of watching the burgh by night. It could be argued that this service was a condition of burgess-ship rather than of the tenure of a burgage, but the two were so closely related that such a distinction would probably not have been drawn by contemporaries. Moreover, the burgess's status was based on the possession of land just as was the laird's. Second, there has been a tendency among burgh historians to lump together all burgh landholding under the term 'burgage tenure' thus giving an impression of a uniform tenure common to all burghs. This is to ignore the true complexities of the situation. While direct tenure of the burgh overlord in return for a money rent may have been the rule in the early days of the settlement, it was not long before an active market in burgh land had changed the situation. Different landlords, the various uses to which the lands were put, and the frequent transfers of property combined to create new forms of occupancy, often with services additional to those required by traditional burgh custom.

Variety of tenure seems to have been more characteristic of royal burghs than of baronial or ecclesiastical ones. There were fewer outside lords or institutions interested in having lands in these towns which in general were smaller and less important in trade than the royal burghs. Moreover, the burgh superior could keep a stricter eye on conditions in his one town than the king could on his many burghs. This more personal relationship, probably not always appreciated by the townspeople, meant that more control might be exercised by the burgh superior over landholding patterns and tenure.

Ironically, it was probably the abbeys, those institutions which held burghs where uniform tenure was the rule, which introduced into the king's burghs a type of tenure differing most markedly from the others. Arbroath Abbey had at least one property in most of the important towns in Scotland and thus the service of hospitality which it required of its tenants was known in many royal burghs. Moreover, charters by Arbroath relating to these properties include the clause 'saving to us the *iusticia regalitatis* and all other pleas we wish to hold in the said land'.[26] It is difficult to determine how extensive this jurisdiction was, but the use of the term 'regality' seems to indicate that the abbey reserved the right to hear both criminal and civil causes relating to the land. As most of these lands were granted to the abbey by the king in the twelfth century when burghal administration of justice was not very developed, it seems likely that he could simply set aside any claims to jurisdiction over the properties by those who were after all *his* burgesses. There were also other restrictions placed on the tenure of these lands as the tenants were not allowed to sell, pledge or grant them without the consent of the abbey. Thus any transfer of the lands had to take place in an ecclesiastical rather than a burgh court. This limited the participation of the other towndwellers in such transactions and served to emphasise the distinctive tenure by which the lands were held.

Those townspeople who were tenants of the church in royal burghs found their lands more heavily burdened than those who held directly of the king. On top of the rent to the church, they also had to pay the king's ferme, so they were in effect paying two rents. Although in the later medieval burgh, increasing rents made the 6d paid to the king an almost nominal amount, this was of little comfort to the landholder who had also to pay the larger rent. Nor was the church backward in making the most of its opportunities. In the fourteenth century Scone Abbey ensured that it would benefit from a period of rising property values in Perth. In 1354 it granted to John and Andrew Mercer a land in Saddlers' Street; in the first year of possession, they were to build a house, then the following year they were to pay 3s 4d rent. Up to this point, the grant echoed the practice of kirset in its provisions, but the canniness of the abbey was then revealed. In the third year the Mercers were to pay 6s 8d, in the fourth year 10s, and so on with the rent increasing by 3s 4d annually until it reached 26s 4d in the ninth year, from which time it remained stable. And just in case the Mercers attempted to ease the burden by delaying construction of the house, the abbey ensured that it would receive the stipulated sums by imposing a penalty of £6 if the house was not erected by the ninth year, this amount being equal to the total of the rents over the nine-year period. Other religious houses might require rent to be paid in a more practical form, such as wax for the lights of the church or foodstuffs such as herring.[27]

References to burgh lands held of the nobility show rents varying from 30d to one merk. Money rents appear to have been the rule. The tenants of such lands were an integral part of the burgh community. A burgh law states that burgesses holding a land of a baron were to be subject to the burgh officials in all civil cases and it seems safe to assume that they were also responsible for the duties which accompanied the possession of a burgage, at least if they wished to enjoy the privileges of burgess-ship. In this respect the Scottish burghs seem to have retained much more jurisdiction over their inhabitants than many English towns where the conflicting rights of a variety of noble and ecclesiastical holders of urban property could easily lead to confusion and complexity.[28]

The purchase and alienation of lands by the townspeople themselves also affected the picture of burghal tenure. If property was alienated *a me*, then the recipient held the land directly of the king, as had the granter. In grants made *de me*, the recipient became the tenant of the granter, but it is not always clear who was responsible for the payment of the king's ferme or the fulfilment of burgh duties. Those charters which do mention the payment to the king usually assign responsibility for it to the new tenant.[29] Perhaps where such a clause was not included the payment continued to be made by the original holder. It may have depended on whether or not the new tenant wished to claim the privileges of burgess-ship which might be associated with the land.

Burgh land could be held in free burgage, feu and heritage, for life, in free marriage or at will. Free burgage involved payment of the stipulated rent, performance of duties required by the burgh, and freedom to alienate the land. Land grants in feu and heritage were somewhat more restrictive. The granter's permission might be required to alienate the land, and the succession to the property might be restricted to the tenant's heirs of the body. Feu and heritage grants were common in the countryside and show the influence of feudal forms on burgh landholding. Grants for life were also found in both urban and rural areas, the recipients being women, who were thus guaranteed some property after the death of their husbands. The burgh laws provided for the widow by stating that she was entitled to the flett, the inner half of the family house, for the rest of her life after her husband's death.[30] Grants for life supplemented this provision and also any terce or dower which might have been agreed on at the time of the marriage. Several of the grants were made by husbands to wives – perhaps a recognition of their contribution to the increased prosperity of the family, or an attempt to ensure that they would be able to make a good second marriage. The interests of the women might also be provided for by grants of land by a relative to a bride and her new husband in free marriage. As with grants made to the church in free alms, no render was required in return. If there were no children of the marriage, however, the property reverted to the granter or his heirs on the deaths of the recipients.

The least secure form of tenure was that by which the land was held at the will of the granter. It was unlikely to be very popular and indeed it does not seem to have been very common. One of the few examples is found in Glasgow, where Emma Dulle held a tenement at the will of John de Govan, burgess of Glasgow, for 3s rent.[31] Emma was probably not a burgess and it seems likely that this form of tenure may have been more usual among non-burgesses who generally held their lands of the wealthier burgesses. Unfortunately, the sources remain silent about the terms on which most non-burgesses held their lands.

Tenure could also be granted for part of a property. In 1411 John Whitton, burgess of Edinburgh, granted to Martin Wright the whole fore part of his tenement on the High Street.[32] Presumably such grants would not include burgess rights as unless the recipient held other lands he would not have the necessary amount to make up one burgage rood. If he did have sufficient land scattered through the burgh, he may have been able to claim burgess-ship. One burgage in Aberdeen apparently consisted of two separate pieces of land.[33] Just as the integrity of the burgage rood could break down, so probably could the requirement that the land be held of the king. As the burgh assumed more control over its own affairs, it is possible that the fact that someone had land that would bind his interests to the burgh was seen as more important for burgess-ship status than from whom he held it. Indeed, if the burgess's immediate superior was another burgess, this might tend to bring him even closer to the burgh community.

Although historians should be careful not to use the term 'burgage tenure' to produce an over-simplified picture of the tenurial situation in the medieval Scottish burgh, this is not to deny that such a concept existed in the minds of contemporaries. In 1384 John Hossok, burgess of Inverness, granted a land in Inverness to William de Dunbar, burgess of Aberdeen. Perhaps because of the inter-burghal nature of this grant, John was careful to stress that William was to hold the land 'as freely as any burgage is held in the kingdom'.[34] Perhaps it was an achievement of the medieval mind that somehow all the gradations and variations of tenure in a society which was very conscious of such things could still form a unified whole, just as the different laws, customs and privileges of the different burghs did not detract from the central essence of the 'burgh'. 'Burgage tenure' did exist, but as an abstract concept rather than as a strict legal definition.

By the late thirteenth century and increasingly in the fourteenth century many burgesses had accumulated enough wealth through trade and industry to be able to invest money elsewhere and diversify their interests. Land proved to be an attractive investment for many. Duncan notes this urban tendency to acquire land in the thirteenth century, but concentrates mainly on rural property. A similar development was taking place within the burgh itself, part of a European trend.[35] Burgess grants to the church and inquisitions on heirs' succession rights are among the evidence which shows that some burgesses of the late medieval burghs were able to amass substantial amounts of urban property, usually spreading their holdings throughout the burgh. Sometimes there might be an attempt to consolidate them, but this tended to occur more with arable lands where consolidation could increase the value of the holdings.

It was the economic value of these lands which attracted the burgess investors. The ownership of several burgages did not confer any more trading privileges than did the possession of a single burgage, and could in fact result in the burden of extra services due to the community. Status was much more enhanced through the holding of rural properties than of urban ones. The main incentives for acquiring burgh lands were the rental revenues and their usefulness as a source of capital which could be mobilised relatively quickly through a sale or pledge. Unlike many rural properties which produced rents in kind, the rents from burgh lands were almost always in cash, a very useful commodity in the commercial world of the burgh and of overseas enterprises. Indeed, by the fourteenth century, there may be the beginning of a rentier class in the burghs,[36] although the evidence is too patchy for this period to determine whether or not there were some burgesses who derived their entire income from rents.

One of the best examples of these landholding burgesses is John Crab of Aberdeen. His properties in the burgh included a land in Upperkirkgate, some booths in Gallowgate, two lands in Netherkirkgate, one in Castlegate, one in Shiprow, four in the Green, and various other lands, including extensive holdings in the burgh's croft territories. In 1382 he granted £9 4s annually to the Carmelites from a group of his properties.[37] The rents varied from 40d to 2 merks. Some of the lands were his and were rented to tenants, while others were held by him of other burgesses and then sublet. The apothecaries' booths on Gallowgate and a newly-built-on property in the Netherkirkgate probably represent an investment of capital in his lands to make them more profitable. A land in Castlegate which Crab held of William Reid and which rendered a 2 merk rent to the Carmelites was presumably sublet by Crab unless he lived there himself, which, given the prestige of the area and the high rent, would be quite feasible. Crab also granted an 8s rent from a land in the Green, held by Nicholas de Etale of Thomas Reid. This could represent an annual rent which Thomas had granted to him from his own land or perhaps Crab was the ultimate owner of the property which had then been let and sublet.

The tenants of the investors included both burgesses and non-burgesses. Thomas Reid was a burgess and may represent a less wealthy group, who entered the urban property market by leasing land to rent out rather than actually purchasing it. Whether the subletter then paid the rent due to the owner of the property directly or as part of the payment to his immediate superior, is not clear.

Booths appear occasionally in these documents, suggesting an investment in the commercial potential of the property. Booths could be rented to merchants or craftsmen after they had been built by the owner of the land. There would probably be no shortage of takers, especially if they were conveniently sited near the market. For an individual whose own land was not so ideally sited, the renting of such a booth would be a cheaper alternative to purchasing property near the market. Richard Johnson, burgess of Elgin, believed in the commercial viability of booths as he built thirteen of them in the market-place of his town. John Wigmer, burgess of Edinburgh, was able to grant 13s 4d annual rent to an altar in St Giles from his booths.[38] Often these speculators were among the most prominent men of the burgh. Burgesses such as Adam Forrester and Roger Hogg of Edinburgh and John Mercer of Perth, held substantial properties in their burghs and were also important in national affairs. Others such as John de Kilmarnock of Ayr, Thomas Baxter of Irvine, and William Pop of Elgin,[39] appear in the records only because of the properties which they held.

It was not only urban land which was a source of wealth. Just beyond the burgh gates were other lands which could also be exploited for profit. The farming activities of many burgh inhabitants meant that land was needed by the burgh for the growing of crops and the pasturing of animals, as well as to supply peats for fuel and wood for building. Most burghs were given an allotment of land by their overlord to be used for agricultural pursuits. The *terra prepositure* found beside the northern towns of Elgin, Inverness, Banff, Cullen and Forres, the Boroughmuir of Edinburgh, the burgess acres of Ayr, and the croft territories of Aberdeen were used for this purpose.[40] With the exception of Ayr, where the burgesses paid an augmented rent of 12d for each burgage and the six acres of land pertaining to it, there is no indication of any rent paid to the king.As they were therefore of little financial interest to the crown, it seems likely that their administration was entrusted to the burgesses at an early date.

The king sometimes granted additional lands to the burgh at a later date. William granted the land of 'Croc' to the burgesses of Inverkeithing and the Burgh Haugh to Inverness, while Alexander II granted the five pennylands of Kyle to Ayr in 1236. In 1313 Robert I granted the care and custody of the Forest of Stocket to the burgesses of Aberdeen and in 1319 he included it among the possessions which they were to hold of him in feu-ferme. Usually the grant was stated to be 'for the support' of the burgh, leading Mackenzie to suggest that it was intended to replace the need for extra taxation to pay for local administration.[41] The revenue from these lands might therefore represent the origin of the 'common good'.

The way in which the lands were used varied depending on their nature. Pastoral and waste land were given over to common use. Here, the townspeople could pasture their animals, probably under the supervision of a common herd as at Aberdeen. In Glasgow, the *terra communis* was divided into three parts, one probably mainly for winter fodder, another for summer grazing and the third for timber and fuel. Some burghs such as Peebles might also be granted the right to resources such as peat and wood from lands not actually belonging to them.[42]

Lying closest to the burgh was the *terra campestris*, the arable land. It was usually divided up between the burgesses, with each individual being allocated a certain number of rigs scattered through the area. The rigs averaged about 200 metres in length and five metres in width, although topographical features could lead to wide variations. Four rigs usually made an acre, giving to each burgess of Ayr twenty-four rigs pertaining to their burgages. In Elgin in 1351 two burgages had four acres each of the *terra prepositure* pertaining to them. At first, the system of run-rig was apparently used, the rigs being reallocated at intervals to provide equal access for all to land of good quality. By the fourteenth century, if not earlier, this system had virtually disappeared and had been replaced by permanent ownership of specific rigs.[43]

In Elgin, the holding of arable land was still connected with the possession of a burgage, but in some other burghs this relationship was no longer in force. Aberdeen provides a particularly good example: the alienation of croft lands as complete in themselves strongly resembled the alienation of property within the burgh, with crofts being sold, granted and pledged in the same manner as urban properties. Several of those burgesses who figured prominently among the urban landholders had an equal interest in the croft territories, John Crab among them. Crab had considerable holdings in the croft territory of the Denburn to the west of the burgh, amounting to twenty-two pieces of land in 1350, as well as lands in the croft territory of the Gallowgate to the north. The Crabstane, lying west of the Denburn, and first appearing in the records in 1421, may be named after him. Another burgess, Adam Pingle, acquired three crofts at the end of the Gallowgate from his co-burgesses, one of them still known as the Aediepingle Croft in the seventeenth century; he also had a croft in the Denburn territory. The third croft territory was at Footdee to the east. Nor was Aberdeen unique. A 1348 grant by John de Kilmarnock of Ayr included sixty-four acres of land from the burgh territory. As with the lands within the burgh, much of the arable land was rented to other towndwellers.[44]

These lands were held like the burgages within the burgh, with their holders equally free to alienate them. The Aberdeen crofts figure frequently among the property transactions of the burgh, and it is apparent that, for some croft-owners at least, the crofts had become less important for their agricultural potential than for their value in terms of capital. In some cases they were even divided and rented to more than one tenant. Laurence de Foty's land in the Denburn territory was held of him partly by Thomas de Mar and partly by William Chalmer in 1399. Those who had several holdings in the burgh territory could make a sizeable income from renting the lands, although some individuals may also have directly exploited part of their holdings. John de Govan granted to the Friars Preachers of Glasgow three rigs in the field of 'le Croupis' for which 30d rent was paid, one rig in the field of Broomielaw which yielded 5s rent, and another seven rigs in Broomielaw for which no rent was stated. Perhaps John had used these lands himself as there is no tenant named.[45]

Fishings pertaining to the burgh might be leased to individual burgesses by the burgh administration, sometimes in shares as small as $^1/_{32}$ of a net. In 1399 the fishings of Aberdeen included 'the Raik', leased for 60$^1/_2$ merks, 'Mid Chingle' at 24 merks, 'Pot' at 30 merks, 'Fords' at 37$^1/_2$ merks and the north water (River Don) which was leased by forty-one different individuals at amounts ranging from 13s 9d to 55s for a total of £44. The rents show that fishings were considered to be a valuable possession. If a burgh had mills as part of its property, they too could be leased to individuals.[46]

According to the *Articuli Inquirendi*, the chamberlain on his yearly visit to the burgh was to inquire if there had been just setting and return of the common good and account made to the community in the last year, implying that leasing of the burgh agricultural lands was commonplace. The burgesses of the fourteenth and early fifteenth centuries seem to have shown more foresight than their successors who later engaged in large-scale feuing of the burgh lands. They rarely leased the land on other than short-term leases. Three years was the usual lease in Aberdeen, thus anticipating an Act of Parliament of 1491 which stated that no burgh land was to be let for more than three years – that such an act needed to be passed implies that the practice of feuing was becoming more common in the fifteenth century. The short-term leases also include provisions to safeguard the rights of the community. When Aberdeen let the land of Rubislaw to William Chalmer in 1399 for an annual rent of £3, it was stipulated that the inhabitants of the burgh should continue to have common pasture for their animals there.[47] Despite the increasing commercial investment in the burgh's agricultural lands, the town-dwellers' connection with the activities of the countryside continued.

Townspeople interested in properties outside the burgh did not confine themselves to the burgh territories. They also acquired rural estates and thus became partially integrated into the feudal system of landholding which prevailed in the country at large. As Duncan has pointed out, there was little investment needed in burgh industry during this period and therefore land provided an alternative. Even in Flanders, with its highly-developed urban industry, there was a similar expansion of burgess landholding into the countryside in the fourteenth century.[48] The charters reveal little of the motives for the acquisition of rural property, but they would have been various. Financial gain would result from renting portions of the land and from selling the produce in a market where the burgess landlord enjoyed several privileges, including freedom from tolls. Such land was also free from the collective restraints imposed by the burgh on its own agricultural lands.[49] The land could be used as collateral for business enterprises, could be exchanged for other land, and if pledged to a creditor, could provide the interest on a debt. And, probably never far from the townsdweller's mind, such land provided social status, enabling the burgess to mix and marry with landowning families on a basis of equality.

There were several ways of acquiring such properties. Royal grants accounted for some, but most common were grants by the nobility, ranging from powerful national figures to local landowners. There was probably a similar motivation for many of the granters. The burgess had the cash needed for the purchase of luxuries befitting noble status, and the sale of land to him provided a quick way of obtaining money for a landowner whose rents were paid mostly in kind. These transactions had a two-way effect. Not only were the burgesses beginning to participate actively in the feudal system, but the lords were increasing their participation in a cash-based market economy.

Land might also be granted for 'service', although unfortunately the nature of the service is rarely specified. Sometimes land was given to burgesses who had been active in such services to the crown as negotiating David II's ransom, arranging commercial treaties with Scotland's trading partners, and participating in royal government through fulfilling the duties of various crown officials. Often the king would grant revenues from the burgh fermes, promising to later grant the recipient lands rendering an income of equal value. The church also rewarded service with land grants. Scone Abbey gave John Mercer the lands of Kincarrathie for his help with obtaining the church of Blairgowrie, while Adam Forrester was granted the land of Fingask by the bishop of Aberdeen for help which was not specified, but may have been his aid to the bishop in a dispute with the lord of Forglen over the second tithes of the wardship of the land of Meldrum. In one case, practical considerations seem to have dictated the form of such a reward. Robert I granted Peter de Spalding, burgess of Berwick, who had betrayed the town to the king in 1318, in exchange for all his lands in Berwick, the lands of 'Ballourthy' and 'Petmethy' in the sheriffdom of Forfar, possibly near the place of origin of his family and certainly far removed from those burgesses of Berwick who might harbour a grudge against him.[50]

Many burgesses acquired control of lands through direct payments or loans. Nicholas de Lidell, burgess of Aberdeen, bought the lands of 'Athinwyokis' in the Mearns for 27 merks sterling. Alexander Abercromby of Murthlie leased certain lands to John Mercer for eight years for £40. Pledges could result in permanent possession. In 1375 John McKelly pledged the lands of Echline in the sheriffdom of Edinburgh to John de Cairns, burgess of Linlithgow, to hold until McKelly paid £80. McKelly must have had trouble meeting his payments as the Cairns family still held the land in the 1420s.[51] The incomplete nature of the records for most pledged lands makes it difficult to determine how often they were redeemed, but it seems likely that some of the grants of land may have been the result of earlier pledges.

Marriage was another avenue to the acquisition of lands. In late medieval Scotland, burgess status, especially if it was accompanied by wealth, was no barrier to marriage with the landowning class. Burgesses were seen as suitable husbands for lairds' daughters, while the marriage of a laird's son to a burgess's daughter would almost certainly bring a sizable tocher or dowry, a welcome addition to the family finances. There is more evidence of marriage between townsmen and noblewomen than between townswomen and noblemen, but this may be partly due to the nature of the marriage agreements. Because a laird's daughter was likely to bring land to the marriage, her permission was required if it was to be alienated and she therefore appears in charters of alienation along with her husband. A burgess's daughter was more likely to bring money to the marriage and therefore was less likely to appear in land grants, unless they related to burgh lands which she might have inherited. A grant by Robert III to William Dubrelle of all the lands which Elena Tollare had held in Inverkeithing before she married William implies a burgh origin for Elena.[52]

Burgesses marrying into landowning families usually acquired land with the marriage, either as a marriage portion granted by the bride's father or through the wife's inheritance on the decease of her father. These lands were usually held in conjunct fee, that is, in joint possession. Adam Pingle of Aberdeen married Marjorie Blackwater and was infeft in conjunct fee with Marjorie in the lands of 'Knock and Gelestan' in the sheriffdom of Kincardine. John Mercer married into the family of Tullibardine and by 1352 had acquired the lands which the earl of Sutherland had granted to the late Sir William Murray of Tullibardine. William de Spens, burgess of Perth, married Isabel Campbell, heiress to the lands of Drummond, Bohapple, Glendouglas and Tarbert. As this marriage shows, a burgess's land interests could extend far beyond the bounds of the burgh. At the other end of the scale was the marriage of Adam de Melville, burgess of Linlithgow, to Elizabeth, one of three daughters of Henry del Orchard, by which he acquired a third of Henry's lands in Upper Lamberton.[53]

Rural properties could also be acquired from other burgesses. Adam de Melville sold his third of land to John de Raynton, burgess of Berwick, in 1332. John eventually consolidated the holding by acquiring the other two thirds from Elizabeth's sisters. In the 1390s Thomas Kymbdy of Aberdeen was granted the land of 'Athquhorthy' in the lordship of Findon by his co-burgess William Chalmer. Grants of such lands from father to son were also common. Chalmer granted the lands of Methlick to his son Thomas in 1400, while John Crab granted his son Paul the land of Kincorth which had been pledged to John by the abbot of Arbroath.[54] In both cases the recipient was apparently a younger son and therefore a specific grant was necessary if his elder brother was not to inherit the property.

As did their fellow landholders, the burgesses held these lands in some form of feudal tenure. The most common service asked was suit of court, that is, attendance at the head courts held by the land's superior lord. This might be combined with other renders. John de Raynton of Berwick held the lands of Billie in Berwickshire for the payment of a rose upon the feast of St James the Apostle and 8s sterling to the lord of Bunkle with ward and customary suits of court at Bunkle. Even when land passed to a burgess in the form of a pledge which might mean only temporary possession, services such as suit of court might be required. John de Cairns was to hold the land pledged to him by John McKelly in chief of John de Dundas, lord of Dundas, rendering service and suit of court until McKelly repaid the money.[55]

Some of the lands were granted in blenche-ferme (that is , with only a nominal yearly render) with the *reddendo* being only 1d if asked. In 1359 Thomas, earl of Mar, granted William de Leith of Aberdeen the lands of Rothens, 'Harebogge' and 'Blakeboggys' in the regality of Garioch for 1d in blenche-ferme, while in 1351 John Crab was granted by Adam de Gardropa, lord of Rubislaw, all the lands in his lordship of Denburn for one pair of white Parisian gloves or 2d silver.[56] Blenche-ferme grants were usually made to the most prominent burgesses of the period. Others might be expected to render various services to the feudal superior. Peter de Spalding was responsible for the portion of knight service due from the lands granted to him by Robert I, while John de Raynton was to render homage and other customary services to the earl of Angus for the lands of Billie. Special service to the king, forinsec service, might also be required. Duncan Kymbdy of Aberdeen was granted lands in feu-ferme, saving forinsec service to the king, about 1317, while William Pilch, burgess of Inverness, who was granted lands in blenche-ferme in Inveralyne, also rendered forinsec service.[57]

Some lands were held for what appears to be an economic rent. John Mercer rendered 53s 4d to Scone Abbey for the land of Kincarrathie, although in this case the abbey was somewhat more generous in its terms as Mercer had ten years in which to build on the land before paying rent. William Chalmer paid ten merks per year for the barony of Murtle granted to him by the bishop of Aberdeen in 1388, while Patrick Forrester, burgess of Dundee, paid 40s for his lands in Fife.[58] Economic rents were especially common in one situation: when the grant of land was made by the community of the burgh. Several burgesses made grants of a country property to an altar of the burgh church. Responsibility for maintaining the grant usually passed to the burgh after the granter's death. The most effective way for the burgh to carry out the wishes of the granter was to grant the land to another burgess in return for an annual rent which would then be applied to the altar. For example, John de Allincrum, burgess of Edinburgh, granted his lands of Craigcrook to the altar of the Virgin Mary in St Giles. In 1377, the community of the burgh granted Craigcrook to Patrick and John Leiper, burgesses of Edinburgh, in return for an annual payment of £6 6s 4d to the community to be used to maintain the altar.[59]

Because there are few references to burgesses actually inhabiting their lands, whether urban or rural, it is difficult to determine what effect the ownership of country property had on an individual's place of residence. It seems quite likely that many continued to live in the burgh, at least for part of the time. Certainly several of the early royal charters to the burghs laid stress on residence in the burgh as a prerequisite for the enjoyment of burgess privileges.[60] In most cases the lands acquired were fairly close to the burgh in which the new owner held his burgage (see map), and could probably be reached easily when necessary. Only a few burgesses held lands a long way from the burgh, and these tended to be men such as Adam Forrester who were heavily involved in national affairs and would travel over much of the country in the course of their duties. In Edinburgh, many of the country properties held by the burgesses are now within the boundary of the modern city. Men such as William Chalmer of Aberdeen and John Gill of Perth continued to be active in burgh life even after the acquisition of several rural properties and their

frequent appearance in the burgh records suggests that they may
have continued to live in the burgh. Roger Hogg of Edinburgh had
a number of lands outwith the burgh, but in 1363 he lived in a
tenement on the High Street.[61]

Not all burgesses followed this pattern, however. Some may have
divided their time between their country estates and the burgh, while
the fact that some preferred their country lands is suggested by a
1317 list of Aberdeen burgesses *rure manentes*, living in the country.[62]
There are thirty-seven names, which probably represented a sizable
proportion of the burgess population but this may have been an
exception because of the troubled times through which the kingdom
and burgh had just passed. As peace returned, and with it the
likelihood that the burgh would not be attacked, many burgesses
may have returned to take up residence. Thirteen of the names are
scored through, and it may be that these were men who had returned,
although the lack of burgh records until 1398 means that this cannot
be verified. It is also possible that they went elsewhere, that they
forfeited their burgess privileges in some way, or that they had died.
That the residence requirement was not strictly observed in all
burghs by the fourteenth century is shown by a 1359 reference to two
burgesses of Dundee, who were described as *extramanencium* and
did not even have any possessions in the burgh.[63] Here are the first
traces of the development of a burgess status based entirely on the
payment of a fee rather than on the holding of a burgage. The
problems which could arise from this situation made themselves felt
even at this early stage, for the debts of these two men could not be
recovered as they had no possessions within the burgh or even within
the sheriffdom.

The problems of non-residence were to increase in the later
fifteenth and sixteenth centuries, especially with the practice of
creating honorary burgesses, but it seems that in the fourteenth and
early fifteenth centuries most burgesses who held country lands were
able to combine the two roles of burgess and feudal landholder. Even
men such as Adam Forrester, with his properties scattered through
eastern Scotland, still devoted time to burgh affairs. This ability to
reconcile landholding within and outwith the burgh had important
ramifications, for by bringing country properties under the control
of men used to a commercially-based economy, it had the dual effect
of introducing burgh ways to the country and the ways of the country
to the burgh. The possession of property, while it helped to define
the burgh, was also one of the means of integrating it with the
countryside.

Illustrations

Map 1. Burghs appearing in the records before 1430.

Wick

Cromarty Elgin Banff
Dingwall Nairn Cullen Rattray
Rosemarkie Forres
Auldearn
Inverness
Fyvie

Newburgh
Inverurie Kintore
Aberdeen

Inverbervie

Forfar Montrose

Dundee Arbroath

Perth

St. Andrews
Auchterarder Cupar
Newburgh Crail
Dunblane
Stirling Kinghorn Kirkcaldy
Dunfermline North Berwick
Dumbarton Edinburgh Dunbar
Linlithgow 2 1 Haddington
Tarbert 3 4 5
Renfrew Langton Berwick
Glasgow Kirkintilloch
Rothesay Dalkeith Lauder
Rutherglen Peebles Kelso
Irvine Lanark Roxburgh
Prestwick Selkirk
Newton-upon-Ayr Jedburgh
Ayr Crawford
Sanquhar

Staplegorton

Lochmaben
Dumfries
Buittle Annan
Innermessan Wigtown Urr
Kirkcudbright
Whithorn

1 Queensferry
2 Inverkeithing
3 Canongate
4 Musselburgh
5 Seton

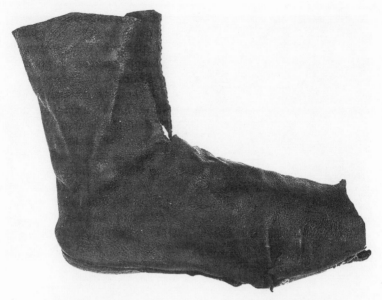

1. Leather shoe from Perth. The archaeological photographs are reproduced with permission of the Scottish Urban Archaeological Trust.

2. Lathe-turned wooden bowls from Kirk Close, Perth.

3. Wooden lavatory seat from Kirk Close, Perth.

4. Clay metal-working mould from Perth.

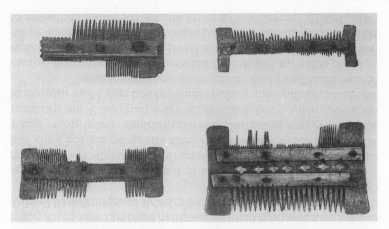

5. Decorated bone combs from High Street, Perth.

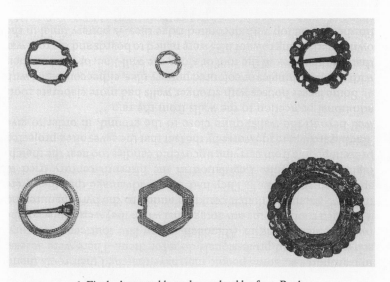

6. Finely decorated brooches or buckles from Perth.

7. Medieval Perth local pottery jug from Mill Street, Perth.

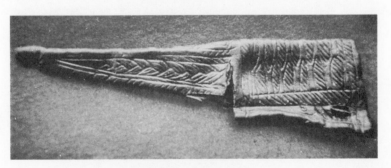

8. Leather sheath from Perth.

9. Elgin aerial view, showing a typical medieval plan of one long main street, widening in the centre for the market, the long narrow burgages, and the castle at one end. (RCAHMS).

10. Glasgow Saltmarket. The timber-framed houses of the burgesses would have resembled these later examples. (RCAHMS).

11. Fordell's Lodging, 18 Church Street, Inverkeithing. One of the oldest surviving secular urban buildings, part of it dates from the fifteenth-century. (RCAHMS).

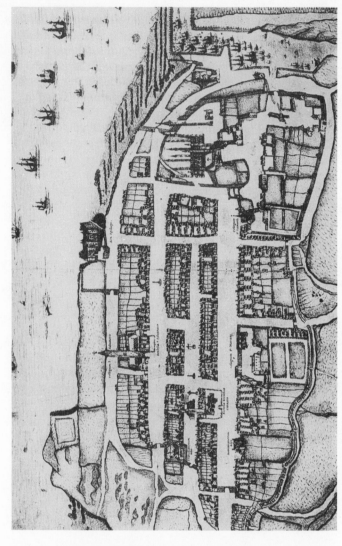

12. Sixteenth-century bird's eye view of St. Andrews. The plan shows a typical layout of the medieval burgages. (Trustees of the National Library of Scotland).

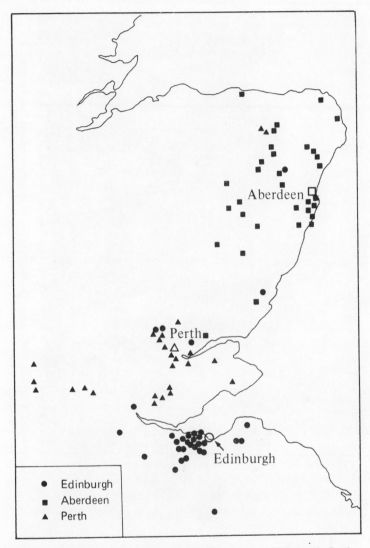

Map 2. Properties held outside the burgh by burgesses of Edinburgh, Perth, and Aberdeen in the fourteenth-century.

13. St Michael's Church, Linlithgow. This nineteenth-century drawing shows the medieval church and its tower, which is now topped by a modern steeple. (RCAHMS).

14. Effigy in St John's Church, Corstorphine, of Adam Forrester, one of the most prominent burgesses of the late fourteenth-century. (RCAHMS).

15. The Battle of Bannockburn from fifteenth-century manuscript of Scotichronicon, Corpus Christi Cambridge MS 171, f.265, showing Stirling houses. (The Master and Fellows of Corpus Christi College, Cambridge).

5 The Burgh in the Kingdom

Historians discussing the Scottish medieval burgh have often tended to see it as an enclave of monopolistic privilege, cut off from the rest of society by the regulations designed to maintain and foster its commercial prosperity.[1] This view considers the burgh only in terms of its legal status, however, neglecting economic and social considerations. The townspeople may have been governed by a separate code of law (although in many respects it was not so different from that which governed the rest of the country) and enjoyed certain trade monopolies, but at the same time they forged close ties with those groups which made up the kingdom outside the burghs.

From the early days of urban life, the dependence of the townspeople on the hinterland ensured that the burgh gates symbolised entry to, rather than exclusion from, the burgh. With the growth of trade, the interdependence of town and country increased. While the expanding burghs depended ever more on the resources of the countryside, those living in the hinterland increasingly relied on the trade of the burgh to dispose profitably of their surplus produce and to provide manufactured goods, both of a cheap and a luxurious variety.

Burghs were dependent on the countryside for the basic resource of population. Lack of evidence makes it impossible to determine the relative proportion of foreign and native settlers in the early burghs, but even if a town was at first largely settled by foreigners, its continued growth and prosperity would depend on attracting new settlers from the local country population. Medieval towns were unhealthy places, unable to replace their populations without constant recruitment from outside. In England it has been estimated that urban families often survived only three generations,[2] and a similar pattern emerges for medieval Scotland. By the fourteenth century, surnames suggesting a local origin were common in most burghs, indicating the links between the new towndwellers and their relatives in the countryside. Young people from the country could come to the burgh to work as servants for town kinsfolk while the burgh, for example, could supply the surplus labour required at harvest time.[3]

The market was the main source of supply for basic foodstuffs for the burgh population, but, as is not surprising for a people only recently separated from a rural way of life, urban families were also capable of exploiting the countryside for themselves. That this was expected is shown in the burgh charters which mention common lands, mills and fishings. Dundee's feu-ferme charter states that the burgh could use its common lands for all types of agriculture. Burgh mills processed the grain. Garden produce could also be grown in small plots in the long rigs stretching back from the frontages. Finds of medieval garden earth at sites in Aberdeen, Perth and Inverness suggest that small-scale cultivation within the burgh itself was not uncommon. As in many medieval European towns, agricultural activity remained of some importance, with many Scottish burghs retaining a distinctly rural appearance.[4]

Many of the plants and animals found outside the burgh were to be found within the burgh as well, although in smaller quantities. Burgage plots often lay unbuilt on and waste for some time and during this period weeds and wild plants might flourish there. Seeds could be blown from nearby fields and marshes into the back yards of inhabited burgages and could flourish there as well if a family neglected to weed its garden. Certain vegetables and plants were cultivated by the townspeople: cabbage, turnip, swede and kale have all been found in excavations. Blaeberries, rowanberries, brambles and raspberries also supplemented the grain-based diet of the majority of the inhabitants.[5]

The frequent appearance of garden earth at many urban sites, as well as later maps showing gardens stretching behind the frontages indicates that small-scale gardening was a common feature of town life. Areas associated with religious houses often had especially large gardens, which could provide a good proportion of the food for the members of the house and perhaps even a surplus for sale at the market. At one site in Aberdeen there is even evidence of possible land reclamation by the Carmelites in the rather marshy area of the Green.[6] Perhaps market gardening was proving a valuable enough occupation to make it worthwhile expanding the area under cultivation, or possibly the population of the institution was increasing. In either case, it seems likely that the brethren, who were meant to be vegetarian, were able to contribute much of their own food requirements from land within the burgh.

Animals were also kept within the burgh. Each of the wealthier burgesses of late thirteenth-century Berwick was expected to have a horse, and Scottish merchants of the fourteenth century travelling to

England went on horseback if they did not go by sea.[7] What appear to be property boundaries running across some excavated burgage plots may in fact be stock barriers, separating the livestock from the inhabitants' living area, although animals were sometimes kept in one part of the house in backland areas. Hay found at some sites may have been used for wintering animals. In Aberdeen in 1400, the lands of Rubislaw were used by the townspeople to pasture their animals.[8]

Food supplies could also be supplemented through hunting and fishing. Animal remains uncovered so far suggest that the percentage of venison in the local diet increased the more northerly the burgh, implying a possible erosion of hunting rights in the more southerly burghs, or a lack of deer due to deforestation.[9] Most burghs also had fishings granted to them, thus allowing them to exploit a valuable natural resource both as a source of income and as an additional food source.

The hinterland supplied the additional foodstuffs required by the burgh population, but also the raw materials for almost every aspect of burgh life, from house-building to heating and industry: even the styles of the backland houses reflected the traditional rural buildings. The wattle and daub houses demonstrate especially well the reliance on the hinterland – for a small house of about three metres square, the builders needed about 1000 wattles, timber posts, clay or animal dung for daub, and heather, broom, or similar material for thatching. Wood might come from riverbanks, hedges or wayside trees. The type of timber available often determined the type of houses built.[10]

The heathland and marsh plants found near many burghs had several uses. Heather, bracken and mosses provided bedding materials. Moss could be used for packing, making ropes,or even as a form of toilet paper. Heather, broom and grasses thatched the roof while other vegetation might be laid down underfoot to help dry up damp floors. The flooring was cleared out periodically and returned to the fields as compost. Sand from nearby riverbeds was also used as flooring.[11]

The raw materials for burgh industry came mainly from the hinterland, although luxury trades might make use of materials imported from abroad. As well as wool for the cloth industry and hides for leatherworking, there was flax for the manufacture of linen and oil, timber for woodworking (although this was becoming increasingly scarce from the fourteenth century), clay for pottery-working and animal bone and horn for the varied articles made from these substances.[12] On market days, some of the finished products of these industries would find their way back to the countryside.

Sometimes documents reflect the lack of practical distinction between town and country. Malcolm Fleming, earl of Wigton in the fourteenth century, granted Newbattle Abbey one acre of arable land in the burgh of Dumbarton.[13] While it is possible that this acre was in the common lands surrounding the burgh rather than among the burgh roods, the phrase 'in the burgh' shows that the burgh was not regarded as a purely urban institution. Indeed, it would be surprising if the concept of a completely urban settlement did exist in such an overwhelmingly rural society. References to 'arable burgage land' and to the arable lands pertaining to tenements and burgages imply that the connection between the townspeople and the country continued to be an important part of their lives throughout the medieval period.[14]

Agricultural pursuits were not the only links between the burghs and the rest of the kingdom. Through the various activities of individual townspeople connections were formed with the crown, the lords and the church, thus making many of the townsfolk an ever more integral part of Scottish feudal society. Although trade might play an important part in a burgess's career, there were other avenues to wealth and status, amongst which service to the crown could prove one of the most rewarding.

As elsewhere in medieval Europe, one of the most useful services which the burgesses could provide to the king was to lend him money. Royal debts were as common a feature of the period as government debts are today, despite, or perhaps because of, the belief that the king should be able to live off his own income. David II was forced to pledge part of the royal jewels to a Flemish merchant and his queen pledged her jewels to an Edinburgh merchant.[15] The reason for the pawning is not clear, although it may have been related to the expenses of setting up a royal establishment once more after the long period of captivity in England. Pawning of royal jewels was not confined to Scotland. The bankrupt English crown did the same shortly after the death of Edward III in 1377.

Repayments of royal debts occur frequently in the accounts. It is often unclear whether these represent repayment of loans or payment for goods sold on credit, but even if they were the latter, they were still in essence loans by the townspeople to the king and as such represented an extra source of revenue for him, albeit one which was supposed to be paid back. It was not only prominent townspeople who loaned the king money. In 1361 the widow of Alexander Bell, an Edinburgh burgess about whom almost nothing else is known, was paid 53s 4d for an old debt owed by the king to her husband.[16] Although in the fourteenth century the average debt was £27, about half the debts recorded were under £10.

Some urban businessmen, however, invested large amounts of capital in royal loans. The largest creditors tended to come from the most prosperous burghs. Between 1359 and 1364 Roger Hogg of Edinburgh was repaid £172 9s owed to him by the king. The debts owed to John Mercer totalled over £224 at the time of his death; Andrew Mercer continued his father's pattern and was owed £400 in 1385. In these circumstances, it is not surprising that Roger Hogg and John Mercer were the men entrusted by the crown with supervising David II's early ransom payments to the English king, handling large amounts of capital being one of their areas of expertise. The burgess Adam Forrester became one of the main royal creditors of Robert II and of his son, both as earl of Carrick and as Robert III.[17]

As with many trading ventures, some of the loans were funded by a partnership, sometimes based on work contacts. In 1364 Adam Tore, master of the Edinburgh mint, and James the moneyer were repaid £400 for a loan. Two burgesses of Aberdeen lent the king £45 some decades earlier.[18] Indeed, there may have been many more partnerships than are evident in the records,as although most repayments were made to only one person, this does not rule out the possibility of joint funding for the loan.

Money-lending did not always prove to be the wisest investment for Scottish businessmen. In a number of cases, debts were not repaid until after the creditor's death, as the example of Alexander Bell shows. The debt was probably contracted quite some time before Alexander's death, as when it was repaid to his widow, it was stated to be 'an old debt'. John Mercer's loans to the crown were repaid to his executors, while part of a debt owed to Alan de Balmossy, burgess of Dundee, was paid to his sons after his death, in 1362. In these cases at least the lender's heirs benefited, but it seems quite likely that many other debts were simply allowed to lapse after the creditor's death. Another drawback became apparent in 1370 when all royal debts contracted before 1368 were repudiated, an action which seems to have led to a dramatic decrease in the amount of credit extended to the king by the burgesses.[19] Confidence was apparently restored by the 1380s, however, when the amount of money repaid roughly equalled the repayments of the 1360s.

The amount contributed by burgess loans to royal revenues cannot be calculated before the return of David II from his English captivity because of the incomplete nature of the Exchequer records to this time. However, in the years 1357–71 over £950 was paid to burgess creditors. The nineteen-year reign of Robert II saw £923 2s 6d paid for burgess loans, over £900 of the total being paid in the 1380s. Altogether for the fourteenth century the recorded debts to individual burgesses totalled just over £2500. Taking into account the incomplete records, and the fact that this amount represents only the repayment of the debts, not the debts themselves, it is apparent that the real value of this source of revenue was much higher than these figures suggest.

As well as providing money to the king, the townspeople supplied him and his family with furnishings, victuals and clothing. The return of David II from England produced a new demand for such articles and the burgesses were quick to take advantage of the expanded market for both imports and domestic products. In 1357–71 almost £1500 was paid to individuals for such goods. The visits of the itinerant medieval kings to the various burghs gave the townspeople the chance to make connections and contracts with the royal household.[20]

With their monopoly over foreign trade and their commercial enterprises, the burgesses were well-qualified to provide the foreign goods required by the court of which wine was one of the most important. In England, wine was the main drink of the upper classes and one of that country's major exports, and it seems that the drinking habits of the English were echoed by the Scots, despite the English habit of sending to Scotland wine which was considered unfit to drink in England. The royal household was the most important consumer of wine in the kingdom. In the fourteenth century payments for wine made up over 15% of the payments to individual burgesses for household supplies. The price varied – a pipe usually cost between £4 and £5, and a tun between 10 merks (£6 13s 4d) and £8. Usually the wine went to provision the royal family and its guests but occasionally it was sent to others as a gift from the king. In 1379 one tun of wine was sent to Sir John de Danielston on the king's mandate. The burgh laws and guild regulations show that the burgesses also purchased wine for themselves; fines for misdemeanors often consisted of a specified amount of wine rather than a money payment.[21]

The royal kitchen and the royal palate benefited from the townspeople's provision of foodstuffs, especially fish which might come from the burghs' fishings. Victuals might also come from the burgesses' country properties. It is likely that the oats supplied to the king in 1397 by William Crumby, burgess of Haddington, were from his own lands, as he had corn fields near the burgh. The king's horses had in fact damaged some of the crop, so possibly William's sale was partially due to an uneasy royal conscience.[22]

Exotic foods such as spices and sugar were brought from abroad, as were supplementary supplies of wheat and malt when needed. In 1369 a Scottish merchant, Henry de Dunbar, was given an English safe-conduct to bring back to Scotland forty quarters of malt for David II. Such safe-conducts were necessary, although not always effective. In 1328, two hundred and forty quarters of wheat shipped by a burgess of Berwick from Picardy for the royal wedding was plundered on its way to Scotland, while victuals bought for the king by a burgess of Aberdeen in 1364 suffered a similar fate.[23]

A safer source of supply was the burgh market. Goods were often purchased there, sometimes with an arrangement for them to be carried to the king's residence. In 1359, Laurence de Garvock, burgess of Aberdeen, was paid for carrying wheat to Monymusk, while in 1389 John de Cairns, burgess of Linlithgow, was paid for several carriages of wine and other commodities for the king's use. An individual might also be given the responsibility of provisioning the royal household when the king visited his burgh. John Mercer was repaid for the king's expenses at Perth during two stays there in 1359 and 1360. Matthew Ferrour, burgess of Stirling, received £3 in 1388 for victuals which he supplied to the king while he was at Stirling.[24]

Clothing was often bought from burgesses. For David's wedding in 1328 most of the cloth was supplied by Flemish merchants, but as the century progressed, Scottish merchants took an increasing part in this trade. In the 1360s William de Leith, burgess of Aberdeen, was supplying cloth and velvet to the crown. Cloth was probably among the purchases described simply as 'divers things for the wardrobe'. The burgesses also provided furs. In 1342 Richard Rokpot of Aberdeen was paid £6 10s for 1½ pieces of cloth and four furs of white budge. The ill-defined line between craftsman and merchant is shown by a payment to Bridinus the butcher at Banff for cloths and furs bought for the king in the same year.[25]

Other townsfolk dealt in more specialised goods. Jousting equipment and armour were supplied to David shortly after his return from France, and Laurence de Spens, burgess of Perth, provided divers necessities for another tournament held in 1380. The provision of munitions for the royal castles showed the burgesses combining business interests with a contribution to the defence of the realm.

£27 worth of supplies for Edinburgh Castle were ordered from Patrick de Lumley, burgess of Lanark, probably in anticipation of the English attack of 1385. Among the items were saltpetre and sulphur, suggesting an early use of firepower.[26] In 1370 John Crab of Aberdeen was paid £15 11s 5d for buying munitions in Flanders for Edinburgh Castle; he also made an unintended monetary contribution to the kingdom's defence for in that year all payments to royal creditors were made at a deduction of one third.[27]

Unfortunately, the terms 'divers things' and 'furnishings' obscure the nature of most of the goods supplied by the burgesses. Payments in this category account for over half the total sum expended on such goods, and individual payments are among the highest ones made. Patrick de Innerpeffer, burgess of Dundee, received £108 9s 9d for 'furnishings' in 1388, while John Mercer was paid £238 6s 10d in 1364. The terminology tends to support the idea that most Scottish merchants of this period dealt in a variety of commodities rather than specialising in one particular article. Among the items included in furnishings were brass pots, silver basins, salt-cellars, wax and balances.[28] Some townspeople supplied the king with articles of their own manufacture. John Goldsmith, burgess of Edinburgh, made a mace which was bought for the king in 1359, and other ornaments for the monarch in 1361. Robert Rollo, a baker in Aberdeen, was paid for supplying provisions, probably including bread, for the royal household while it was at Aberdeen, Kindrochit and Glenconglas in the 1380s. Aberdeen craftworkers made armorial bearings for the king in 1364 and clothes for the royal family in 1342.[29]

As well as supplying goods, the burgesses provided a variety of services to the king. Several of them were employed in royal building projects, especially those connected with Edinburgh Castle in the reign of David II. John de Cairns and William Gupild, burgesses of Edinburgh, helped build the new castle tower, the remains of which now lie beneath the Half Moon Battery. Roger Hogg was involved in the construction of a new wall and well-tower in 1361–2, while in 1383 Adam Forrester was paid for the erection of a kitchen and other necessary buildings. The wealth and contacts of these prominent burgesses made them ideal choices to oversee such work, as they would know where to secure craftsmen with the necessary skills. Adam Forrester may have recommended employing the mason John of Scone to carry out the lead-work on the castle, as it was the same John who was one of three masons who contracted with the burgh of Edinburgh to build five new chapels in St Giles. Adam Forrester was one of the leading members of the community in this endeavour.

Sometimes the skills of the burgess himself might prove useful. In 1362 Nicholas Mason, burgess of Stirling, was paid £5 along with other masons for work on Stirling Castle.[30] Probably the best known example of a burgess involved in the king's works is that of John Crabbe of Berwick, who built up the defences of the town for the Scots and then destroyed them for the English. John de Raynton, who unlike his fellow-burgess seems to have stayed on the side of the Scots, also contributed to the defence of the town and castle, and was paid £13 6s 8d for the protection of the walls and the castle in 1330 when there were ominous signs of danger from the south.[31] Other royal building projects also involved burgesses. John Scot of Inverness hired out his ship to carry wood to St Monans in 1365 and 1368 for David II's new church there. In a project of equal interest to the king and a burgh, David Scot, burgess of Montrose, was paid to build a mill by Montrose in 1329. On a more intimate level, burgesses were also involved in the work of preparing royal tombs. Andrew Painter, burgess of Edinburgh, was sent to Flanders to buy black stones for the tomb of David II in the early 1370s, and towards the end of the decade was paid for bringing stones for the tombs of Robert II's mother and father and also for Robert's own tomb from England to Edinburgh.[32]

Although the royal household was usually accommodated in castles or monasteries, burgesses sometimes leased out houses for various members of the court. In 1329 John called Aylbot of Perth was paid for leasing his house for two years to the king's physician. In later years Adam Mercer rented out another house in the burgh to store the king's victuals, while a house belonging to Walter de Strathearn was used for the royal wardrobe. The house of John de Corry in Edinburgh was occupied by the mint in 1359.[33]

The burgesses could also serve their royal master in affairs of state. Their contribution to the Scottish resistance in the Wars of Independence, both through securing supplies and carrying out attacks on English shipping has already been noted. Individuals such as Alexander Pilch of Inverness aided William Wallace, while the attack on Edinburgh Castle in 1341 was carried out with the help of three burgesses of Edinburgh, William Bartholomew, Walter Curry and William de Fairley.[34]. Burgesses were also sent on various diplomatic missions: Adam Forrester was particularly active in trying to preserve peace between Scotland and England in the late fourteenth century. John Wigmer, burgess of Edinburgh, was sent to England in 1348 to treat about David II's ransom, while Alexander Wigmer, probably John's son, travelled to England to discuss the method of

payment after David's return. John Dugude, burgess of Perth, was
in Prussia on the king's service in 1383.[35] Adam Tore of Edinburgh,
William Feth of Dundee, William Chalmer of Aberdeen and John
Mercer all served as envoys to Flanders during the fourteenth
century. Burgesses continued to serve as diplomats in the fifteenth
century. As well as their knowledge of foreign countries gained from
trading activities, their wealth and resources were very useful for
fitting out the embassies.[36]

Another way to serve the nation was to undertake the responsibilities of royal office. Indeed, service in the royal household and the
government – and these were often the same thing – could result in
royal favour which would provide the basis of a family's fortunes.
The requirements of commercial enterprise demanded the ability to
supervise accounts, making merchants well-qualified for the position of auditor. Adam Forrester, Patrick de Lumley and John
Ochiltree were among the burgesses who served as auditors of the
Exchequer accounts. John Rollo, burgess of Edinburgh, and Patrick
de Innerpeffer acted as auditors of the earldom of Strathearn in
1380.[37] Burgesses were also effective suppliers of provisions for the
royal household, and therefore a suitable choice for the position of
steward. William de Leith served as steward of the queen's household in 1359, while Andrew Mercer was steward of the king's
household in 1388.[38] The royal official who had most contact with
the burghs was the chamberlain. He often entrusted his more
onerous duties to deputies, who might be chosen from the towns
which he supervised. Patrick de Lumley, as well as filling the post of
auditor of the Exchequer, was also deputy for the chamberlain south
of Forth from 1391 to 1398. A burgess might also be appointed to
fulfil the duties of a chamberlain who had died while in office. John
Mercer was one of two men appointed to render the chamberlain's
accounts after his sudden death in 1376. Eventually, the logical step
was taken and the position was filled by a man from the burgess class.
In the early fifteenth century, Sir John Forrester, the son of Adam
Forrester who had served as deputy-chamberlain in 1388–91 and
1404–6, became the king's chamberlain, an office which he held for
most of the reign of James I.[39]

A royal post apparently reserved exclusively for burgesses was that
of master of the mint. When a new mint was established in Edinburgh in the 1350s, Adam Tore was put in charge of it. The burgess
John the Goldsmith was also heavily involved in the operations of the
mint, although the office of moneyer was filled by a Florentine. A
local man became keeper of the money in Perth when a mint was

opened there in 1373.⁴⁰ Apparently, a burgess, used to handling money, was seen as the person best qualified for such a position.

Government service led to national prominence for some townsmen. The organisation of David II's early ransom payments was largely entrusted to John Mercer, helped by the Edinburgh burgess Roger Hogg. In 1360 Mercer was in Bruges, busily collecting together all the money for that year's payment, and sending messengers to England to arrange the method of delivering the money. Details of his actions are given in the account he rendered to the Exchequer for that year. In 1373–6 he acted as treasurer for the ransom money. His services were considered important enough that in 1378 he was allowed to deduct 2000 merks from the ransom installment as compensation for the losses he suffered when imprisoned by some over-zealous Englishmen in 1376 during a time of truce between the two countries.⁴¹

Adam Forrester carried out a variety of roles in his career in government service. He was clerk of the customs rolls south of Forth in 1363 and 1366. In 1382, by which time he had become a prominent landholder in the area around Edinburgh, he was sheriff of Lothian. After serving as a deputy-chamberlain, in 1391 he was made custodian of the great seal while the king's chancellor was absent. He audited the Exchequer accounts from 1388 to 1404, and then served as deputy-chamberlain for two more years. His high position in government was recognised when he was given a major role in the peace negotiations with England at the turn of the century.⁴²

Government service could also involve offices which were more directly connected with the burgh. The organisation of the customs system required a variety of officers and in many cases it was the townspeople who took on the responsibilities. As well as custumars, there were several other officers whose function it was to supervise the activities connected with customs collections and thus safeguard a major source of royal revenue. For example, early in David's reign, a separate customs rate was imposed on foreign merchants and in some cases separate officers were appointed to collect the tax. In 1332 William Martin who had been a custumar until the previous year carried out this task in Edinburgh in conjunction with Gilbert de Leith, one of the serving custumars. Sometimes extra taxes were imposed on the export of English goods and special collectors were appointed for this too.⁴³ Gilbert de Leith also served as custodian of the cocket. The clerk of the cocket, whose office probably developed from the custodian's, kept a record of all customs paid on exports and all other particulars relating to the export business of the burgh. His book could be checked against that of the custumar by the auditors of the Exchequer. He often held half of the cocket seal and was therefore required to be present when goods were being customed. The office could be a hereditary one. Duncan Rollo, burgess of Edinburgh, succeeded to the post after the death of his father John. Between them, the two Rollos filled the position for forty-eight years, from 1372 to 1420. Those who were appointed to the post were expected to fulfil the duties personally – Richard Scot, clerk in Dundee in 1397 and 1398 required royal permission to appoint a deputy in the latter year.[44]

In 1364 an act was passed for the setting up of a tron or public weighbeam in every port. Here the wool and hides would be weighed before export and the appropriate customs rate charged. The act also provided for a tronar in each burgh and burgesses in Linlithgow, Perth, Dundee, and Montrose are all named as filling this post.[45]

The central figure in the customs system was the custumar whose office was bestowed by royal grant, and it is his accounts which survive in the *Exchequer Rolls*. Usually there were two custumars to a burgh, although the number could vary and sometimes one man served as custumar for more than one burgh. William de Dunbar was custumar for Inverness, Elgin and Forres in 1383–5, while the role of custumar of Haddington and North Berwick was filled by a burgess of Haddington from 1375 to 1381. Sometimes a deputy was appointed, for which apparently, royal permission was not required.[46] Most custumars were burgesses, although others including constables, sheriffs and even clerics could be appointed to the position. Usually the individuals chosen had some connection with the town even if they were not burgesses. In Dundee in the 1320s Marjorie Schireham, who was not styled burgess but was probably the wife or daughter of the burgess Gregory Schireham, played an active part as custumar of the burgh. Those chosen from among the townspeople were usually the most prominent and respected members of the community. Among the custumars are many whose names have been mentioned earlier: Adam and John Forrester in Edinburgh, William Chalmer and Adam Pingle in Aberdeen, Patrick de Innerpeffer in Dundee, John and Andrew Mercer in Perth and John Scot in Inverness.[47] All were prominent landowners and figures of consequence in the community and often beyond it.

The life of the custumar was by no means a sinecure and could even prove hazardous at times. Apart from the anger of merchants who felt they had been overcharged, the custumar had sometimes to deal with problems from a higher source. In the late fourteenth century, the duke of Rothesay was given the power to collect the revenues from the custumars, but abused this right by extorting money from them. He kidnapped the unfortunate custumar of Montrose and kept him prisoner until he paid the sum demanded, even though the poor man had already given the whole balance to the chamberlain.[48] Acting as custumar could prove to be an expensive proposition, for which the fee of 1d per sack of wool[49] might not totally compensate.

The customs also provided another link between the crown and individual townspeople, allowing the king to reward his servants, either through remissions of customs on exports or by annuities payable from the customs revenues. Gregory Chapman, burgess of Stirling, was allowed to export wool without paying customs in 1380. Sometimes only a part of the export duty was remitted. Some merchants were freed from paying the extra duty on English wool which was sent to the Continent from Scottish ports.[50] Most annuities paid to townspeople came from the customs, although a few were paid from the burgh fermes. The amounts ranged from £2 to £13 6s 8d. These pensions did not go just to the custumars, although they figured prominently among the recipients. Among them was Marjorie Schireham, who was well-rewarded for what was a rather unusual occupation for a woman of her time.[51]

Another beneficiary of royal gifts and pensions was the church, townspeople sometimes acting as middlemen. Northern churchmen such as the bishops of Caithness and Orkney were largely dependent on burgesses of Aberdeen to convey their annuities to them, while a payment of tithes by the custumars of Edinburgh to the abbot of Paisley was made with the help of Patrick de Lumley.[52] The most active individual in such work was Adam Forrester who acted as middleman at various times for the bishop of Aberdeen, the Dominican Friars of Edinburgh, the bishop of St Andrews, the abbot of Melrose and the abbot of Dunfermline. The receiving of money for the abbot of Dunfermline seems to have become somewhat of a family business, as Adam carried out this duty from 1383 until his death when the money was received by his son Sir John.[53] Most of the townspeople who carried out this task were also serving the crown, for it was usually in the capacity of bailies or custumars that they took charge of the payments.

Townsmen sometimes served the church by giving aid and counsel to churchmen involved in disputes over lands and rents. In 1386 Adam Forrester helped the bishop of Aberdeen in a dispute with the lord of Forglen over the second tithes of the wardship of the lands of Meldrum. His help proved effective for in 1392 the bishop granted him lands as a reward for his 'council, help and service'. Burgesses also acted as witnesses to agreements made by the church with secular landholders. William Chalmer witnessed an indenture between the bishop of Aberdeen and John Forbes in 1387 and another one between the bishop and the earl of Moray in 1389.[54]

In their capacity of merchants, townsmen supplied the needs of ecclesiastical households much as they did the royal household. The servants of religious establishments bought provisions in the burgh markets. If the records of an episcopal household had survived, burgh merchants would probably have figured prominently among those supplying the rich trappings of the medieval bishops. The church made much of the burgesses' overseas trade possible by providing a large share of the country's exports of wool from its extensive flocks of sheep. Churchmen also watched over the interests of individual merchants. In 1365 the bishop of St Andrews requested the English king to give a safe-conduct to the merchant William Talyfere allowing him to ship grain to Scotland.[55] It seems likely that the grain was for the bishop's household.

A towndweller might supply goods to the church as a merchant, pay it rent as a tenant, contribute money in tithes, and grant it lands or rents for the salvation of his soul. In ecclesiastical burghs, the burgh fermes went to the church while annuities to religious institutions were often granted from the fermes of other burghs. It was therefore in church interests to see the towns and their people prosper. Usually the relationship between the church and the towndwellers was a fairly amicable one. Medieval Scotland saw little of the prolonged and sometimes violent conflict between towns and their ecclesiatical overlords which affected several English and Continental towns. The townspeople were not afraid to stand up for their rights, however, and defended their privileges before parliament in trading conflicts or rent disputes such as that between Newburgh in Fife and Lindores Abbey. Sometimes individuals also came into conflict with the church. John Crab of Aberdeen had a dispute with the bishop of Aberdeen over the lands of Murtle, which he held of the bishop. William Chalmer defended the interests of his co-burgess. Perhaps the bishop was impressed by his defence, for on Crab's death in 1388, he granted the lands to Chalmer.[56]

Occasionally, the church was subjected to more than legal battles. In 1357 a royal mandate to the sheriff of Aberdeen was required to prevent Laurence de Garvock, burgess of Aberdeen, and his adherents from infringing the rights of Arbroath Abbey in the lands of Nigg. In 1366 there was an even more serious attack on church property, when thirty burgesses and fishers of Stirling joined together to wreck the nets and fishings of nearby Cambuskenneth Abbey in the Forth.[57] Apparently, respect felt for the spiritual nature of the church did not always extend to its rights of property-holding.

On the whole, however, relations were peaceful. The links between the townspeople and the church were strengthened further by the recruitment of new religious, both as clergy and as members of religious houses. Education at establishments in the burghs run by the church helped to supply a body of literate young men who might go on to train for the priesthood. Many of the scholars who went to England and Europe (and from the early fifteenth century to the University of St Andrews) for further education and then entered the priesthood seem to have come from urban families, who would have had the wealth to pay for such an education. Among the families who probably produced graduates were the Forresters and the Allincrums of Edinburgh, the Colonias and Reyntons of Berwick, and the Pullars and Mercers of Perth. John Pilmore, bishop of Aberdeen, was apparently the son of Adam de Pilmore, burgess of Dundee. Sons of burgesses became notaries public, a position under the control of the church, masters of hospitals, and chaplains. Not all entered the church: men such as Robert de Gatmilk returned home to take an active part in the administration of their burghs.[58]. Others, both within and outwith the church, made a career for themselves in royal service and thus provided valuable contacts for burgess relatives interested in serving the crown.

Concern for spiritual salvation also kept strong the bonds between the burgesses and the church. Scotland participated in the upsurge of lay piety which marked medieval Europe in the fourteenth and fifteenth centuries, often expressed in the form of gifts of lands, moneys and sacred objects to the church, gifts made in the hope that material contributions might help one's chances of attaining salvation in the afterlife. For those who were wealthy enough, added intercession could be assured through the founding of an altar, where masses would be said for the founder's soul. In some of these gifts, there was also a worldly dimension, as contributions to the parish church, a centre of community life in the single-parish Scottish burghs, increased the donor's status in the eyes of fellow townspeople.

Most of the grants made by the townspeople to the church in this period were directed to the burgh church or to religious houses connected with the burgh. Relationships with the major religious institutions of the kingdom, the bishoprics and the large abbeys, tended to be confined to those of urban tenant and ecclesiastical overlord. The fullest records of burgess grants to the church come from Aberdeen, where the cartulary of the burgh church of St Nicholas and the charters of the religious houses which were preserved by Marischal College show the medieval people of Aberdeen actively supporting their burgh church and the local religious houses of the Carmelites, Trinitarians, and Dominicans. In the case of St Nicholas, it was not just revenues which the burgesses contributed to the upkeep of the church. The building had been badly damaged in an English attack on the burgh in 1336, and the Aberdonians were determined to restore it to its former beauty. Several altars were founded and furnished with religious ornaments such as images of saints, gilt chalices and holy vestments, older altars were given new images, repairs were made to the floor of the church, and the building itself was extended by the alderman William de Leith with the assistance of the community. A burgess was appointed to be in charge of church funds,[59] representing the continuing interest of the community in its church. A similar concern with the parish church is evident in the records of grants to St Giles in Edinburgh. With the exception of major projects such as expanding the existing building, however, most of the grants were made by individuals or small groups. In the fifteenth century, craft guilds began to imitate individuals by founding and maintaining various altars within the burgh churches.

Most grants to religious houses were made on an individual basis and consisted mainly of gifts of lands and rents. In Aberdeen, many of the burgage roods and crofts had part or all of their rents assigned to one or more of the burgh's religious houses. Nor were the friars lax in safeguarding their income. Any default in rent was quickly acted upon. In 1409 the prior of the Carmelites complained before the burgh court that the rents granted to his house by John and William Crab had not been paid. Paul Crab, who was then in possession of these lands, was obliged to resign them to the prior.[60] Such grants were not to be made lightly by the townsfolk, for they affected not only the granters but also their successors.

While some burgesses found employment in service to the church or the crown, others were offering their skills to the lords and magnates of the kingdom in trading activities, administration and government services. Archibald Douglas, lord of Galloway, and John of the Isles were among those who employed merchants to secure provisions for them from abroad.[61] Some individuals may have found full-time employment in this capacity, as about one-third of them appear in the records only in this connection. Other men put their administrative skills at the service of local lords, acting as bailies to give sasine of lands or as procurators and attorneys for those resigning lands. Other townsmen carried out duties as deputies for local officials. Gregory Bowman, burgess of Kintore, rendered the account of the sheriff of Aberdeen to the Exchequer in 1328. Sometimes such service was reciprocated. In 1341, William de Meldrum, sheriff of Aberdeen, acted as attorney to render the burgh accounts of Aberdeen.[62]

Many lords and magnates received pensions from the crown from the burgh fermes or customs. As with the church, townsmen often acted as middlemen for the payment of these sums. Adam Forrester counted many secular as well as ecclesiastical lords among his clients – one historian describes him as a 'financial agent for all and sundry'. Among his noble customers were Sir William Stewart of Jedburgh, the earls of Douglas and Caithness, the earl of Carrick (later Robert III) and the duke of Rothesay.[63] Other burgesses followed suit, although with rather fewer clients.

Nobles sometimes asked townsmen to be arbiters in their disputes. An agreement between the bishop of Moray and the lord of Badenoch was arrived at in the house of Thomas Johnson, burgess of Inverness, while John de Pitscottie of Perth was an arbiter chosen by William de Fenton in his dispute with the Abbey of Cambuskenneth. Andrew Mercer made a judgment in a disagreement over the lands of Logy and Strathgartney between the earl of Fife and John Logie, kinsman of David's second queen, and recorded that they accepted his decision 'strekand thair handys in myne, bodely makand gude fayth that thai sulde halde sekir, ferme, and stable'.[64]

Lords and townpeople also took joint action on occasion. They fought together in many of the campaigns of the Wars of Independence, for example. On a less elevated level, Robert Davidson of Aberdeen and the earl of Mar were companions in piracy and in the early years of the fifteenth century they captured a Prussian ship on its way to Flanders. The resulting diplomatic row led to a number of reprisals and it was some time before normal trade relations with the Baltic cities were resumed.[65] Magnate participation in burgess affairs was not always beneficial.

Foreign trade gave the burgess the opportunity to improve his own standard of living. Men such as John Mercer, whom the English chronicler Walsingham reports as having had 'inestimable wealth', must have lived more comfortably than many a local lord.[66] The burghs, as centres of overseas trade, gave access to imported luxuries for those who could afford them, while the goods produced by urban craftsmen were generally of higher quality than those made by their rural counterparts. For the wealthier towndwellers, therefore, there was little to prevent them from living in a style similar to, or even better than, that of many of their landowning neighbours.

One essential characteristic of lordly status was the ownership of land. In the fourteenth and fifteenth centuries this became an increasingly common part of the lifestyle of wealthy burgesses. As land conferred lordship, the possession of country estates gave burgesses an entree into the class of local lords. Intermarriage between the children of burgesses and local lords was not uncommon and helped to blur the line between the two groups.[67] Although on a national level burgesses were identified with the third estate, in the world of the burgh and its hinterland, the distinctions between second and third estate were far less clearcut.

Some burgesses styled themselves as lords of particular lands after acquiring them. John Gill of Perth often called himself John Gill of Halton when appearing in lists of burgess witnesses after 1370. Adam Forrester was known as lord of Nether Liberton from 1387, but by 1397 was styled lord of Corstorphine. Other burgesses might use such titles only on certain occasions when they were deemed appropriate. Thus William Chalmer of Aberdeen called himself lord of Findon when he appointed a bailie of the barony of Findon; when he himself received grants, he was sometimes referred to as lord of Auchneeve, but when he was involved in burgh affairs, he did not use these titles.[68] Another way of acquiring titles was through royal service. Both Adam Forrester and his son were knighted. William Chalmer, when he went on a diplomatic mission in 1394, was known as esquire. Andrew Mercer was Sir Andrew by 1385.[69] As all these men also had extensive landed possessions, their status among the noble class was assured. Royal service provided the final legitimation for entry into the second estate.

Some burgesses were given possession not only of the land but also of the unfree men who were regarded as belonging to that land. Grants in free barony to William Chalmer, William de Leith and Patrick de Innerpeffer included the ownership of neyfs (bondmen and women) and their progeny. During the 1300s the institution of serfdom was dying out in Scotland and it seems therefore that these grants may not have bestowed much practical power on their recipients in this respect, but were important for what they implied about attitudes towards the burgess recipients. The fact that such grants could be made to townspeople shows not only how highly they could be regarded, but also how completely they could be absorbed into the feudal world beyond the burgh, while yet retaining their burghal identity.

6 The Community

The townspeople of medieval Scotland were more than a collection of individuals, each pursuing his own livelihood. Within their own burghs, within the burghs as a whole, and within the kingdom, they were part of a community. The laws which governed their lives, the interests which dictated their actions, and the conditions of trade and industry within the Scottish society of the time, all led to a sense of community which helped the burgesses exercise far more influence in the nation's affairs than their small number might have implied.

For the townsfolk this sense of community had its roots in the individual burghs. As Susan Reynolds has pointed out, a sense of community was characteristic of all medieval groupings of people from villages to kingdoms,[1] and the burghs were no exception to this rule. Indeed, the early burghs needed unity among their early settlers for their very survival. Trade would not prosper in a town without some degree of harmony and consensus among its members. Common economic interests encouraged unity, while grants of exclusive privileges to the towns also fostered community spirit. Privileges required to be protected and administered and the best way to do this was through communal action and rules.[2]

Physical propinquity also encouraged a sense of community. Residence in the burgh was regarded as an important qualification for burgess-ship. As was common throughout Europe, a serf seeking to become a burgess had to live in the burgh for a year and a day before being allowed to enjoy the privileges of the burgh.[3] Many royal charters lay stress on residence in the burgh as a condition for enjoying the privileges granted. When William I erected the burgh of Ayr, the liberties he granted were given to the burgh and the burgesses dwelling within it. The feu-ferme charter granted by Robert III was likewise made to the burgesses and community of Ayr inhabiting the said burgh. Similar references were made in royal charters to Irvine, Haddington and Lanark. The feu-ferme charter to Banff in 1372 was quite specific in its attitude to those burgesses who did not live in the burgh, stating that they were not to enjoy the grant of the burgh nor any emolument, commodities or liberties. A number of grants gave certain privileges to those who resided in the burgh but were not burgesses. All inhabitants of Dundee were allowed to trade in the market as long as they shared with the burgesses the responsibility of paying royal contributions.[4] Such grants made clear that enjoying common privileges involved assuming common burdens.

One of the problems of discussing the concept of community in the burghs is determining who was included in that community, although this is a question which has concerned historians more than contemporaries.[5] On the status and rights of non-burgesses within the burgh, the records are almost entirely silent. In the early days of the burghs it seems to have been assumed that most adult males would be burgesses – women and children enjoyed trading and other privileges through their husbands or fathers, but did not partake in the political life of the town. As immigration from the countryside increased, the proportion of non-burgesses grew. Many, if not most, of the new inhabitants lacked the resources to purchase the land required for burgess-ship, and found employment as domestic servants and employees for established inhabitants. The backlands buildings excavated in Scottish burghs are generally of a poorer quality than those found on the frontages; probably many of these are the dwellings of the poorer inhabitants of the town.[6] There are few regulations among the burgh laws dealing with the welfare of this segment of the population, but this does not necessarily imply that they were considered to be outside the community.

Two points can be made about the participation of this group in the community as a whole. First, inequality of status does not prevent people from feeling themselves to be part of the community. In medieval society, inequality was an accepted part of life. More-over, most people had economic and social links which united them with the burgesses. Servants, apprentices and workers living in the households of their employers tended to become closely affiliated with those households and felt as much a part of the community as did the families of the burgesses. Even those living elsewhwere, and given the small size of the towns they were never far away, shared much of their waking hours with their employer and would share similar priorities and interests. The family-based organisation of burgh trade and crafts[7] fostered a close relationship between the poorer and better-off members of the burgh.

Secondly, the lack of political privileges did not have the impor-tance in medieval times which it assumes today. For many, attain-ment of burgess status was not a crucial goal – after all, it brought added responsibilities as well as extra privileges. 'Getting and spending, incurring poverty and debt, making profits, ... seeking pleasure and amusement'[8] were of equal importance in life for many. On the whole, it was felt that political leadership was best vested in the hands of the most important members of the burgh, who had both the time and the money to devote to it. If the interests of a group of non-burgesses was threatened, they could appeal to the burgesses for help. In 1366 a group of fishers from Stirling were helped in their attack on the fishings of Cambuskenneth in the Forth by twenty-three burgesses of the town.[9]

On the whole, it was accepted that the burgh government, chosen from the burgesses, would do its best for the community as a whole. Sometimes, of course, it failed to reconcile all the different interests which were the inevitable part of a trading community. This was especially the case with price legislation, where attempts to protect the welfare of one segment of the population by ensuring low prices were sure to meet with protest from the producers of the goods. But even though there might be complaints from those adversely affected, there was no apparent interest in changing the status quo. Nor would change come from below. Those who were ambitious enough to achieve burgess status were far more likely to identify themselves with their fellow-burgesses than the unenfranchised. But again this distinction lays too much stress on legal differences. In the burgesses' minds, they represented the community and therefore they *were* the community.

As the burghs grew, laws were developed to govern urban life. In promoting the interests of the inhabitants, these laws also helped to create a sense of community. The responsibilities laid on the townspeople included many reciprocal duties probably imposed 'to foster the spirit of good neighbourship by the interchange of friendly services'.[10] Various transactions were validated by the witness of neighbours. If a burgess found himself in trouble outside the burgh, his fellow-burgesses would go to help him out. The market was so regulated that no burgess would be able to enjoy special liberties at the expense of another. Weights and measures were inspected to prevent fraud, and 'just prices' for necessities proclaimed so that all could secure supplies. Other laws ensured the welfare of burgesses who were sick or poor, as well as that of families whose provider had died. As burgesses replaced royal officials in local government, those placed in positions of responsibility were reminded that their duty was not only to the king but also to the burgesses.[11]

The administration of the laws was carried out by the burgesses themselves, assembled in the burgh court. Such collective legal activity was common in towns and villages throughout medieval Europe.[12] Here the burgesses heard disputes, imposed penalties, and proclaimed and approved new statutes, as well as admitting new burgesses to their community. It may have been the bailies or town council which initiated such actions, but usually it was the community which gave the action final authority. In some burghs the assent of the community may have been a mere formality, but in others, as suggested by the use of the phrase 'the major part of the community', it seems likely that the motions placed before the community could be the subjects of some debate.As attendance at the burgh court was one of the duties of burgess-ship, the occasion underlined their corporate identity. Sometimes the court even gave scope for non-burgess involvement, especially if it was held out of doors, for even if non-burgesses could not express individual opinions, they could always add their voices to general calls of approval or dissent.[13]

The community was more than an abstract concept in medieval Europe. In the Scottish burghs it was a body capable of initiating actions and assuming responsibilities seen to be in the best interests of the burgh and its inhabitants. It was, to all intents and purposes, what would be called today a corporation; although contemporaries did not call it this, they would have recognised the concept, and they gave legal recognition to craft corporations from the mid-fifteenth century.[14] The symbol of the community, as with the craft corporations, was its seal, the common seal of the burgh. This was usually attached to any record of actions in which it took part, although it is a mark of the lack of concern with exact legal requirements that it was not actually required to validate the action. If the seal was not available, as seems to have been the case on a number of occasions in Aberdeen at the end of the fourteenth century, the seals of the bailies would do just as well.[15]

As Reynolds has shown, the whole idea of collective activity, has very old roots in Europe, going back long before the resurgence of urban life in the eleventh century. Corporate ideas probably existed in the Scottish burghs from the first establishment of local government, although there are no surviving records to show this. Hints of such ideas are first recorded in the mid-thirteenth century, when a sale of burgh land by the prior of St Andrews is witnessed by the whole court of the burgesses of St Andrews, acting as a community, although not yet styled as such. It is significant that the scene of this communal action should have been the burgh court, for here, more than anywhere else, the burgesses were brought together as a community. By 1275, a grant of an annual rent to the abbey of Arbroath could be dated ' in the presence of the community of the burgh of Arbroath', and by 1283 a sale of land in Glasgow included the phrase *teste communitate*, witnessed by the community.[16] By the fourteenth century the form *teste communitate* was used in several burghs, including Dundee, Lanark and Aberdeen.[17] By this time also the crown had formally recognised the existence of 'the community of the burgh' and the majority of royal grants from this time on were made to the burgesses and/or magistrates and the community.[18]

The community dealt not only with the king but also with the church and with local lords on matters affecting burgh interests. By an indenture between the burgh of Irvine and Brice de Eglinton the burgesses and community put at feu-ferme to Brice twenty acres which his brother Ralph had earlier granted to them. Brice was to hold the lands of the burgesses and community, paying 10s annually. As was customary in transactions between two individuals, the burgesses and community warranted the land. A dispute over the £20 owed to the Ayr Blackfriars from the burgh fermes of Ayr was settled by an indenture between the Friars and the burgesses and community of the burgh of Ayr in 1406.[19]

Most interaction between the burghs and the church or local lords had to do with lands, mills and fishings of which the burgesses made use. The grant of feu-ferme charters gave many burghs control over such pertinents but before this the ownership, use and duties owed on these burghal adjuncts were often in dispute, especially as they were often granted to institutions or individuals outwith the burgh. In resolving such issues the burgesses acted as one body and strengthened their sense of community. Mills were especially contentious subjects. In 1330, an indenture between the burgesses and community of Elgin and Pluscarden Abbey resolved their quarrels over multure (the toll in grain or flour) owed by the burgesses and community to the abbey for the use of the mills of Elgin. The dispute between Ayr and the Blackfriars involved mill rents as well as burgh fermes and dragged on for over twenty years.[20]

By granting land to the burgh, the crown gave formal recognition to the community's right to hold land, an important privilege in medieval society. In the later Middle Ages the community not only received land grants, but was an active landholder, setting lands at ferme both for the benefit of the burgh and on behalf of the burgh church. The lands included properties both within and outwith the burgh. In Dumfries, the stone houses known as the Newark were the property of the community of that burgh. The community of

Aberdeen set at ferme to William de Dunbar, burgess of Aberdeen, arable burgage land in one of the crofting territories, for a render of 4s to sustain a mass at the altar of St Mary in the burgh church of St Nicholas.[21]

This last grant illustrates a common reason for the community to set lands at ferme. Just as the community delegated the responsibility for administering the lands, fishings, and other sources of revenue which were granted to it in a feu-ferme charter by leasing them to individual burgesses, in the same way it delegated the task of administering the lands granted to the burgh church. Many of the charters which founded an altar or provided for the maintenance of a priest specified that after the granter's death, the community and magistrates of the burgh were to be responsible for providing a priest. In a sense the burgh community was acting as the government of its parish as well.[22] In 1331, Kelso Abbey and the community of the burgh of Roxburgh jointly provided a priest for the high altar of the burgh church through a grant of Roger de Auldton, burgess of Roxburgh. Such provisions were accompanied by the responsibility to maintain the priest by administering the lands and rents granted by the founder. Setting the lands and rents at tack was seen as the most effective way of doing this. An example of the process appears in the *St Giles Register* which records the 1362 charter by the Edinburgh burgess John de Allincrum granting the lands of Craigcrook near Edinburgh to the altar of the Virgin Mary in St Giles. In 1377, the aldermen, bailies and community put these lands at feu-ferme to the burgesses Patrick and John Leiper, who were to pay annually £6 6s 8d for the sustenance of the altar and its chaplain. A grant of lands and rents by John de Whiteness, burgess of Edinburgh, to both the altar of the Holy Cross and the community of the burgh was probably intended to provide the community with a clear right to administer the grant for the altar. The Edinburgh community's concern for the burgh church was demonstrated in 1368, when it was decided that all such grants were to be recorded in a register in order to safeguard them for the church, and that all entries were to be made under the supervision of the alderman and community.[23]

The administration of church revenues and the provision of priests for altars were only two of the tasks undertaken by the community on behalf of the burgh church. As in towns and villages throughout Europe, the church was the focus of community life and spirit, both secular and religious, a place where the community worshipped together, held meetings, and witnessed transactions by its members. The Elgin churchyard may even have been the site of the burgh market. The church was an object of pride, a visible symbol of a community's confidence in itself. From the mid-fourteenth to the mid-fifteenth century this pride was demonstrated in at least ten burghs, including Haddington, Linlithgow, St Andrews and Dundee as they either rebuilt, repaired or extended their churches. While individuals contributed to the foundation of altars and the maintenance of priests, extensive work on the actual fabric of the church involved the whole community. In 1355 the provost of Aberdeen, with the assistance of the community, extended the choir of St Nicholas to the altar of St Leonard, although whether the money came from the common good funds of the burgh or a special tax for the purpose is not clear. The extension of St Giles church in Edinburgh by the construction of five new chapels was arranged with three masons by Adam Forrester, Andrew Yutsoun the provost, and the community in 1387. The masons eventually received £600 for the work. Some of this money was collected from the guild. In Edinburgh, the dean of guild was also master of the kirk work by 1453 and it may have been in this capacity that Adam de Spot, dean of guild in 1401, collected money from the guild in that year.[24]

The guild had an especial interest in the burgh church as religious activities were an important part of its functions. Just as the church could provide the townspeople with spiritual comfort, the guild could give its members warmth and sociability through feasting and joint religious observances, encouraging 'ferme and sekyr lufe ilk til other'.[25] It functioned as a community within a community, an organisation to which people could belong while still seeing themselves as members of the wider burgh community. The existence of the guild illustrates how people could belong to overlapping communities, just as they do today, without their participation in any community being diminished for it. Thus a wealthy merchant such as John Mercer might be a member of the guild, the community of the burgh of Perth, the parish of St John's Church, and also the local gentry. Townspeople were members of more than just the community of their own burgh.

The idea of community extended beyond the burgh bounds, bringing together the people of different burghs. As Nicholson points out, the strength of the burgesses lay not only in their control over trade, but also in their spirit of co-operation and in the institutions which reflected this spirit.[26] Unfortunately, because cases of conflict between the burghs are more likely to be recorded, they are the ones on which most attention has been focused.[27] Rather than being seen as centres of privilege, each opposed to the others' interests, however, the burghs should be viewed as parts of a cohesive whole, providing a nationwide system of commercial interaction, although in Scotland this never reached the heights of co-operation of such organisations as the Hanseatic League. Individual privileges were to be safeguarded, to be sure, but the infringement of privileges was the result of confusion about their exact nature as often as it was a deliberate attempt to extend one burgh's rights at the expense of another's.

Some conflicts actually involved inter-burghal co-operation as well. In complaining in 1289 that Montrose burgesses were obstructing the fair at Aberdeen, the burgesses of Banff pointed out that the fairs had been established for the benefit of Banff and other burghs north of the Mounth, and that the disturbances injured not just Banff, but also Aberdeen and the whole northern province. Banff was probably supporting a petition made by Aberdeen, as two years earlier, the Guardians had appointed a commission to settle a dispute about fairs between Aberdeen and Montrose. In the final judgment, the claims of the northern burghs were recognised as justified.[28] Similarly, the market privileges granted to Brechin had the effect of uniting the nearby burghs of Dundee, Forfar and Montrose against this non-burghal intruder on their trading rights. When David II granted the freedom of the Tay and the Southesk to the merchants of Brechin in 1370, the burgesses of Dundee and Montrose were ordered not to obstruct them. In 1372 the merchant guilds of Montrose and Forfar took counteraction against the Brechin privileges by granting each other reciprocal trading rights and specifically excluding Brechin.[29] There may have been earlier collusion between Dundee and Montrose in sending representatives to the crown about the usurpation of burghal privileges at Brechin and elsewhere. On 5 March 1352, as a result of issues raised at the chamberlain ayre held at these places, David II issued two very similar letters, one forbidding the holding of fairs at Brechin or Fordoun or anywhere else within the bounds of Montrose, the other forbidding fairs at Coupar Angus Abbey, the church of Alyth, the towns of Kettins or Kirriemuir or anywhere else in the bounds of Dundee.[30] As David was at this time home from England for a short period, it seems likely that the burgesses hastened to bring their petitions to his attention.

Cohesion among the burghs was a royal policy as well, as an early grant by William I to the burgesses of Aberdeen and 'the burgesses of Moray' suggests. In the early thirteenth century a grant of privileges to Aberdeen had stated that these rights were not to prejudice those granted to other burghs in the bailiwick of Aberdeen. When David II made Inverbervie a burgh, he specified that its privileges were not to prejudice those of Aberdeen, Montrose, Dundee or Arbroath. When a 1370 grant to Dunbar gave the burgh a trading area which conflicted with the bounds of Haddington, the burgesses of each were granted reciprocal trading rights in the other burgh.[31] Perhaps this arrangement influenced the agreement which was made between Montrose and Forfar two years later. The practice of allowing one burgh trading rights in another was also to be found in the case of Cupar, where the burgesses of St Andrews were given royal permission to trade. In this case, some friction arose as the merchant guild of Cupar complained about the rights of the St Andrews traders, although unsuccessfully.[32]

Most disputes occur in the records after David's 1364 grant confirming the burgesses' rights of trading within the liberties of their respective burghs. Possibly this act gave the burghs a firm legal position on which to base their claims, making any infringement more likely to be reported. The resolution of such disputes also resulted in the liberties of particular burghs being more closely defined. The judgment in a dispute between Ayr and Irvine enabled Irvine to have its rights in the baronies of Cunningham and Largs confirmed.[33] On the other hand, the act may also have encouraged inter-burghal agreements such as that between Forfar and Montrose, but because these were not made a matter of government record, most have not survived, whereas the disputes which came before the crown have.

Burgh cooperation took many different forms. Cupar and St Andrews were both parties to an indenture with Bruges in 1348, while Edinburgh, Perth, Dundee and Aberdeen spoke with one voice as the 'four great towns of Scotland' in another letter to the same city. Perth and Dundee were probably jointly involved in at least one trading venture.[34] In 1325, when Robert I wished to know the privileges which anciently belonged to the burgh of Dundee, the issue was decided by an inquisition of landed men and burgesses of Berwick, Aberdeen, St Andrews, Forfar, Arbroath and Montrose.[35] Nor was there any attempt to rob the burgh of its privileges, as the inquisition declared that it had the same privileges as other burghs in the kingdom.

This inquest demonstrates another feature which contributed to burghal solidarity in this period. Here were the burgesses of both royal and ecclesiastical burghs working together. Moreover, their conclusion implies that there was little difference seen between the privileges of royal and non-royal burghs. The reciprocal trading privileges given to Dunbar and Haddington suggest a similar view. That this situation was beginning to change might be implied by the dispute between Cupar and St Andrews, but as yet there was little distinction made. The controversy between Irvine and Ayr was decided on the basis of immemorial rights rather than of status.[36] In the fifteenth century, such distinctions would become more important.

The co-operation between the burghs was sometimes reinforced on an individual level by burgesses who had interests in more than one burgh. Just as certain religious houses such as Arbroath Abbey held properties in several burghs, so too did burgesses. Hugh de Selkirk, burgess of Edinburgh, held a tenement in Haddington, and by 1371 the burgh had granted him land in the burgh common in order to extend his tenement. Individual burgesses could also make grants to burgesses of other burghs. On 16 September 1384, John Hossok, burgess of Inverness, sold a piece of land in Inverness to William de Dunbar, burgess of Aberdeen. William was to render 3s to the heirs of a late burgess of Inverness. A man of this name served as custumar of the burgh from 1382 to 1386. If this was the same man, perhaps the sale was intended to provide accommodation for him when he visited the burgh in his capacity of custumar. The interest of the burgh in this sale is implied by the presence of the provost and two bailies among the witnesses, as well as the appending of the burgh seal. The witness list included the names of burgesses from both the burghs involved.[37]

In 1387, Richard de Strathearn, burgess of Perth, granted a burgess of Dundee property in Perth, for which he was to render 40s to Richard and the burgh ferme owed to the king.[38] Did the payment of the burgh ferme mean that burgess-ship went along with the property? It was possible for an individual to be a burgess of more than one burgh. Gregory Chapman appeared as both burgess of Stirling and burgess of Dumbarton, although never as both at once. He granted to his son John Palmer all his lands lying in the burghs of Stirling and Dumbarton and in the city of Glasgow. If John died without legitimate heirs, the lands were to go to the burgh churches of Stirling and Dumbarton, a stipulation which implied that Gregory had had active interests in both these burghs. John was also burgess of the two towns.[39] Perhaps the best example of burgess-ship of more than one burgh is to be found in a grant of 10 April 1374 in which John Gardner, burgess of Linlithgow, granted land in that burgh to John son of Clement, 'burgess of the said burgh and of Dumbarton'.

In 1385 John son of Clement rendered to the Exchequer the account of the bailies of Dumbarton. The fact that all three of these men were burgesses of Dumbarton suggests that they may have wished to attain burgess-ship of another burgh in order to participate more directly in the trade of the east coast.[40]

The burghs were united not only by common interests and by individual burgesses but also by common privileges and laws. This was emphasised in the fifteenth century by a wave of parliamentary legislation affecting all the burghs, but it had also been illustrated earlier in some charters which used the privileges of one burgh as a model for the rights granted to another. Alexander II gave Aberdeen the rights and privileges granted by his predecessors to the burgh of Perth, while Dingwall was granted privileges as at Inverness. Robert I granted to Dundee the right to have a merchant guild as at Berwick.[41]

The body of burghal law which developed to regulate life in the burghs also helped to create a sense of community. Although local conditions might result in variations in such laws, references to 'the laws of the burghs' in a number of documents imply that there was a general acceptance of the main principles of the burgh legal system. The supervision of the chamberlain on his ayre also helped to reinforce the basic similarity of the burgh laws, by providing a set of guidelines for administration. In theory the ayre was held annually, but in practice the disruption caused by war and plague prevented this in many years. When the visitations did occur, however, they served to remind the burghs of their special relationship with the king and reinforced their common sense of identity. In baronial burghs the relationship of the burgesses with their overlord seems to have imitated that of the king's burghs with the crown, as at least in some cases a chamberlain was appointed to supervise burgh affairs.[42] The chamberlain presided over the burgh institution known as the Four Burghs, which may have developed from the practice of one burgh asking another for advice on particular points of law. Originally comprising four burgesses each from Berwick, Roxburgh, Edinburgh and Stirling, the Four Burghs acted as a court of appeal from the burgh courts and the chamberlain ayre. Interpretation of burghal law could be referred to the judgment of the Four Burghs, as happened in a case in Edinburgh in 1292. The court also had the power to impose fines; Simon Gelchauch of Aberdeen was fined 50s in 1330.[43] Such amercements went to the king, as did the issues of the chamberlain ayre, presumably because they were counted among the issues of burgh justice which were payable to the crown.

The usual meeting-place of the Four Burghs was Haddington, although war conditions resulted in it meeting elsewhere. At least one meeting took place at Stirling. In 1369, Lanark and Linlithgow replaced Berwick and Roxburgh, which were held by the English, as two of the burghs. By the beginning of the fifteenth century, there is evidence that the court was making an attempt to extend its powers, when it was enacted that two or three commissioners from all the king's burghs south of Spey should attend the 'parliament' of the four burghs 'to trait, ordaine and determe vpon all things concerning the vtilitie of the common well of all the Kings burghs, their liberties and court'.[44] There were two sides to this development, for while in one sense it represented an even greater cohesion among the king's burghs, it also had the effect of emphasising the distinction between royal and non-royal burghs.

The Four Burghs perhaps provided the earliest forum where the burgesses could meet together. The burgesses of Berwick, Roxburgh, Stirling and Edinburgh were here given the experience of working together to determine cases of burghal law and to formulate rules concerning burgh life. Burgesses of other burghs came into contact with the body by bringing cases before it. As early as 1211 it may have acted as a meeting place for the burghs to discuss the contribution of 6000 merks which they agreed to give the king. Trade agreements such as the 1347 establishment of a staple at Middelburg, would have been made largely on the collective advice of the merchant burgesses, and it seems likely that the Four Burghs was the place where the burgesses discussed such matters before presenting their counsel to the king, especially in the years before 1357, when burgess attendance at parliament and general councils was apparently very sporadic. The Four Burghs thus foreshadowed the powers of the later Convention of Royal Burghs, which was formally constituted in 1487.[45]

The sense of community between the burghs which was expressed in the working of the Four Burghs found new expression in the fourteenth century with the emergence of the burgesses as an officially recognised political entity, one of the three estates which made up the Scottish parliament from the 1350s onwards. As early as 1296, the seals of six burghs, Aberdeen, Perth, Stirling, Roxburgh and Berwick, had been attached to a treaty with France. The phraseology of the reference to these burghs, the *communitates villarum*, communities of the towns rather than communities of the burghs, suggests French influence and it is probable that the seals were procured largely at the request of the French king. The occasion, however, marked the first recorded use of the burgh seals on a document of national importance, and probably introduced, if it did not actually put into effect, the idea of burgess involvement in national affairs. Later in the same year, burgesses again took part in an affair of national importance, although not of national pride, when burgesses from several burghs, or at least their representatives, went to Berwick to swear fealty to the conquering Edward I.[46]

The resistance to English rule during the early years of the fourteenth century strengthened the ties of burgesses, clerics and barons fighting for the same cause, and there may have been some burgesses present at a small gathering of national importance, the crowning of Robert I in 1306. There is some indication that they were present, at least as petitioners, at a parliament of April 1312 when the king and council ordained that the burghs were to discuss taxes and army service only through the chamberlain. This may have been an attempt at setting up some formal procedure for burgess participation in parliamentary meetings. Grants of burgh privileges in 1313, 1317 and 1319 hint at the presence of burgh representatives as petitioners and it seems, as Dickinson suggests, that by the 1320s the burgesses must certainly have been familiar with the institution of parliament.[47]

Medieval government was based on the ideal of consultation and from the thirteenth century onwards, the range of those with whom the king consulted on a regular basis broadened in several countries. New needs for money and military service, caused largely by the increasing costs of war, led rulers to consult with and ask help from the increasingly prosperous and populous towns. The Scottish kings were no exceptions to this. The first parliament at which burgesses apparently took a major role occurred in 1326 at Cambuskenneth, at which the king was granted an annual contribution of a tenth to help sustain his household, impoverished by the hardships of war.[48] To this agreement, burgh commissioners were party. Two years later another parliament was held to arrange the payment of the peace contribution which the Scots had agreed to pay England by the Treaty of Edinburgh-Northampton. This time there is much better evidence of the participation of the burgesses, as the form of the summons to the parliament has survived. Summons were sent to the usual members of the kingdom and also to 'six sufficient persons from every burgh community'. The indenture of 1326 was confirmed and a contribution to the peace agreed. The participation of the burgesses in this parliament marked a development in the theory of burgh representation, because the burgh commissioners were given the power to agree to a tax of any amount on behalf of those remaining at home.[49]

The 1328 parliamentary summons and Exchequer records which show the burgesses participating in two parliaments in 1341 disprove the old theory that the 1326 parliament was an aberration and that the burgesses did not reappear in parliament until the later years of David's reign. The importance of the burghs was again recognised in 1352 when King John of France addressed a letter to the prelates, earls, barons and communities of the towns and provinces. From 1357 the Scottish king showed a similar attitude towards the burghs, based largely on the realisation of the central role which the burgesses had to play in the raising of money for the royal ransom.[50]

In early 1357 a general council was held to discuss the question of the ransom and to appoint representatives to send to London. The record of the proceedings included the seals of Aberdeen, Dundee, Perth and Edinburgh, in the name of all the burgesses and the whole community. On 26 September, the clergy, nobility and burgesses (soon to be recognised officially as the three communities or estates) met separately and appointed representatives to participate in ransom discussions with the English. Burgesses of seventeen burghs chose eleven representatives who were empowered to make contracts in the name of all the communities of the burgesses and merchants of the kingdom. Here the concept of representation was taken even further, for these burgess commissioners were to represent all the burghs of the realm, not just those of which they were the burgesses. In the event, it does not appear that any of the burgess delegates did go to Berwick as negotiators, but it seems likely that they sat in the general council which appointed those who did go.[51]

The ransom treaty was ratified in Berwick on 5 October, and in a general council at Scone on 6 November. The ratification was made with the assent of 'the three communities', the first recorded use of the term. Nor were the burgesses only present to give assent to the royal actions. Provisions to maintain burghal privileges and to protect the export trade imply the active participation of the burgesses in this council, as well as the fact that their assent was not automatic and may have had to be bargained for. Five days later a parliament was held and it seems likely that the same burgesses who had attended the council attended the parliament as well, especially as it was here that it was agreed to raise the customs and to provide additional revenue through a tax similar to those of 1326 and 1328.[52]

Financial needs may have helped bring the burgesses into parliament, but it was not only taxation which ensured their continued

participation in parliaments and general councils after 1357. Scotland was comparatively lightly taxed, especially compared to England, and taxation never became almost automatic, even under
David II and the needs of the ransom.[53] The burgesses were there to
provide consultation and advice on other matters as well. 'The old
community of the realm had become a trinity in which the burgesses
figured, alongside churchmen and barons, as a political entity, an
"estate" whose approval must be sought for any government measure that relied upon a consensus of opinion'.[54] In March 1364 David
proposed accepting Prince Lionel of England as heir if he had no
children, in lieu of paying the rest of the ransom. The suggestion was
rejected outright by the three communities, the burgesses having a
special interest in this affair because they were largely responsible for
the ransom payments that would result. An embassy was sent to
London to renegotiate the ransom, and burgess members of parliament were on hand to meet the embassy when it returned.[55]

In May 1366 the king's council decided that a land valuation
should be discussed in parliament and in July the bishops, earls,
barons, tenants-in-chief and 'from every burgh certain burgesses'
were summoned and called 'in the due and accustomed manner', to
treat on certain matters. The burgesses were also present at the parliament of September 1367, when a new constitutional development
took place. It was decided to delegate the responsibilities of parliament to a small group, while the rest of the members went home for
the harvest. To be truly representative, the committee had to include
all those elements seen as integral to the parliament. Thirteen
burgesses were appointed to the committee, representing Edinburgh, Aberdeen, Perth, Dundee, Montrose, Haddington and Linlithgow. A similar committee in 1370 included seven burgesses. This
development led in the fifteenth century to the institution known as
the Lords of the Articles, who considered petitions and drafted
legislation for parliament.[56]

A reference to the three communities suggests burgess involvement in the parliament of March 1369. The three communities
elected the earl of Fife as Guardian in a general council of 1388, and
in 1399 they granted £2000 Scots to be raised for messengers to
arrange treaties with England and France. It seems likely that the
burgesses were represented in most, if not all, the general councils
and parliaments from the 1360s until the end of the century,
although the lack of records of attendance for every meeting makes
this impossible to prove. For the last two years of the 1390s, the local
records of Aberdeen give some suggestion of burgess involvement in

national affairs. The accounts of the provost for 1398–9 include a payment to two burgesses to attend a council at Linlithgow. This may have been a parliament or general council, although there is no evidence of it in the scanty records of the period. A 2s payment to William Chalmer at Perth seems more likely to have implied a national gathering, as great councils were held in Perth in April 1398 and January 1399. By 1437, Aberdeen regulations which may have echoed earlier legislation of the 1390s, provided for the election of two commissioners to parliaments and general councils.[57]

Burgess participation in parliament represented not only a political development but also a further extension of the idea of community among the burghs. In order to have influence in the general councils and parliaments, it was necessary for the burgesses to provide a united front. Probably the pattern of 1357 when the burgesses met first in a separate group to choose their delegates for the ransom negotiations was repeated at future councils and parliaments with the burgesses working out first the issues they wished to raise and the actions they wished to take. Co-operation rather than conflict was the keynote to relations within the third estate, and their recognition as one of the three 'communities' showed that the political cohesion of the burgesses was recognised by the rest of the political groupings of the realm. Although they achieved this political recognition as a separate community, it did not exclude the burgesses from being an integral part of the wider community which made up the kingdom of Scotland. Parliament itself formed a link between the centre and the localities, helping to promote unity. The townspeople's contribution to the kingdom might sometimes be made in unique ways because of their particular privileges and occupations, but they participated with all the other groups in the country in the responsibilities, misfortunes, and prosperity characteristic of life in medieval Scotland.

When royal contributions were called for from the kingdom, the burghs paid their share along with everyone else. Sometimes, as in 1211, a lump sum was agreed upon, in which case the organisation of its collection probably involved burgesses, who decided how the burden was to be shared out among the burghs. At other times, as in 1326, the tax took the form of a tenth, which did not commit the burghs as a whole to find a particular sum of money and required less complicated arrangements. In 1328, however, the burgesses preferred to have the collection of their contribution under their own control, and in lieu of a second tax, compounded for their share and offered to pay a total of 1500 merks in three separate instalments.[58]

It was in the demands produced by David II's ransom, however, that they were really to prove their value to the kingdom.

From the late thirteenth century, those burgesses involved in the export trade had contributed to the crown's revenue through the customs dues. In 1357, parliament, faced with the need to find 100,000 merks for the ransom, decided to double the customs duty as one method of raising the necessary money. This was a new way of obtaining additional revenues, as the customs rate had remained steady since it was first introduced in the late thirteenth century. The idea to make use of the customs in this way may have been largely based on practice in England where it was common to alter the customs rate when additional revenues were required, but it also represented an extension of the idea of taxation on moveable goods. Where it differed from ordinary taxes of the period was that it continued to be in force even after the original reason for it, the ransom, was no longer being paid. The ransom payments ended in 1377, shortly after the death of Edward III, with 24,000 merks still unpaid. The customs, which had been quadrupled in 1368, thus benefited the crown,[59] and led to an even stronger link between the king and the burgesses, as it continued to be in the royal interest to promote the activities of the overseas merchants.

One of the measures proposed to raise the ransom money was that the king should be empowered to buy all wool and fleeces in Scotland at a price of 4 merks per sack or per 200 woolfells. This represented about two-thirds of the market price. The wool could then be sold outside the country and the profit put towards the ransom. In the event, the actual price paid was usually 5 merks, but the exercise appears to have been moderately successful, probably raising about £1000. Some burgesses offered their services as middlemen for this collection; several payments for wool were made to burgesses rather than directly to producers. Wool was bought both from individuals such as Roger Hogg, and from the communities of the burghs.[60] It seems that the burgesses at home were willing to combine to carry out to the best of their ability measures agreed upon by their representatives at a national level. On a less altruistic level, it may also have been hoped that by providing the king with fairly large amounts of wool on a communal basis, the individual merchants might be left some produce of their own with which to carry on their trade. Certainly it was not in the king's interests to buy all the wool as this would then have drastically decreased the receipts from the customs. Money was raised for the king's purchase of wool by the doubling of the customs rate on wool from early 1358, but soon such taxation itself was recognised to be a far more effective way of securing revenue than the requisitioning of the wool crop. At Michaelmas 1358 the woolfell customs was tripled, and the duty on hides and wool followed suit on Martinmas 1358 and Whitsunday 1359 respectively. The entire triple custom was to go towards the ransom.[61]

The part played by the burgesses was not simply that of taxpayer, however. After the customs rate had been tripled, it became common to sell part of the custom to the burgesses. Edinburgh burgesses paid £76 7s 4 ½d for a share of the customs. Precedents for the purchase of the customs could be found in the leasing to the burghs of their fermes, and also in the futures purchases made by many merchants in their acquisition of wool. In England, it was common for the king to receive loans in return for the right of the creditor to future customs receipts. The purchase of the customs by the Scottish burgesses involved collective action on two levels, as not only did the community of each burgh advance a certain sum to the king, but there was obviously an inter-burghal agreement about the proportion contributed by each burgh, as the total payment came to the round sum of 5000 merks. There was also co-operation between individual burghs, as one combined payment was received from the burghs of Inverness, Elgin, Banff and Forres, and another from the burgesses of St Andrews and Cupar.[62]

The importance of the burgesses to the ransom payments was further attested to by the appointment of two of their number to supervise the payment of the second instalment to the English in 1359. John Mercer, the most prominent Scottish merchant of his time, and Roger Hogg, an Edinburgh burgess with close links to government, acted as royal agents and paid the 1359 instalment at three different dates to the agent of the English king in Bruges. Mercer's account shows that the entire 10,000 merks was expected to come from the combined customs receipts and the sale of half the customs to the burgesses, although the sums might be supplemented by the chamberlain to a certain extent. As it turned out, enough money was raised, but not all of it arrived in time for the payments and Mercer had to pay £115 5s interest on a loan of £1166 13s 4d to make up the correct amount, as well as £62 penalty for delay and for messengers to England to arrange the payments.[63] Where the loan came from is not clear, but it seems likely that a merchant such as Mercer would have relatively easy access to credit facilities, especially in a banking centre such as Bruges, and this may have been a consideration when he was appointed to his post.

Such detailed evidence of the arrangements for raising the ransom money unfortunately only survives for the second instalment, so that it is not possible to determine how the first instalment was raised or to discover much about the organisation behind the collection of later payments. Political factors resulted in various re-negotiations of the ransom treaty, including an agreement made in 1365 after the three communities refused to accept Edward III's son as heir to the Scottish throne. The yearly instalments were decreased to 6000 merks. It was probably in July of that year that it was decided to have the customs from 19 June to January of each year paid exclusively to the ransom, and also that a contribution to the king's expenses should be made by the three estates. The contribution from the burghs of 1000 merks appears to have been pre-arranged and paid in one lump sum,[64] once again implying inter-burghal co-operation and organisation.

Financial difficulties led to the decision for a sweeping revocation of royal grants in 1367 and once more the use of the entire triple customs for the ransom. As one-third of this was crown property, however, the king and council also had the power to levy a contribution to that extent when the amount was known. In June 1368 this system was replaced by a quadrupling of the customs, the additional rate going to the king's expenses. Later, this reservation was given up and the entire customs was paid to the chamberlain for the expenses of both king and nation. The ransom had thereby proved a way of bringing immense additional sums into the king's hands, largely at the expense of the burgesses.[65]

Payment of the ransom was not the only action in which townspeople particpated with the rest of the kingdom. Many also took part in the defence of the realm against the English. Perhaps Edward I recognised their potential in any resistance against his rule, as he required the representatives of nine burghs to do homage to him at Berwick in 1296. Certainly, the burgesses of Berwick had shown open defiance to the English forces earlier that year. On 30 March the English took their revenge, indiscriminately slaughtering the townspeople. Throughout the conflicts of the fourteenth century, the burghs suffered their share of burning and looting by both English and Scottish armies, experiencing with the rest of the country the fortunes of war, and for some, the problem of divided loyalties.[66]

During Edward I's occupation, it was generally the people of the northern burghs, more remote from the English centre of power, who took the lead in burghal resistance. Alexander Pilch of Inverness, although he made peace with Edward and served as keeper of Inverness Castle for the English from 1304, was among the supporters of Bruce in 1306. Three other northern burgesses, Andrew Slegh, Andrew Bishop and Adam Chapeu, all from Aberdeen, also figure in an English list of Bruce supporters.[67] Aberdeen was an important centre for those fighting the English by sea, and it was here that many of the overseas supplies which were so important to the Scottish resistance were brought into the kingdom. Perhaps it was because the northern burghs did not suffer the effects of such intensive English occupation and administration as the burghs further south that they were able to take such an effective part in the defence of the realm. This is not to say that the northern burghs escaped unscathed – several were burned in the punitive northern expeditions made by both Edward I and Edward III – but the English policy seems to have been to destroy the buildings of the burghs, rather than to make a prolonged effort to destroy the spirit of the inhabitants through occupation by a garrison. In the event, the burghs proved very resilient, soon rebuilding and getting on with everyday life. In one instance, war was actually of benefit to some burghs. The loss of Berwick to the English for much of the fourteenth century resulted in an expansion of the export trade of the Lothian ports and, above all, of Edinburgh.[68]

Because contemporary and near-contemporary Scottish chroniclers, in common with most of their fellows, concentrate mainly on the deeds of a glorious few, the townspeople of the period share the same fate as the majority of the population, and fail to have their part in the Scottish resistance recorded. And yet the defiance shown by the burgesses of Berwick was not a unique phenomenon. The story of the storming of the English-held castle by the men of Aberdeen in 1308 may be legend, but in 1336 Edward III took revenge for the death of one of his followers at the hands of the people of Aberdeen by setting the entire town alight.[69] Indeed, although the records give little specific detail about the activities of the burgesses in the wars, 'the overriding picture is of burghal solidarity in the patriotic cause'.[70] The friendship shown to the burghs by Robert I once he was in a position to reward them implies that they must have played no small part in his eventual victory. The royal favours which the burghs obtained helped them to overcome the damages caused by war and to recover some of their former prosperity.[71]

The profits of successful warfare as well as £7000 of a tenth granted for the crusades were put to use by Robert I, to pay those seamen and traders who ran the English blockade with imports from

Flanders and attacked English shipping. Flemish and German traders were active in this business, but Scottish merchants also took part.[72] The Scottish traders had an important effect on diplomatic relations between Scotland and her allies, as the demand for Scottish wool, especially in those countries temporarily deprived of English supplies, ensured that help would continue to be given to the Scots from many directions. Scottish merchants on the Continent were able to secure supplies and keep open the lines of communication between Scotland and the countries which they visited.

The towns' military role did not end with the Wars of Independence. Adult males aged 16–60 were liable for military service in defence of the realm if summoned by the king, although they were sometimes able to gain exemptions by paying for other men to be hired instead. The demands could be quite high. A brieve to one burgh stated that it was to provide 120 armed men for sixty days with six sufficient men of the burgh to lead them. The burgesses were to possess weapons, and by the fifteenth century, and probably earlier, were expected to hold regular wapinschaws (weapon-showings) on nearby fields. They could also contribute to the security of the realm through their regular activities; James I encouraged all merchants to bring back military supplies from their trading ventures overseas.[73]

After David II's return from captivity, the interests of the burgesses coincided with the interest of the crown in desiring peace with England. Trade was an important element in easing relations between the two countries, and provided at least one issue of on which they could agree. Increased commercial contacts encouraged the development of cultural, social and diplomatic links and this perhaps helped to resolve disputes by negotiation rather than by force. Burgesses took part in some of the diplomatic missions to England. John Wigmer, burgess of Edinburgh, was involved in negotiations for David's release in 1348, while Adam Forrester played a major part in talks with the English in the closing years of the century. The burgesses were also willing to send representatives to negotiate the ransom treaty in 1357. Diplomatic treaties with other countries, strengthening links and increasing commercial interdependence also involved burgess negotiators,[74] who were thus able to serve both their own interests and those of the community.

Because the burghs were the focus for the institutions of government, the burgesses came into frequent contact with members of the other two estates, often within their own burghs. Justiciar's courts, ecclesiastical courts, sheriff courts, the Exchequer and the supreme court, the parliament, were usually held in the burghs. Some burghs had especially close links with the sheriff as many royal burghs were the heads of sheriffdoms. William de Meldrum, sheriff of Aberdeen, lived in Gallowgate, and on one occasion was one of those who rendered the accounts of the *prepositi* on their behalf to the Exchequer. Co-operation is shown in a list of forestallers, in which certain names were marked 'to the provost' and others 'to the sheriff'. When Perth was granted the right to arrest forestallers, the sheriff of Perth was ordered to provide any assistance necessary.[75] As well as the help provided by the sheriff, church courts enforced contracts involving oaths, matrimonial cases, slander and any other cases perceived as involving faith and morals.[76]

In theory, the king's burghs were to be entirely independent of the control of all royal ministers with the exception of the chamberlain. In 1344, David II granted the burgesses of Inverness that no king's official except the chamberlain could supervise weights and measures in the burgh. Ecclesiastical and baronial burghs appear to have been more subject to interference by the burgh superior. Even the king's burghs, however, although they generally maintained their independence in the control of their internal affairs, could not remain isolated from the other authorities which carried out the government of Scotland. In some cases the lands which were later granted to the burghs were under separate jurisdiction. For the five pennylands granted to Ayr, the burgesses were to render one suit of court before the sheriff of Ayr for every plea held there. Certain privileges were allowed, however, for it was stipulated that the burgesses were not to be called to serve with the army, unless summoned with other burgesses by the king. In 1417, the burgesses complained in the sheriff court that the sheriff was ignoring this privilege.[77]

Where the burgesses of a burgh were accused of wrongdoing to an individual or institution outside their authority, the king ordered his own ministers to ensure that right was done. In many cases this was because the burgh officials were being treated as officers ultimately responsible to the crown. Thus John Balliol could order his sheriff and bailies of Perth to compel the *prepositi* of the burgh of Perth to render to Kelso Abbey six merks owed from the burgh fermes. William de Meldrum, sheriff of Aberdeen, was presumably carrying out royal instructions when he wrote to the *prepositi* and bailies of the burgh of Crail in 1348 that he had inspected the charter of the chamberlain about the privileges of the men of Arbroath Abbey, and ordered them to make redress for molesting them and extorting customs. The powers that could be given to a non-burghal authority over the burgesses were demonstrated in 1386, when the earl of Carrick commanded the sheriff and bailies of Ayr to distrain the goods of the burgessses of Ayr if the burgh fermes owed to the Blackfriars were not paid by the provost and bailies.[78] This represented a further step in the interference in burgh affairs as the burgesses were being made responsible for the failure of their magistrates in their capacity as royal officials and foreshadowed more widespread interference in the burghs by the crown from the fifteenth century onwards.[79]

The king's ministers also helped the burghs by enforcing their privileges outwith the bounds of the town. In 1401 the sheriff of Banff was ordered to arrest Malcolm de Drummond, lord of Mar, and any others who troubled the burgesses and community of Banff in their fishings. A dispute between the burgesses of Peebles and Robert Cruik over the moss of Walthamshope in 1262 was ordered by the king to be heard at an inquisition held by the sheriff of Peebles.[80] Through the pertinents which belonged to the burghs they were brought into contact with the laws and courts which governed the rest of the kingdom.

The townspeople shared in other aspects of life in medieval Scotland. They were not immune from the effects of bad harvests, although the fact that they were more easily able to import grain may have helped cushion them against the worst of the famines. On the other hand, the crowded and unsanitary conditions of many burghs may have resulted in higher mortality from the plague, with losses of perhaps one-sixth to one-third of their population in the series of outbreaks from 1349 to the mid-fifteenth century, although the lack of evidence means that this can only be an estimate. The strict measures imposed in Aberdeen to prevent the plague coming to the burgh in 1401 suggest that the town had some previous experience of the sickness.[81]

Burgesses were major participants in the wide-spread travels of the medieval Scots. Trips abroad were made in the company of scholars, churchmen, nobles and pilgrims. Pilgrims were a major feature of medieval life and burgesses were frequently to be found among their number. There are records of several merchants who went on pilgrimages or at least applied for safe-conducts in order to do so. Among them were some of the most prominent burgesses of the time, including Roger Hogg and his wife Margaret, John Goldsmith and William Fersith, all of Edinburgh. Favourite destinations were the Holy Land, the tombs of Peter and Paul at Rome and the shrine of St James at Compostella. Those going to Compostella usually sailed from Dover or Plymouth to Galicia or a French port, while those going to Rome might go through England or sail from Scotland across the North Sea to Bruges or some other North Sea port. Canterbury was another popular destination, while within Scotland Whithorn and St Andrews were a common goals for pilgrims, both Scottish and foreign.[82] Pilgrim traffic also benefited towns fortunate enough to be sited beside or on the route to holy sites – North Berwick, for example, was a common stopping-off point on the way to St Andrews. Townspeople also provided ships to take pilgrims overseas, financial facilities, security for the homes of urban pilgrims while abroad, and accommodation for those who came to visit local shrines.

The contributions of the townspeople to the community of the realm took many forms. As markets, the burghs provided a place of exchange where country people could bring cash crops and exchange them for manufactured goods, where nobles could purchase imported luxuries and where the king could collect essential customs revenues. They provided meeting-places for the councils and institutions which governed the realm as well as sites for more local justice forms such as the sheriff court. The inhabitants of the burghs contributed to the culture of Scotland by producing or importing manufactured goods, by encouraging the growth of literacy, by providing schools and by patronising works of architecture and art. The burghs also provided places for the interchange of ideas, the intermingling of different levels of society, and the meeting of foreign visitor and native Scot.

The townspeople were an integral part of the kingdom at many different levels. Many engaged in agricultural pursuits and lived in houses little different from those of their fellows in the countryside. During the fourteenth century, some townspeople introduced commercial practices into the countryside by speculating in arable lands while they also bought country estates and integrated with the local nobility through intermarriage and emulation of their lifestyle. Others participated in the government of the kingdom and carried out the duties of some of the highest officers of the realm, as well as winning official political recognition for the third estate. Wherever the townspeople went, whatever they did, they usually managed to become a part of the community, whatever that community might be: the government of the kingdom, the landholding elite or the common people of Scotland. Towns are sometimes seen as an anomaly in medieval society but the townspeople of Scotland were not an anomaly in the society of their kingdom, they were an integral part of the community of the realm. It has recently been suggested that it was their very success in integrating so well with the community of the realm that eventually led to the breakup of the medieval burgh community.[83] But at the beginning of the fifteenth century, that development still lay in the future.

Notes

INTRODUCTION

1. See Ian Adams, *The Making of Urban Scotland* (London,1978), 16-22 for a summary of the various theories.
2. R. M. Spearman, 'Early Scottish towns: their origins and economy' in *Power and Politics in Early Medieval Britain* eds. S. T. Driscoll and M. R. Nieke (Edinburgh,1988).
3. *Excavations in the Medieval Burgh of Aberdeen 1973-81 [Aber.Exc.]* ed.J. C. Murray (Edinburgh,1982); *Excavations in the Medieval Burgh of Perth 1979-1981 [Perth Exc.]* ed. P.Holdsworth (Edinburgh, 1987). Three more monographs are forthcoming, one on more of the Perth excavations, one on excavations of Carmelite friaries in Scotland, and the third on excavations in St. Andrews. The Perth High Street Excavations [PHSE] have not yet been published. Unpublished reports for other sites in Perth are held by the Scottish Urban Archaeological Trust [SUAT].
4. Adams, *Urban Scotland; Scottish Urban History* eds. George Gordon and Brian Dicks (Aberdeen,1983). *An Historical Geography of Scotland* eds.G. Whittington and I. D. Whyte (London, 1983) also contains some material on towns.
5. *The Scottish Medieval Town* eds. M. Lynch, G. Stell and R. M. Spearman (Edinburgh, 1988). This volume also contains an excellent bibliography of primary and secondary sources on medieval towns.
6. *Tolbooths and Townhouses* ed.G. Stell (RCAHMS, forthcoming).
7. There are reports by the Scottish Burgh Survey [SBS] from 1977 to 1982. The work of the survey has now recommenced and further volumes on Glasgow, Aberdeen and Dundee are forthcoming.
8. E. P. Torrie, 'The Gild of Dunfermline in the Fifteenth Century', PhD thesis (Edinburgh, 1984); H. Booton, 'Burgesses and Landed Men in North-East Scotland in the Later Middle Ages: A Study in Social Interaction', PhD thesis (Aberdeen, 1988). An exception to the concentration on the fifteenth century is the short study of Perth by A. A. M. Duncan, 'Perth: The First Century of the Burgh' in *Transactions of the Perthshire Society of Natural Science*, Special Issue (1974).

CHAPTER ONE: LIFE IN THE BURGH

1. *CDS*, ii, no. 508; Ranald Nicholson, *Scotland: The Later Middle Ages* (Edinburgh, 1974), 265; M. Spearman, 'The Medieval Townscape of Perth' in *Scottish Town*, 56; *Abdn. Chrs.*, p. 312. For problems of urban demography see Jan de Vries, *European Urbanization 1500-1800* (Camb., Mass., 1984), 17-19 and Edith Ennen, *The Medieval Town* tran. N. Fryde (Amsterdam, 1979), 185-7. Most Scottish burghs probably had less than 2000 inhabitants. In Europe probably about half the urban population lived in towns of this size, Paul M. Hohenberg and Lynn Hollen Lees, *The Making of Urban Europe 1000-1950* (Camb., Mass., 1985), 51.
2. *RMS*, i, no. 196; G. Stell, 'Urban Buildings' in *Scottish Town*, 62; R. Gourlay and Anne Turner, *Historic Dumfries* (SBS, 1977), 8; Stirling Chrs., no. 17. For other bridges see Harry R. Inglis, 'The Roads and Bridges in the Early History of Scotland', *PSAS*, xlvii (1912-13), 307. Few towns prospered without good

communications, Henri Pirenne, *Medieval Cities: Their Origins and the Revival of Trade* tran. F. Halsey (Princeton, 1975), 154-7; John H. Mundy and Peter Riesenberg, *The Medieval Town* (Huntington, 1958), 12-13.

3. *RRS*, vi, no. 483; Harold Booton, 'Inland Trade: A Study of Aberdeen in the Later Middle Ages' in *Scottish Town*, 148; S. McGrail, 'Medieval boats, ships, and landing places' in *Waterfront Archaeology in Britain and Northern Europe*, eds. Gustav Milne and Brian Hobley (London, 1981), 19. For more detailed discussion of some individual harbours see Angus Graham, 'Archaeological Notes on Some Harbours in Eastern Scotland', *PSAS*, ci (1968-69); G. Stell, 'Urban Buildings', 62-3.

4. *Arb. Lib.*, ii, no. 42; Anne Turner Simpson and Sylvia Stevenson, *Historic Arbroath* (SBS, 1982), 35; *Edin. Chrs.*, no. 20; Nicholas M. McQ. Holmes, 'Excavation south of Bernard St., Leith, 1980', *PSAS*, cxv (1985), 403; D. Palliser, 'The Medieval Period' in *Urban Archaeology in Britain;* eds. John Schofield and Roger Leech (London, 1987), 64. Graham, 'Harbours', 227.

5. Aberdeen University Library [AUL], MS. M. 390, Mass 1/11; C. M. Brooks, 'Shore Brae' in *Aber. Exc.*, 38-42. More such excavation is needed as it can tell us about not just the waterfront but also the origins and development of the town, continuity of settlement, shipping and trade, B. Hobley, 'The London waterfront – the exception or the rule?' in *Waterfront Archaeology*, 1.

6. Duncan, 'Perth', 32, 41; Anne T. Simpson and S. Stevenson, *Historic Perth* (SBS, 1982), 22.

7. William Dodd, 'Ayr. A Study of Urban Growth', *CAAS*, 2nd ser., x (1972), 306-8, 318-320; St Andrews also had a port at the river Eden, St Andrews University Library [St AUL], B65/22/6.

8. Graham, 'Harbours', 217; A. E. Herteig, 'The medieval harbour at Bergen' in *Waterfront Archaeology*, 82.

9. *ER*, iii, 1, 48, 203, 250; *Elgin Recs.*, i, 16, 19; Anne Simpson and S. Stevenson, *Historic Elgin* (SBS, 1982), 2.

10. *Early Travellers in Scotland*, ed. P. Hume Brown (Edinburgh, 1891), 26. For a list of town defences and later walls see M. J. Jones and C. J. Bond, 'Urban defences' in *Urban Archaeology*, 92, 98-104. Ennen states that most European towns were walled but points out that there were exceptions such as the towns of the Tyrol which were generally unwalled, *Medieval Town*, 85-7. For other unwalled European towns see Robert Dickinson, *The West European City* (London, 1961), 310, 312.

11. *RRS*, ii, no. 213; *Leges Burgorum* in *Ancient Burgh Laws*, c. 81; Spearman, 'Perth Townscape', 52. The possible fourteenth-century Edinburgh wall shown by Adams, *Urban Scotland*, 38, fig. 2.4 would have defended the castle precinct rather than the burgh. The situation in Scotland seems to have differed from that in Europe where towns faced more threats to their security and were building walls from the eleventh century, Pirenne, *Medieval Cities*, 154-7, although some historians have argued that early Scottish towns also faced turbulent neighbours, Dickinson, *European City*, 284.

12. J. C. Murray, 'Conclusions' in *Aber. Exc.*, 247.

13. *Edin. Chrs.*, no. 12; *RMS*, ii, no. 615.

14. *Assisa de Tolloneis* in *Ancient Burgh Laws*, nos i, iii; Walter Bower, *Scotichronicon*, viii ed. D. E. R. Watt [Watt, *Bower*] (Aberdeen, 1987), 6; E. Ewan, 'The Community of the Burgh in the Fourteenth Century' in *Scottish Town*, 236-7.

15. Dodd, 'Ayr', 320. For various types of town plans see Jeremy W. R. Whitehand and Khan Alauddin, 'The Town Plans of Scotland: Some Preliminary Considerations', *Scottish Geographical Magazine*, lxxxv (1969).

16. N. P. Brooks and G. Whittington, 'Planning and growth in the medieval Scottish burgh: the example of St Andrews', *Trans. Inst. Brit. Geographers*, n. s., ii, no. 2 (1977), 290; R. Cant, 'The Medieval Kirk of Crail' in *From the Stone Age to the Forty-Five*, Studies Presented to R. B. K. Stevenson eds. Anne O'Connor and

D. V. Clarke (Edinburgh, 1983), 374-6.

17. Jonathan Wordsworth, 'The Archaeological Investigation of Medieval Inverness' in *The Middle Ages in the Highlands*. The Inverness Field Club (Inverness, 1981), 75.

18. *Spalding Misc.*, v, 250; Anne Turner Simpson et al, *Historic Edinburgh, Canongate and Leith* (SBS, 1981), 29; Robert Gourlay and Anne Turner, *Historic Haddington* (SBS, 1978), 4; J. Wordsworth et al,'Excavation of the settlement at 13-21 Castle Street Inverness, 1979', *PSAS*, cxii (1982), 388; J. Wordsworth, 'Inverkeithing', *Discovery and Excavation* [*D&E*] (1981), 10.

19. Geoffrey Stell, 'The earliest tolbooths: a preliminary account', *PSAS*, cxi (1981), 445-6; *Irvine Muniments*, no. 6. In most European towns public buildings were relatively modest.'Their designs and architectural details were meant to impress and reassure, not overwhelm strolling citizens.' Hohenberg, *Urban Europe*, 129.

20. *Familie of Innes*, 54-6; *Moray Reg.*, no. 235; *Abdn. Recs.*, 10, 238; *Abdn. Chrs.*, no. 15.

21. *APS*, i, 497; *Edin. Chrs.*, no. 7; *Abdn. Recs.*, 37.

22. Ian B. Cowan, 'The Emergence of the Urban Parish' in *Scottish Town*, 82, 93; *CDS*, ii, nos 1115, 1324. My thanks to Dr E. P. Torrie for the information about St Mary's which will appear in the forthcoming Scottish Burgh Survey on Dundee.

23. James Barbour, 'The Greyfriars' Convent of Dumfries and its Environs', *TDGAS* (1910-11), 25; J. C. Murray and Judith Stones,'45-59 Green 1976' in *Aber. Exc.*, 90. For a list of religious houses in Scottish towns see Laurence Butler,'Medieval urban religious houses' in *Urban Archaeology*, 169.

24. *Abdn. Counc.*, i, 37; E. Ewan,'The Age of Bon-Accord: Aberdeen in the Fourteenth Century' in *New Light on Medieval Aberdeen* ed. J. S. Smith (Aberdeen, 1985), 35; Ian Cowan,'Church and Society' in *Scottish Society in the Fifteenth Century* ed. J. Brown (London, 1977), 124.

25. John Durkan, 'Care of the Poor: Pre-Reformation Hospitals' in *Essays on the Scottish Reformation 1513-1625*, ed. D. McRoberts (Glasgow, 1962), 116-20, 126-7; *Abdn. Reg.*, ii, 283-4; *Moray Reg.*, no. 117; Derek Hall, *Excavations at St Nicholas Farm St Andrews 1986-87. Interim Report* (SUAT, 1987).

26. *APS*, ii, 14; *Leges Burgorum*, c. 85.

27. Khan Alauddin, 'Scottish Burghs: Some Aspects of their Origins, Development and Plan', B. Litt thesis (Glasgow, 1968), 112; M. Spearman,'Perth Townscape', 46 (illustration), 48; *Fragmenta Quaedam Veterum Legum et Consuetudinum Scotiae Undique Collecta [Frag. Coll.]* in *Ancient Burgh Laws*, c. 54; *Leges Burgorum*, c. 119. For medieval European town plans see Dickinson, *European City*, 302-7.

28. Brooks, 'Planning and Growth', 288; *Abdn. Recs*, lvi, n. 2; Spearman,'Perth Townscape', 55-7.

29. M. Spearman,'Canal Street II' in *Perth Exc.*, 68, 71; Hilary Murray,'Excavation at 45-47 Gallowgate, Aberdeen', *PSAS*, cxiv (1984), 312.

30. N. Brooks, 'Urban Archaeology in Scotland' in *European Towns: Their Archaeology and Early History*, ed. M. W. Barley (London, 1977), 29; St AUL, SL110/6/7. For other references to boundaries see E. Ewan,'The Burgesses of Fourteenth-Century Scotland: a Social History', PhD thesis, Edinburgh University (1985), 24, n. 33.

31. L. Blanchard, 'Kirk Close, 86-100 High St.' in *Perth Exc.*, 29; Spearman,'Canal St. II', 82-3.

32. National Library of Scotland [NLS], Adv. MS. 9A. 1. 10., f. 45; *Arb. Lib.*, ii, no. 13.

33. Julian Munby, 'Medieval domestic buildings' in *Urban Archaeology*, 156.

34. G. Stell, 'Urban Buildings', 69, 73. See illustration on dust jacket.

35. Hilary Murray, 'Medieval Wooden and Wattle Buildings Excavated in Perth and

Aberdeen' in *Town Houses and Structures in Medieval Scotland: A Seminar*, eds. Anne Turner Simpson and Sylvia Stevenson (SBS, 1980).

36. L. Blanchard, 'The Excavated Buildings' in *Perth Exc.*, 87; Malcolm Atkin and D. H. Evans, 'Population, Profit and Plague: The Archaeological Interpretation of Buildings and Land Use in Norwich', *Scottish Archaeological Review*, iii (1984), 92-4. An Aberdeen tax roll of 1408 shows rich and poor townspeople living in the same neighbourhoods, *Abdn. Chrs.*, 312.

37. *Ayr Chrs.*, no. 6; Barrow, *Kingship and Unity*, 91; Watt, *Bower*, 64, 74, 80; *Early Travellers*, 10.

38. *Early Travellers*, 10; H. Murray, 'Medieval Bldgs', 44; A. Crone and J. Barber, 'Structural Timbers' in *Perth Exc.*, 87.

39. H. Murray, 'Medieval Bldgs', 39-43; John A. di Folco, 'Roof Furniture and Floor Tiles' (PHSE), 11.

40. Blanchard, 'Excavated Buildings', 85-6.

41. Wordsworth, 'Castle Street', 381; H. Murray, 'Medieval Bldgs', 42-3.

42. H. Murray, 'Excavated Secular Buildings' in *Aber. Exc.*, 226, 227. The transition to timber framing is not clear, Stell, 'Urban Buildings', 73-6.

43. *Ayr Friars*, nos 10, 12; *Abdn. Recs.*, 11; H. Murray, 'Wooden and Clay Buildings from Perth High Street' (PHSE), 81; J. Schofield, 'Excavations south of Edinburgh High Street 1973-4', *PSAS*, cvii (1975-76), 180. There were also stone foundations at Canal Street, Blanchard, 'Excavated Buildings', 86. Stone houses began to appear in European towns in the twelfth and thirteenth centuries, Dickinson, *European City*, 322.

44. Duncan, 'Perth', 39-40; Scottish Record Office [SRO], GD79/5/1; *Arb. Lib.*, i, no. 322.

45. Munby, 'Domestic Buildings', 156; Stell, 'Urban Buildings', 73; H. Murray, 'Aber. Bldgs', 225; *RMS*, i, no. 146. Jettied buildings also helped protect the lower storey from the weather, Margaret Wood, *The English Medieval House* (New York, 1965), 222.

46. H. Murray, 'Aber. Bldgs', 225. I would like to thank Geoffrey Stell for his helpful discussion of the tenement tradition in Scotland.

47. Alexander Fenton, 'Thatch and Thatching' in *Building Construction in Scotland. Some Historical and Regional Aspects*. Scottish Vernacular Buildings Working Group (Edinburgh and Dundee, 1976), 39; *Abdn. Recs.*, 90, 91; G. Whittington et al, 'Discovery of Medieval Plough-Marks in St Andrews', *Scottish Studies*, xx (1976), 113.

48. *APS*, ii, 12; H. Murray, 'Medieval Bldgs', 47-8.

49. di Folco, 'Roof Furniture', 1-5, 11, 13. The finial is illustrated in N. Q. Bogdan and J. W. Wordsworth, *The Medieval Excavations at the High Street Perth 1975-76. An Interim Report* (Perth, 1978), 32. For English roofs see Wood, *Eng. House*, 296-8. In London, attempts were made to enforce the use of shingles or tiles from 1212, *ibid*, 297.

50. H. Murray, 'Medieval Bldgs', 46-7; Murray, 'Perth Bldgs', 67; Blanchard, 'Excavated Buildings', 86.

51. B. Ford, 'Window Glass' in *Perth Exc.*, 152; *Moray Reg.*, nos 226, 241; J. Stones ed. *A Tale of Two Burghs The Archaeology of Old and New Aberdeen* (Aberdeen, 1987), 13. Window glass could only be afforded by the wealthy for most of the Middle Ages, Wood, *Eng. House*, 351, 358. Oiled parchment was a common substitute, Joseph and Frances Gies, *Life in a Medieval City* (New York, 1969), 37.

52. Wordsworth, 'Castle Street', 386; D. Robinson, 'Botanical Remains' in *Perth Exc.*, 209.

53. Elizabeth Eames, 'The plain glazed floor tiles' in Schofield, 'Edinburgh High Street', 211-12. For references to other floor surfaces, see Ewan, 'Burgesses', 40, n. 67.

54. H. Murray, 'Medieval Bldgs', 44; H. Murray, 'Perth Bldgs', 71. There is also

evidence of early terraced buildings at York, Colin Platt, *The English Medieval Town* (London, 1976), 67.

55. *Perth Blackfriars*, no. 34; Wordsworth, 'Castle Street', 385; Blanchard, 'Kirk Close', 29; Wood, *Eng. House*, 216. Houses might also be subdivided, Atkin and Evans , 'Population', 94.

56. *Stirling Chrs.*, no. 10; H. Murray, 'Perth Bldgs', 49; Blanchard, 'Kirk Close', 20.

57. M. Fraser and J. H. Dickson, 'Plant remains' in *Aber. Exc.*, 240; *Leges Burgorum*, c. 116; N. L. MacAskill , 'Pottery' in *Perth Exc.*, 91.

58. *Leges Burgorum*, c. 116; A. Curteis, 'The Worked Wood' (PHSE), 67.

59. Stones, *Two Burghs*, 29.

60. R . M. Spearman, 'Metalworking Evidence' in *Perth Exc.*, 158; *Chron. Froissart*, i, 24.

61. L. Laing, 'Cooking-Pots and the Origins of the Scottish Medieval Pottery Industry', *Archaeological Journal*, cxxx (1973), 199; N. MacAskill et al, 'Pottery' (SUAT), 7, 20; S. A. Moorhouse, 'The medieval pottery industry and its markets' in *Medieval Industry* ed. D. W. Crossley (London, 1981), 114.

62. MacAskill, 'Perth Pottery', 91-5; Curteis, 'Worked Wood', 25-7, 33-8; John Barber, 'Medieval Wooden Bowls' in *Studies in Scottish Antiquity presented to Stewart Cruden* ed. David J. Breeze (Edinburgh, 1984), 133.

63. J. C. Murray, 'The Pottery' in *Aber. Exc.*, 123; Curteis, 'Worked Wood', 1. The porringers found at Perth may be the earliest example of what became a very popular vessel in Scotland, Curteis, 'Worked Wood', 7. Woodworkers also produced high-quality goods, Barber, 'Wooden Bowls', 144.

64. A. C. MacGregor, 'A Report on Worked Bone, Antler and Ivory' (PHSE), 16; C. Thomas, 'Leather' in *Perth Exc.*, 182; *Leges Burgorum*, c. 116; Stones, *Two Burghs*, 30, 29 fig. 24; Gies, *Life in City*, 38-40.

65. Stones, *Two Burghs*, 14; Curteis, 'Worked Wood', 14-15.

66. H. Murray, 'Aberdeen Bldgs', 224.

67. *Peebles Chrs.*, no. 3; *Stir. Chrs.*, no. 11; *Abdn. Chrs.*, no. 8; *Irvine Muniments*, no. 2. Coal was sometimes used as fuel but less commonly than peat, Torrie, 'Gild of Dunfermline', 226, 304.

68. *Leges Burgorum*, c. 18; H. Murray, '42 St Paul Street 1977-8', in *Aber. Exc.*, 53, 55; *Arb. Lib.*, ii, no. 38. Fire was a constant risk in the towns. In 1425 Parliament ordered every burgh to equip itself with firefighting equipment, *APS*, ii, 12.

69. *De Articulis Inquirendis in Burgo in Itinere Camerarii Secundum Usum Scocie [Art. Inq.]* in *Ancient Burgh Laws*, c. 43; *Statuta Gilde* in *Ancient Burgh Laws*, c. 19.

70. *Abdn. Recs.*, 116, 174; H. Booton, 'Burgesses and Landed Men', 7; Evan M. Barron, *Inverness in the Fifteenth Century* (Inverness, 1906), 18. For refuse disposal at Dunfermline see Torrie, 'Gild of Dunfermline', 292-7.

71. Matthew Livingstone, 'A Calendar of Charters and Other Writs Relating to Lands or Benefices in Scotland in Possession of the Society of Antiquaries of Scotland', *PSAS*, xli (1906-7), 312-13; L. Blanchard, 'An Excavation at 45 Canal Street, Perth, 1978-79' (SUAT).

72. H. Murray, 'Perth Bldgs', 49; Blanchard, 'Kirk Close', 23-5; Schofield, 'Edinburgh', 162, 170; Wood, *Eng. House*, 385.

73. Blanchard, 'Excavated Buildings', 86; H. Murray, '45-47 Gallowgate', 308; H. Murray, 'St Paul Street', 66; H. Murray, 'Perth Bldgs', 64.

74. SRO, RH1/2/628; Blanchard, '45 Canal Street', 7; Spearman, 'Canal St. II', 65-73.

75. N. McGavin, 'Lanark' in *D&E* (1979), 38; *Moray Reg.*, no. 240; Whittington, 'Plough-Marks', 116; Derek W. Hall, *Excavations at Market Street St Andrews 1985. Interim Report* (SUAT, 1985), 5.

76. H. Murray, 'St Paul Street', 57-8, 81; Blanchard, 'Kirk Close,' 20; *Hadd. Chrs.*, 1-3.

77. *Leges Burgorum*, c. 102; *Statuta Gilde*, c. 21; *Frag. Coll.*, c. 20; G. W. I. Hodgson, 'The Animal Remains from Mediaeval Sites Within Three Burghs on

166

Notes

the Eastern Scottish Seaboard' in *Site Environment and Economy* ed. Bruce Proudfoot (London, 1983), 14; Raymond E. Chaplin and Linda Barnetson, 'The Animal Bones' in Schofield, 'Edinburgh High Street', 231; G. W. I. Hodgson and C. Smith, 'The Animal Remains' in Wordsworth, 'Castle Street' ['Inverness Animal'], 375.

78. See Ewan, 'Burgesses', 21-2 and ch. 4 below; Spearman, 'Perth Townscape', 52; David Bowler, personal communication.
79. M. Lynch, 'Towns and Townspeople in Fifteenth-Century Scotland' in *Towns and Townspeople in the Fifteenth Century* ed. J. A. F. Thomson (London, 1988), 181; N. Shead, 'Glasgow: An Ecclesiastical Burgh' in *Scottish Town*, 119.
80. S. A. Moorhouse, 'Medieval pottery and its markets' in *Medieval Industry* ed. M. W. Crossley (London, 1981), 96-108; *APS*, ii, 12; Spearman, 'Perth Townscape', 55; R. M. Spearman, '29-30 South Methven Street' in *Perth Exc.*, 58.
81. Information on Rattray comes from a BBC Radio Scotland interview of J. C. Murray, 13 July 1988, and J. C. Murray, *The Deserted Medieval Burgh of Rattray, Aberdeenshire. Interim Report on the Excavations* (Aberdeen, 1986), 3-4, 5.
82. R. M. Spearman, 'Workshops, Materials and Debris – Evidence of Early Industry' in *Scottish Town*, 145, 136; Ennen, *Medieval Town*, 68. For more detailed references to archaeological evidence of urban industry see Ewan, 'Burgesses', 51-80.
83. Hodgson, 'Three Burghs', 9, 12.
84. Hodgson, 'Inverness Animal', 377; *Leges Burgorum*, c. 64; G. W. I. Hodgson, 'Report on the animal remains excavated during 1975-76 from the mediaeval levels at the High Street, Perth' (PHSE), 5.
85. Hodgson, 'Perth High Street animals', 17-18.
86. A. W. K. Stevenson, 'Trade with the South 1070-1513' in *Scottish Town*, 191-2.
87. Duncan, 'Perth', 43-4.
88. *Leges Burgorum*, c. 103, 20; *Modus Procedendi in Itinere Camerarii infra Regnum Scocie [Iter Cam.]* in *Ancient Burgh Laws*, c. 28; *Stir. Chrs.*, no. 7; SL, B59/23/2. My thanks to Dr E. P. Torrie and Mrs Marion Stavert for information on the Perth and Dunfermline guilds.
89. H. Bennett, ' Textiles' in *Aber. Exc.*, 198.
90. H. Bennett, 'Textiles'(PHSE), 2-4.
91. H. Murray, 'St Paul Street', 83; L. Blanchard, 'Kirk Close – A Backland Excavation' in *Town Houses and Structures*, 37.
92. Bennett, 'Textiles' (PHSE), 11-14, 22; Stones, *Two Burghs*, 26; *Leges Burgorum*, c. 42; *Assisa de Tolloneis*, no. vii.
93. Bennett, 'Aberdeen Textiles', 198; Spearman, 'Workshops', 138.
94. A. A. M. Duncan, *Scotland: The Making of the Kingdom* (Edinburgh, 1975), 510, n. 24; E. M. Carus-Wilson, *Medieval Merchant Venturers* (London, 1954), 183-210; Bennett, 'Textiles' (PHSE), 25, 27, 37.
95. *Assisa de Tolloneis*, xi; *Aberdeen's Hidden History* ed. G. G. Simpson (Aberdeen, 1972), 21; Bennett, 'Textiles' (PHSE), 18.
96. Bennett, 'Textiles' (PHSE), 19.
97. *Ibid*, 23-4, 58.
98. *Ibid*, 84; John Hunter, 'Report on the Medieval Glass from the Perth High Street Excavation' (PHSE), 6.
99. Duncan, 'Perth', 36-7.
100. Spearman, 'Workshops', 139; Dave Evans, *Digging up the 'Coopie'. Investigations in the Gallowgate and Lochlands* (Aberdeen, 1987), 12-14; *Abdn. Recs.*, 229, 230. A documented site will be examined in Dunfermline – my thanks to Philip Holdsworth of SUAT for this information.
101. Blanchard, 'Kirk Close', 27; J. Stones, 'The Small Finds' in *Aber. Exc.*, 194.
102. A. C. MacGregor, 'Perth Bone, Antler and Ivory', 6, 19.
103. Spearman, 'Workshops', 140-1; A. MacGregor, 'Bone, Antler and Ivory Objects' in *Aber. Exc.*, 180-4.

104. Robinson, 'Perth Botanical Remains', 206-9.
105. *Leges Burgorum*, c. 36, 59; *Abdn. Recs.*, 93-5; A. Grant, *Independence and Nationhood:Scotland 1306-1469* (London, 1984), 63; *Leges Burgorum*, c. 18, 116.
106. Spearman, 'Workshops', 142; Hall, *Market Street, St Andrews*, 3; J. R. Hunter, 'Medieval Berwick upon Tweed', *Archaeologia Aeliana*, 5 ser., x (1982), 81; Canal Street III at Perth – my thanks to P. Holdsworth for this information; Spearman, 'South Methven St.', 58; *Lind. Lib.*, no. 10. See Spearman, 'Workshops', 142-3 for description of how the ovens functioned.
107. *Leges Burgorum*, c. 63; *Statuta Gilde*, c. 43; *Art. Inq.*, c. 15; *Abdn. Recs.*, 21; *Leges Burgorum*, c. 60; *Frag. Coll.*, c. 5.
108 *Statuta Gilde*, c. 22; Spearman, 'Workshops', 142; P. A. Rahtz, 'Medieval milling' in *Medieval Industry*, 2. For references to burgh mills see Marinell Ash, *List of Medieval Mills in Scotland* (typescript, 1980) under burgh names, and ER, i-iv.
109. *Camb. Reg.*, no. 55; Fenton Wyness, *City by the Grey North Sea*, 2nd ed. (Aberdeen, 1972), 15; Stevenson, 'Trade with the South', 186.
110. Stones, 'Aber. Small Finds', 180.
111 *ER*, i, 6; Duncan, *Scotland*, 478; C. Martin, 'The Boat Timbers' (PHSE), 93, 101; J. Stones , 'Iron Objects' in *Aber. Exc.*, 188.
112. Curteis, 'Worked Wood', 43, 57-8, 65; Crone and Barber, 'Structural Timbers', 88; Wordsworth, 'Castle Street', 381. It is possible that coopers may have worked outside the burgh in adjacent woodlands as no evidence of waste blocks has been found, Spearman, 'Workshops', 143.
113. *St Giles Reg.*, no. 14; *Abdn. Recs.*, 85; D. Wright, 'The Baskets' (PHSE), 102-3.
114. *Angels, Nobles and Unicorns*, exhibition catalogue, National Museum of Antiquities of Scotland (Edinburgh, 1982), 68; *Edin. Chrs.*, no. 14; *Arb. Lib.*, ii, no. 43; *Abdn. Recs.*, 68; N. H. Trewin, 'The Stone Objects' in *Aber. Exc.*, 184.
115. See *Angels, Nobles*, 37-8, 39 for illustrations.
116. *ER*, i, 616-7, ii, 65, 160; Colvin Greig, 'Queen St Midden Area 1973' in *Aber. Exc.*, 23; *Abdn. Reg.*, i, 284-6.
117. MacAskill, 'The Pottery' in 'Castle Street', 368, 370; R. M. Spearman, 'Metalworking Evidence' in *Perth Exc.*, 157-8; Alison R. Goodall, 'The medieval bronzesmith and his products' in *Medieval Industry*, 63; Spearman, 'Workshops', 144.
118. R. M. Spearman and E. Slater, 'Physical Analysis of the Metalworking Debris' in 'Castle Street', 354; *Early Travellers*, 11; R. F. Tylecote, 'The medieval smith and his methods' in *Medieval Industry*, 44; Stevenson, 'Trade with the South', 186.
119. Stones, 'Aberdeen Iron Objects', 188; W. F. H. Nicolaisen, 'Tension and Extension: Thoughts on Scottish Surnames and Medieval Popular Culture', *Journal of Popular Culture*, 14:1 (1981), 123.
120. C. J. Tabraham, 'Kelso Abbey', *D&E* (1975), 50-1; *Arb. Lib.*, ii, no. 43; J. D. Bateson, 'A Medieval Pewter Token' (PHSE), 1-2. Trade tokens probably circulated before 1280 when Alexander III introduced halfpennies and farthings, and possibly again in the fifteenth century as they did in England, Palliser, 'Medieval period', 64.
121. Barrow, *Kingship and Unity*, 1, 97; I. H. Stewart, *The Scottish Coinage* (London, 1955), 18-19. Continental mints were also concentrated in towns, Ennen, *Medieval Town*, 134-5.
122. *ER*, i, 615-6, ii, 159-60. Bonagius of Florence worked in the Durham mint before coming to Edinburgh, Stewart, *Coinage*, 26.
123. Watt, *Bower*, 12.
124. Lloyd Laing, 'Cooking-Pots', 192, 193; MacAskill, 'Pottery' (SUAT), 8, 19. Perth Local pottery was not found on the twelfth-century King Edward Street site – my thanks to Peter Clark of SUAT for pointing this out.
125. MacAskill, 'Pottery' (SUAT), 20-1; MacAskill, 'Inverness Pottery', 366.

126. Stevenson, 'Trade with the South', 189.
127. MacAskill, 'Perth Pottery', 110; Lloyd R. Laing, 'Excavations at Linlithgow Palace, West Lothian 1966-7', *PSAS*, xcix (1966-7), 131 ; Moorhouse, 'Medieval pottery and its markets', 96, 100, 105; Colvin Greig ,'Virginia Street Steps, Castle Lane 1974' in *Aber. Exc.*, 107.
128. N. MacAskill, 'Pottery' in Holmes,'Leith', 416; MacAskill, 'Pottery' (SUAT), 21; Lloyd R. Laing and Eric J. Talbot, 'Some Medieval and Post-Medieval Pottery from South West Scotland', *Glasgow Archaeological Journal*, iii (1974), 44.
129. Moorhouse, 'Medieval pottery and its markets', 107-8.
130. Curteis, 'Worked Wood', 70; John di Folco, 'Roof tile fragments from the Isle of May', *PSAS*, cxi (1981), 524.
131. Stones, *Two Burghs*, 32; J. Stones,'Copper Alloy Objects' in *Aber. Exc.*, 186.
132. H. Bennett,'Textiles' in *Perth Exc.*, 159, 174; *ER*, i, 142; *APS*, ii, 18.
133. Gies, *Life in City*, 85; C. Thomas,'Leather', 174-5; Curteis,'Worked Wood', 65; *Abdn. Recs.*, 39; St AUL, SL110/6/9.
134. *Early Travellers*, 27; Hodgson, 'Three Burghs', 9, 11; G. W. Hodgson and A. Jones, 'The Animal Bone' in *Aber. Exc.*, 235-6; Hodgson, 'Perth High Street animals', 2, 28. Townspeople tended to eat the meat of older animals, a pattern recognised outside Scotland as well, John Schofield,'Recent approaches in urban archaeology' in *Urban Archaeology*, 2.
135. Stones, *Two Burghs*, 29-30; Fraser, 'Botanical Remains', 242, 243; *ER*, i, 483.
136. Grant, *Independence*, 74. A research project by Juliet Cross at the University of Aberdeen on skeletal remains from several Scottish sites is summarised in Stones, *Two Burghs*, 32-7, from which the following information on health is mainly drawn. The forthcoming report on Carmelite friary sites will also contain information on skeletal remains.
137. *Ibid*, 36-7; Fraser, 'Plant Remains', 240-1. For the ills suffered by the townspeople of Dunfermline see Torrie,'Gild of Dunfermline', 287-90.
138. *Abdn. Recs.*, 211; *APS*, ii, 16; Gies, *Life in City*, 117. For a description of the leper's life in the fifteenth century see Robert Henryson's poem, *The Testament of Cresseid*.
139. Fraser, 'Plant Remains', 242; Gies, *Life in City*, 115.
140. A. MacGregor,'Bone, Antler and Ivory Objects' in *Aber. Exc.*, 182; MacGregor, 'Perth Bone, Antler and Ivory', 4-5; Curteis,'Worked Wood', 62; W. Norman Robertson, 'The Game of Merelles in Scotland', *PSAS*, xcviii (1964-66), 321-2; Murray, radio interview.
141. *APS*, ii, 5-6; Murray,'Archaeological Evidence', 18. See illustrations in Stones, *Two Burghs*, 34.
142. Watt, *Bower*, 8-10, 76-8.

CHAPTER TWO: THE GOVERNANCE OF THE BURGH
1. William Mackay Mackenzie calls into question the validity of the laws as an accurate reflection of burgh society, William Mackay Mackenzie, *The Scottish Burghs* (Edinburgh, 1949), 21-30. While recognising that they should be taken as an *indication* of the social conditions rather than as gospel, they are useful in helping to draw a picture of life in the medieval burgh, especially when they are used in conjunction with other documentary evidence. For further discussion, see Iain Flett and J. Cripps, 'Documentary Sources' in *Scottish Town*, 20 and M. Lynch, 'Towns and Townspeople', 179. For the dates of the Burgh Laws, see Hector MacQueen and William Windram, 'Laws and Courts in the Burghs' in *Scottish Town*, 209-11.
2. *ESC*, no. 169. Duncan suggests, however, that the strong foreign element in burghs such as Perth and Berwick would be likely to assert its financial

independence from the sheriff immediately, Duncan, *Scotland,* 159.

3. *Abdn. Recs.*, xix-xxi. For the sheriff as farmer of the burgh see Duncan, *Scotland,* 483.
4. George S. Pryde ed. *The Court Book of the Burgh of Kirkintilloch, 1658-1694* (SHS, 1963), xxxiii.
5. Fraser, *Eglinton,* ii, no. 8(3).
6. Mackenzie, *Burghs,* 96; M. Lynch et al, 'Introduction' in *Scottish Town,* 7-9. Lynch also argues against the appearance of uniformity implied by royal legislation on the burghs in the fifteenth century, pointing out that such legislation was often passed in response to the situation in one particular town, Lynch, 'Towns and Townspeople', 174-5.
7. *Abdn. Recs.*, lxxi, n. 1
8. Duncan, *Scotland,* 483.
9. *Iter Cam.,* 132-54. For a description of the chamberlain's ayre in one burgh see W. Croft Dickinson, 'A Chamberlain's Ayre in Aberdeen 1399x1400', *SHR,* xxxiii (1954).
10. *Abdn. Recs.*, cii-ciii.
11. Mackenzie, *Burghs,* 99; *ND,* no. 234.
12. *Leges Burgorum,* c. 70.
13. *Leges Burgorum,* c. 4, 3, 76, 59, 112; *Statuta Gilde,* c. 37.
14. By the fourteenth century the bailies had taken over this duty, Cosmo Innes, 'Notes of Some Curiosities of Old Scottish Tenures and Investitures', *PSAS,* iii (1857-8), 87.
15. SRO, RH6/142A.
16. MA, M/W1/1; NLS, Adv. MS. 20. 3. 9, ff. 153-4; *APS,* i, 536-7.
17. *St Giles Reg.,* no. 15; SRO, GD79/5/1.
18. *Abdn. Recs.,* 34.
19. *Abdn. Recs.,* passim; NLS, Adv. MS. 9A. 1. 10, f. 38.
20. *St Nich. Cart.,* i, 16-17; *A. B. Ill.,* iii, 43-4; *Edin. Chrs.,* no. 14.
21. *Abdn. Recs.,* 101; *A. B. Ill.,* iii, 43-4.
22. *St Giles Reg.,* no. 1.
23. *Ibid,* nos 8, 14.
24. *Glas. Reg.,* i, no. 295.
25. *Edin. Chrs.,* no. 14.
26. SL, B59/23/4; SRO, GD79/5/5; SRO, GD79/5/6. For other burghs see *An Historical Atlas of Scotland,* rev. ed. (forthcoming). For powers of the sheriff, see *Fife Ct. Bk.,* xxxviii-ix.
27. *Peebles Chrs.,* no. 5; *Iter Cam.,* c. 4, 29.
28. *Statuta Gilde,* c. 37.
29. *Abdn. Recs.,* cxviii, n. 7; *St Giles Reg.,* nos 15, 19.
30. *Leges Burgorum,* c. 70; *Juramenta Officiariorum* in *Ancient Burgh Laws,* 130; *Art. Inq.,* c. 63.
31. *Abdn. Recs.,* passim; *Art. Inq.,* c. 4, 59, 48, 49.
32. *Abdn. Recs.,* 92; SRO, RH1/2/614.
33. *Banff Annals,* ii, 377-8.
34. *Abdn. Recs.,* 34, 39, 41; *Aberdeen Friars,* 21.
35. *Leges Burgorum,* c. 37; *Arb. Lib.,* ii, no. 22.
36. NLS, Adv. MS. 20. 3. 9, ff. 153-4.
37. *Ayr Friars,* nos 17-19.
38. *Leges Burgorum,* c. 87; David Murray, *Early Burgh Organization in Scotland* (Glasgow, 1924-32), i, 332.
39. *Juramenta Officiariorum,* 128.
40. *Abdn. Recs.,* 7, 23; *Leges Burgorum,* c. 44
41. *Leges Burgorum,* c. 57: W. C. Dickinson, 'Burgh Life from Burgh Records', *AUR,* xxxi (1946), 221-2; *Abdn. Recs.,* 22, 23.
42. *Frag. Coll.,* c. 31; *Moray Reg.,* no. 149.

43. *Abdn. Recs.*, 21; *Iter Cam.*, c. 6, 8.
44. *Leges Burgorum*, c. 105, 119; *Reg. Brieves*, no. lxviii, cf. no. xxv. The 1398 Aberdeen entry is left blank, possibly to allow for later entries. In 1399 there were eleven liners, in 1400 nine, *Abdn. Recs.*, 21, 100, 196.
45. *Leges Burgorum*, c. 119.
46. See Brooks, 'Planning and growth', 287-9 for evidence of town planning, albeit under the bishop's control.
47. *Abdn. Counc.*, i, 392; *Abdn. Recs.*, 101, 196-7; W. E. K. Rankin, 'Scottish Burgh Churches in the Fifteenth Century', *Records of the Scottish Church History Society* (1941), 69. In 1358 the Aberdeen burgess John Fichet was described as 'in charge of church funds', *St Nich Cart.*, i, 17.
48. Charles Fraser-Mackintosh, *Invernessiana* (Inverness, 1875), 78; *Lanark Recs.*, 347; SRO, GD79/5/2; John Durkan, 'The Early Scottish Notary' in *The Renaissance and Reformation in Scotland: essays in honour of Gordon Donaldson*, eds. I. B. Cowan and Duncan Shaw (Edinburgh, 1983).
49. *Ayr Friars*, no. 12. Dickinson suggests that custody of the seal may have been given to one of the members of the council, *Abdn. Recs.*, lxxxix.
50. *Leges Burgorum*, c. 107; *Pais. Reg.*, 385-6.
51. *Statuta Gilde*, c. 37; *Leges Burgorum*, c. 112. The council was often known as 'the dusane' but this did not necessarily imply that it had twelve members, Mackenzie, *Burghs*, 107-8.
52. *APS*, ii, 95; *Abdn. Recs.*, 100, 196.
53. *Dundee Chrs.*, 135; *Abdn. Recs.*, 99; *Melr. Lib.*, ii, no. 488. Dickinson equates the prima with the guild court. For an argument against this see below, pp. 58-62.
54. *Statuta Gilde*, c. 37; Dickinson suggests that the town council framed the statutes in Aberdeen, *Abdn. Recs.*, lxxxii-iii.
55. *Moray Reg.*, no. 235.
56. Susan Reynolds, *Kingdoms and Communities in Western Europe, 900-1300* (Oxford, 1984), 63-4. A common seal was in use in Oxford in 1191, Platt, *English Town*, 129.
57. *Pais. Reg.*, 399-401.
58. *Cross. Chrs.*, 20-2; SRO, RH6/175.
59. SRO, GD4/226; *Arb. Lib.*, ii, no. 42; Montrose Archives [MA], M/W1/1.
60. *RMS*, i, no. 196; *Edin. Chrs.*, no. 14; *Abdn. Counc.*, i, 392; *Ayr Friars*, no. 26; *Arb. Lib.*, ii, no. 22.
61. *Edin. Chrs.*, no. 6; *APS*, i, 453.
62. G. H. Martin, 'New Beginnings in North-Western Europe' in Barley, *European Towns*, 412, 413; *St Giles Reg.*, no. 15; *Abdn. Recs.*, 212-5. For the transition from oral tradition to written records in England at this time, see M. T. Clanchy, *From Memory to Written Record: England 1066-1307* (London, 1979). In Scotland a similar increase in central government records has been noted by Bruce Webster, *Scotland from the Eleventh Century to 1603* (London, 1975), 203 and G. G. Simpson, 'The Use of Documentary Sources by the Archaeologist. A Viewpoint from Scotland', *Archives*, xiii, no. 60 (1978), 208. A study of fifteenth- and early sixteenth-century Aberdeen has shown an increase in notaries there, Booton, 'Burgesses and Landed Men', ch. 3.
63. Symbolism has not completely died out in modern Scotland; several border burghs still carry out the common riding each year to indicate the boundaries of each burgh's common lands. A film of the Langholm common riding has been made by the School of Scottish Studies.
64. *Art. Inq.*, c. 48, 59; *Iter Cam.*, c. 1, 2; *Abdn. Recs.*, 180-4.
65. *Fife Ct. Bk.*, lxi. The burgh records of Aberdeen strongly ressemble the record of courts and assizes.
66. *APS*, i, 466; *St Giles Reg.*, no. 1; *Ayr Chrs.*, nos 4, 6, 12. For the security associated with registers and cartularies, see Clanchy, *Written Record*, 79-82.
67. *St Giles Reg.*, no. 15; *Abdn. Recs.*, cxvi. With the increasing bulk of records in the

fifteenth century, however, an attempt was made in some burghs to record the proceedings of different bodies separately, Flett, 'Documentary Sources', 25-6.

68. The guild book of Dunfermline has recently been published by E. P. D. Torrie. Booton's thesis on Aberdeen makes extensive use of the town records of that burgh. An edition of the guild book of Perth is being prepared by Marion Stavert.

69. Reynolds, *Kingdoms*, 155, 332.

70. *Kel. Lib.*, ii, no. 459.

71. Duncan, *Scotland*, 482, n. 30. Mackenzie suggests that it may have developed from the inquest whose main function was to determine the inheritance of lands but which could also set the watch, issue ordinances for the protection of the town and control market prices, Mackenzie, *Burghs*, 109-10. For an argument for a fairly late date of development see MacQueen, 'Laws and Courts', 213.

72. *Melr. Lib.*, i, no. 27; *St A. Lib.*, 284-5; *Scone Lib.*, no. 95; H. M. Cam, 'From Witness of the Shire to Full Parliament', *TRHS*, 4ser. xxvi (1944), 28-9.

73. MacQueen, 'Laws and Courts', 212 details the similarities between 'burgh law' and 'feudal law'. For more information on the legal system of medieval Scotland, see W. C. Dickinson, 'The Administration of Justice in Medieval Scotland', *AUR*, xxxiv (1952) and *An Introductory Survey of the Sources and Literature of Scots Law* (Stair Society, 1936).

74. *RRS*, vi, no. 2; MacQueen, 'Laws and Courts', 215.

75. There were exceptions to this. No Yule head court was recorded at Aberdeen in 1399 and a Perth head court in 1369 was held on 9 February, *Abdn. Recs.*, passim; SRO, GD79/5/1.

76. *Leges Burgorum*, c. 40; *Abdn. Recs.*, 210.

77. SRO, GD52/293; Dundee Archives [DA],TC/CC10 no. 5; SRO, GD79/5/1.

78. *Abdn. Recs.*, 35, 139. It is also possible that this phrase meant that those who best knew the facts of the case were not present.

79. *Abdn. Recs.*, cxxiii, passim. The following account of court procedure is based largely on Dickinson's account, *Abdn. Recs.*, cxxix-cxl.

80. *RMS*, i, app. 2, nos 374, 396; *Abdn. Recs.*, cxxvii. There was a cuckstool in Aberdeen from at least the late thirteenth century, *Abdn. Reg*, i, 35-6.

81. *Abdn. Recs.*, 34, 113. It has been suggested that the chamberlain's judicial role might imply that he was the antecedent to the burgh court, David Robertson and Marguerite Wood, 'Burgh Court Records', in *Intro. to Scots Law*, 102. Appeals from both the burgh court and the chamberlain ayre could go to the Court of the Four Burghs, see below, pp 144-5 (on this text).

82. Sandeman Library [SL], B59/23/4; *RMS*, ii, no. 615.

83. Dickinson suggests that this was a meeting of the guild assembly, possibly with the town council in attendance, *Abdn. Recs.*, cx, n. 5. Nicholson, basing his evidence on Dickinson, identifies it with the guild court, Nicholson, *Scotland*, 263. For an argument against identifying it too closely with the guild, see Ewan 'Burgesses', 128-9.

84. *Abdn. Recs.*, 211, 164, 179, 215.

85. For a list of burghs with guilds in the Middle Ages see Ewan, 'Burgesses', 130, and *Historical Atlas* rev. ed. General merchant guilds are recorded in Europe from the eleventh century, Ennen, *Medieval Town*, 96-9.

86. M. Lynch, 'Whatever happened to the medieval burgh?', *Scottish Economic and Social History*, iv (1984), 12-13. See also Susan Reynolds, *An Introduction to the History of English Medieval Towns* (Oxford, 1977), 181-7 and E. P. D. Torrie, 'The Guild in Fifteenth-Century Dunfermline'in *Scottish Town*, 247-8. The older view is expressed in Nicholson, *Scotland*, 263 and Grant, *Economic Life*, 135-6.

87. Murray, *Burgh Org.*, i, 462 argues for the applicability of the *Statuta* to other burghs. Mackenzie argues against it, Mackenzie, *Burghs*, 100. For the description of thirteenth-century Berwick see *Chron. Lanercost*, 185.

88. This tradition is probably based on William's charter granting the burgesses of

Perth the right to have a guild merchant, *RRS*, ii, no. 467.
89. My thanks to Dr E. P. Torrie and Mrs Marion Stavert for this information. For comments on waulkers and weavers, see Barrow, *Kingship and Unity*, 102; Charles Gross, *The Gild Merchant* (Oxford, 1890), 108-9.
90. *Iter Cam.*, c. 28; *Abdn. Recs.*, 27.
91. A recent statement of this idea is R. G. Rodgers, 'The Evolution of Scottish Town Planning' in *Scottish Urban History*, 76.
92. Duncan, 'Perth', 43; *Abdn. Chrs.*, no. 3; *APS*, i, 536; *Dunf. Gd. Bk.*, xviii.
93. *RRS*, vi, nos 464, 334; MA, M/W1/1.
94. SL, B59/23/6; SL, B59/23/14.
95. *St Giles Reg.*, no. 163. Duncan, *Scotland*, 494 and J. Marwick, 'The Municipal Institutions of Scotland', *SHR*, i (1904), 128-9 interpret the term alderman this way. E. P. Torrie refutes this, *Dunf. Gd Bk.*, xx.
96. *Dunf. Gd. Bk.*, xxi; Torrie, 'Guild in Dunfermline', 255-6.
97. *Dunf. Gd. Bk.*, xxii; Torrie, 'Guild in Dunfermline', 256-7.
98. *Dunf. Gd. Bk.*, xxii, 164. Reynolds also emphasises the importance of the guild's social function, Reynolds, *English Towns*, 167-8. Publication of the Perth Guild Book may further illustrate this point.

CHAPTER THREE: TRADE AND TRADERS
1.   *Regiam Maiestatem* in *Ancient Burgh Laws*, c. 35.
2.   There were some exceptions. Perth's petty customs in 1341-2 were £4 8s 2d, *ER*, i, 484.
3.   Reynolds, *English Towns*, 59; Ennen, *Medieval Town*, 73-4. For the importance of regional trade to one such burgh, see Anne Turner Simpson and Sylvia Stevenson, *Historic Forfar* (SBS, 1981), 1-2, 5, 20. R. Dickinson argues that most small Scandinavian towns which developed in the fourteenth and fifteenth centuries did so mainly for purposes of local trade, Dickinson, *European City*, 287.
4.   Brechin was the only non-burghal market for much of the fourteenth century and it had to struggle to keep its privileges, *RRS*, vi, nos 120, 334, 369; *Brech. Reg.*, i, nos 5, 16.
5.   For a conjectural map of the trading liberties, see J. M. Houston, 'The Scottish Burgh', *Town Planning Review*, xxv (1954-55), 116. For specific burghs see *An Historical Atlas of Scotland*, rev. ed.
6.   *RRS*, vi, no. 305; SL, B59/23/6; *Abdn. Recs.*, 180-4.
7.   *RCRB*, i, 538-40. Pryde sees this grant as completing the evolution of the burghs' market monopoly, George Pryde, 'The Origin of the Burgh in Scotland', *Juridical Review*, xlvii (1935), 274.
8.   For example, Dundee, DA, TC/CC 17. According to the burgh laws, widows who traded along with burgesses were liable to pay aids, *Leges Burgorum*, c. 104.
9.   *Kel. Lib.*, ii, no. 459.
10. *Leges Burgorum*, c. 66, 72, 73; *Statuta Gilde*, c. 32; *Abdn. Recs.*, 222-4, 58.
11. *Leges Burgorum*, c. 9, 65; *Abdn. Recs.*, 79, 118.
12. *Leges Burgorum*, c. 37; *Abdn. Recs.*, 83; Lynch, 'Towns and Townspeople', 181.
13. *Abdn. Recs.*, 41, 115.
14. *ER*, i, pp xcv, cxxxviii, 521, ii, 599.
15. *RRS*, vi, nos 120, 121; *Edin. Chrs.*, no. 8.
16. Duncan, *Scotland*, 472, 512; *Leges Burgorum*, c. 86-8; Sir James Marwick, *List of Markets and Fairs* (Glasgow, 1890).
17. *Arb. Lib.*, ii, no. 22.
18. I. F. Grant, *The Social and Economic Development of Scotland before 1603* (Edinburgh, 1930), 118; G. W. S. Barrow, 'Land Routes: The Medieval Evidence' in *Loads and Roads in Scotland and Beyond* eds. Alexander Fenton and

Geoffrey Stell (Edinburgh, 1984), 50-6, 58. The custumars' accounts distinguish between ships and little boats (*batella*). The latter may have been used for coastal trade.

19. *Melr. Lib.*, i, no. 14; Stevenson, 'Trade with the South', 187-8, 189-94, 198-202.

20. *CDS*, v, no. 584; W. Stanford Reid, 'Trade, Traders and Independence', *Speculum*, xxix (1954), 215-20; David Ditchburn, 'Trade with Northern Europe 1297-1540' in *Scottish Town*, 162.

21. *Foedera (H)*, II, i, 98.

22. *Calendar of the Patent Rolls preserved in the Public Record Office* (London, 1893-1982) [*CPR*], *1313-17*, 269; James Dilley, 'The German Merchants and Scotland 1295-1327', PhD thesis (UCLA, 1946), 87-9. See also his 'German Merchants in Scotland, 1297-1327', *SHR*, xxvii (1948).

23. *APS*, i, 480; *CPR, 1324-7*, 23, 115.

24. *ER*, i, 119, 342-4, 314-22; Ranald Nicholson, *Edward III and the Scots* (Oxford, 1963), 60.

25. *Foedera (H)*, II, ii, 92-3.

26. *CPR, 1340-43*, 212.

27. Rooseboom, *Staple*, 5; *APS*, i, 514-15; Nicholson, *Scotland*, 153.

28. *Hansisches Urkundenbuch* [*Hans. Urk.*] ed. K. Hohlbaum (Halle, 1879-96), iii, no. 131; *CPR, 1350-4*, 281, 417; *Calendar of the Close Rolls preserved in the Public Record Office* (London, 1902-1963) [*CCR*], *1354-60*, 386; *CPR, 1354-8*, 292.

29. *Rot. Scot.*, i, 798; T. H. Lloyd, *The English Wool Trade in the Middle Ages* (Cambridge, 1977), 144. Robert I was aware of the usefulness of wool as a source of revenue for war, Nicholson, *Scotland*, 107.

30. John Davidson and Alexander Gray, *The Scottish Staple at Veere* (London, 1909), 98. See *Rot. Scot.*, i, ii, passim for safe conducts.

31. *RRS*, vi, no. 316.

32. James Campbell, 'England, Scotland and the Hundred Years War in the Fourteenth Century' in *Europe in the Late Middle Ages* eds. J. R. Hale, J. R. L. Highfield and B. Smalley (London, 1965), 204.

33. Campbell, 'Hundred Years War', 204; *Hans. Urk.*, iii, no. 579; A. W. K. Stevenson, 'Trade between Scotland and the Low Countries in the later Middle Ages', PhD thesis (Aberdeen, 1982), 14; Lloyd, *Wool Trade*, 225.

34. Rooseboom, *Staple*, 9.

35. *CDS*, iv, nos 387, 481.

36. *ER*, iii, 659; *Hanserecesse. Die Recesse und andere akten der Hansetage von 1256-1430* ed. Karl Loppmann (Leipzig, 1870-77), iii, no. 404.

37. Nicholson, *Scotland*, 266; Fischer, *Germany*, 238-9; Ditchburn, 'Trade with the North', 164-7.

38. Rooseboom, *Staple*, app. no. 10.

39. Rooseboom, *Staple*, app. nos 12-14; James Yair, *An Account of the Scotch Trade in the Netherlands, and of the Staple Port in Campvere* (London, 1776), 27-33.

40. Stevenson, 'Low Countries', 22-5; *CDS*, iv, no. 462; *APS*, i, 571; Lynch, 'Towns and Townspeople', 176.

41. J. Donnelly, 'Thomas of Coldingham, merchant and burgess of Berwick upon Tweed (died 1316)', *SHR*, lix (1980), 105-20.

42. Duncan, *Scotland*, 428-9.

43. Francesco Balducci Pegolotti, *La Pratica Della Mercatura* ed. Allan Evans (Camb., Mass., 1936), 258-69; Duncan, *Scotland*, 429-31; Lloyd, *Wool Trade*, 316.

44. Bennett, 'Textiles' (PHSE), 83.

45. Lloyd, *Wool Trade*, 312, 315-16.

46. *Ibid*, 303; *Statuta Gilde*, c. 31.

47. Stevenson, 'Low Countries', 151; *Family of Rose*, 112-3.

48. Stevenson, 'Low Countries', 152.

49. *ER*, i, 366-8, 425-7; *ER*, ii, pp xli; *APS*, i, 504.

50. *APS*, i, 496, 497; *ER*, ii, 234, 267, 275, 375. In Aberdeen in 1317 there were two 'keepers of the cocket seal'. These may have been the custumars, *CDS*, v, no. 632.

51. *ER*, iii, 66.

52. *ER*, ii, 381, 314-5.

53. *Ibid*, 374, 378, 471, 515.

54. Carus-Wilson suggests that about two-thirds of the wool trade was handled by foreign merchants in late thirteenth-century England, Carus-Wilson, *Med. Merchant*, xxi, although this estimate has been questioned, Reynolds, *English Towns*, 76-7.

55. A. O. Anderson, *Scottish Annals from English Chronicles*, 295, n. 2; *Chron. Bower*, i, 130.

56. *The Chronicle of Walter of Guisborough* ed. Harry Rothwell, Camden Series, 89 (1957), 275; *CDS*, iii, no. 1128; Duncan, *Scotland*, 516. For doubts about the Whitehall as a factory see Ditchburn, 'Trade with the North', 162.

57. *Rot. Scot.*, i, 926: M. M. Postan, *Medieval Trade and Finance* (Cambridge, 1973), 119.

58. *CPR, 1367-70*, 424; *CDS*, iii, nos 713, 1586.

59. Davidson, *Staple*, 8.

60. *Foedera (H)*, II, i, 98; W. Stanford Reid, 'Sea-Power in the Anglo-Scottish War, 1296-1328' in *The Mariner's Mirror*, xlvi (1960), 13-17; *Foedera (H)*, II, iii, 153.

61. *ER*, ii, 243, 329; *APS*, ii, 16.

62. *CPR, 1367-70*, 471; *CCR, 1364-8*, 440-1.

63. *Rot. Scot.*, i, 948; *ER*, iii, 51.

64. *CDS*, iv, no. 300.

65. Stevenson, 'Trade with the South', 188-9 suggests that the staple was at Bruges for most of the century.

66. Davidson, *Staple*, 337-49; Stevenson, 'Trade with the South', 188-99.

67. *Bronnen Tot de Geschiedenis van den Handel met Engeland, Schotland en Ierland 1100-1485* ed. H. J. Smit ('S-Gravenhage, 1925) i, no. 310; Stevenson, 'Low Countries', 177-81; Rooseboom, *Staple*, app. nos 8, 9, 13.

68. Yair, *Scotch Trade*, 27-33.

69. Stevenson, 'Low Countries', 181-2.

70. Rooseboom, *Staple*, app. nos 8, 12, 13.

71. *Hans Urk.*, iii, no. 579; Rooseboom, *Staple*, app. nos 8, 10.

72. Yair, *Scotch Trade*, 29; Ditchburn, 'Trade with the North', 171.

73. Donnelly, 'Thomas of Coldingham', 111-2; Lloyd, 'Wool Trade', 307; Pirenne, *Medieval Cities*, 123-5. However, solo ventures seem to have been more common in the Baltic trade, Ditchburn, 'Trade with the North', 170.

74. *Rot. Scot.*, i, 716, 724, 815, 823.

75. *Ibid*, i, 832; *RMS*, i, no. 443.

76. *Rot. Scot.*, i, 867, 897, ii, 19.

77. *Ibid*, i, 960.

78. *CDS*, iv, no. 460; *Rot. Scot.*, ii, 135, i, 865, 978; *ER*, ii, 450, 463. Thomas de Ballon also appears in the English records as a Scottish merchant, Edna Hamer, 'Anglo-Scottish Relations in the Reigns of Robert II and Robert III', M. Litt. thesis (Glasgow, 1971), 115. Such partnerships probably reflected the family partnerships common to European rural society, Mundy, *Medieval Town*, 38-9.

79. *Formulary E, Scottish Letters and Brieves 1286-1424* ed. A. A. M. Duncan (Glasgow, 1975), no. 62. The factor of an Edinburgh merchant arranged passage to France for the bishops of St Andrews and Dunkeld in 1295, *Chron. Lanercost*, 168-9. Merchants' sons often served as factors to learn their fathers' business. See Fritz Rörig, *The Medieval Town* (Berkeley, 1967), 134-8.

80. *ER*, ii, p. xlii, n. 4; *Hans. Urk.*, iii, no. 131.

81. *CPR, 1324-7*, 354; *CCR, 1337-39*, 172; *CCR, 1327-30*, 186-7.

82. *Rot. Scot.*, i, 836.

83. *Rot. Scot.*, i, ii, *passim*, i, 907.
84. *ER*, i, 342-4; *Rot. Scot.*, i, 945, 959.
85. Rooseboom, *Staple*, app. no. 8.
86. *CDS*, iii, nos 149, 736, 1030.
87. *CDS*, iii, no. 1639; *Rot. Scot.*, i, 933, ii, 2, 7, 119.
88. *Rot. Scot.*, i, 839-40, 854; *CDS*, iv, nos 322, 324.
89 *CDS*, iv, no. 324; *Rot. Scot.*, i, 932, 933, 848.
90. *ER*, i, pp c-ci.
91. Nicholson, *Scotland*, 82; Fischer, *Germany*, 5; *CDS*, iii, no. 549; *CPR, 1313-17*, 235; H. S. Lucas, 'John Crabbe, Flemish Pirate, Merchant and Adventurer', *Speculum*, xx (1945), 338. Despite Nicholson's contrast of the law-abiding Scottish merchant and the less restrained noble, *Scotland*, 267, the merchants of Scotland seem to have been no less averse than merchants of other countries to privateering.
92. *CPR, 1313-17*, 8, 334. See Reid, 'Traders' for an assessment of the merchants' contribution to the Scottish resistance to Edward III.
93. *CDS*, iv, no. 250; *CCR, 1377-81*, 39; *CDS*, v, no. 504.
94. Reid, 'Traders', 213-14.
95. *CPR, 1343-45*, 170. Some of the wealthiest merchants in Newcastle were involved in such activities, J. B. Blake, 'Medieval Smuggling in the North-east: Some Fourteenth-century Evidence', *Archaeologia Aeliana*, 4th ser., xliii (1965), 252.
96. *CPR, 1343-45*, 280; *Calendar of Inquisitions Miscellaneous (Chancery) preserved in the Public Record Office* (London, 1906-37), iii, no. 972.
97. Isabel Guy, 'The Scottish Export Trade, 1460-1599 from the Exchequer Rolls', M. Phil thesis (St Andrews, 1982), 18; Blake, 'Smuggling', 247-52.
98. *CDS*, iii, no. 1396.
99. Blake, 'Smuggling', 245; Constance Fraser, 'Medieval trading restrictions in the North East' *Archaeologia Aeliana*, 4th ser., xxxix (1961), 141-2.
100. Campbell, 'Hundred Years War', 204-5. Most of the wool was shipped from the southern burghs such as Edinburgh and Haddington.
101. *CDS*, iii, no. 698; *Rot. Scot.*, ii, 31, 91. For more about John Hull, see Denys Hay, 'Booty in Border Warfare', *TDGAS*, xxxi (1952-3), 151.
102. *ER*, passim.
103. Stevenson, 'Low Countries', 219; Stevenson, 'Trade with the South', 189.
104. *CDS*, iv, no. 462. See *Calendar of the Fine Rolls preserved in the Public Record Office* (London, 1911-62), vi, 457-8 for a detailed cargo list and the prices the items would cost in Flanders. Stevenson suggests such cargoes show a peculiarity of the Scottish trade in that most nations imported entire cargoes of one commodity from the Low Countries, Stevenson, 'Low Countries', 225, although Lloyd suggests that not all English merchants specialised as much as is generally thought, Lloyd, *Wool Trade*, 308. See also Duncan, 'Perth', 47.
105. *CDS*, iii, nos 146, 537, iv, no. 151; Nicholson, *Scotland*, 266; Ditchburn, 'Trade with the North', 168.
106. *Rot. Scot.*, i, 911-2, ii, 120; Davidson, *Staple*, 89-90.
107. J. B. Blake, 'The Medieval Coal Trade of North East England: Some Fourteenth Century Evidence', *Northern History*, ii (1967), 16.
108. Nicholson, *Scotland*, 266; *ER*, i, 410, iii, 659; Stevenson, 'Trade with the South', 193. It is unlikely that Scotland was exporting timber by this time as suggested in Grant, *Independence*, 9, as its forests had decreased greatly in size over the previous centuries.
109. MacAskill, 'Perth Pottery', 101, 110.
110. *Rot. Scot.*, ii, 7; Bennett, 'Aberdeen Textiles', 198-9; *ER*, i, cxiv-vi.
111. *ER*, ii, 238; Stevenson, 'Trade with the South', 192; Lynch, 'Towns and Townspeople', 181-2.
112. *CDS*, iii, no. 1451, iv, no. 114.

113. *CCR, 1364-68*, 451; *CPR, 1313-17*, 455; *CPR, 1321-24*, 333; *CDS*, iii, no. 1505; *Rot. Scot.*, i, 881, 915.
114. *ER*, iii, p. lxxxi. Lynch points out that the increasing predominance of Edinburgh in the traditional export trade also forced other burghs to diversify their commercial activities, Lynch, 'Towns and Townspeople', 176-7. For fish exports see Stevenson, 'Trade with the South', 185-6.
115. This is true even if its role has been ignored by historians such as Postan who, in his essay on medieval trade in Northern Europe in *The Cambridge Economic History*, ii (Cambridge, 1952), does not once refer to Scotland.

CHAPTER FOUR: POSSESSION OF PROPERTY

1. Duncan, *Scotland*, 475-6; *RMS*, ii, no. 2378.
2. *Arb. Lib.*, i, no. 346; Duncan, *Scotland*, 480.
3. SRO, GD124/1/411; AUL, MS M. 390, Mass 1/11.
4. *St Giles Reg.*, no. 25.
5. *Leges Burgorum*, c. 42; SRO, GD52/393; DA, TC/CC 10 no. 5.
6. *RMS*, i, no. 629 states the law and refers to Patrick de Innerpeffer; AUL, MS. M. 390, Mass 19/4; *RMS*, i, no. 242.
7. *RMS*, i, no. 65; *RMS*, i, no. 284; *RRS*, vi, no. 80. *RMS* contains many other grants of forfeited land.
8. *Ayr Chrs.*, app. pp xxxv-vi, no. 43; Dodd, 'Ayr', 363. For townhouses see Ch. 1.
9. *RMS*, i, nos 649, 691; *RRS*, vi, no. 288.
10. Wendy B. Stephenson, 'The monastic presence in Scottish burghs in the twelfth and thirteenth centuries', *SHR*, lx (1981), 99-105.
11. *Arb. Lib.*, i, no. 344.
12. *RRS*, ii, no. 282.
13. Judith Stones, '67-71 Green 1977' in *Aber. Exc.*, 94-5.
14. *Leges Burgorum*, c. 23, 24; *RMS*, i, no. 755.
15. SRO, GD52/396; *Abdn. Reg.*, ii, 293-4.
16. *Ayr Chrs.*, no. 41.
17. *Melr. Lib.*, i, no. 354, ii, no. 442.
18. SRO, GD198/221; St AUL, Skene of Halyards Papers, no. 13.
19. *Leges Burgorum*, c. 79, 90; *Frag. Coll.*, c. 4.
20. SRO, RH6/152.
21. *Arb. Lib.*, ii, nos 8, 13. See also *Scone Liber*, no. 177.
22. *RRS*, vi, no. 260; British Library [BL], MS Add 33245, ff 79v-80v.
23. SRO, GD52/391.
24. SRO, GD79/4/106. For example, AUL, MS. M. 390, Mass 10/5; *St Giles Reg.*, no. 14. See discussion below, p. 139 (in this text).
25. Murray, *Burgh Organisation*, i, 36-7.
26. *Arb. Lib.*, i, no. 349.
27. *Scone Liber*, no. 172; Duncan, 'Perth', 46; *Moray Reg.*, no. 160; *Newb. Reg.*, no. 279.
28. *Frag. Coll.*, c. 6; Reynolds, *English Towns*, 97.
29. Fraser, *Colquhoun*, ii, no. 17.
30. *Leges Burgorum*, c. 23.
31. *Glas. Friars*, no. 14.
32. *Camb. Reg.*, no. 94.
33. *Arb. Lib.*, i, no. 347.
34. SRO, GD190/2/2.
35. Duncan, *Scotland*, 503, although he gives some examples of urban land speculation. For England, see Postan, *Medieval Trade*, 15; for Flanders, W. Prevenier, 'La Bourgeoisie en Flandre au XIIIe siècle', *Studia Historia Gandensia* (1979), 409; for Europe in general, Mundy, *Medieval Town*, 37-8.

Notes 177

36. There is similar evidence for Bury St Edmunds, Robert S. Gottfried, *Bury St Edmunds and the Urban Crisis: 1290-1539* (Princeton, 1982), 136-43, although rentiers were still fairly uncommon in England in the fourteenth century, Platt, *English Town*, 181.
37. *RMS*, i, no. 682. See maps of medieval Aberdeen in *Aber. Exc.*, 244-5.
38. *Moray Reg.*, no. 242; *St Giles Reg.*, no. 156.
39. *Ayr Friars*, no. 12; *Irvine Muniments*, 123-4; *Moray Reg.*, no. 241.
40. *Abdn. Recs.*, lxxviii; SRO, GD52/1033. The lands granted to Ayr comprised about 2300 acres, Dodd, 'Ayr', 318. See R. Fox, 'Urban Development 1100-1700' in Whittington, *Historical Geography of Scotland*, 80, for a map of Stirling's holdings. The crofts of Aberdeen as they probably were in the seventeenth century are illustrated in a map by P. J. Anderson at the back of *Abdn. Chrs.*
41. *RRS*, ii, nos 102, 213; *Ayr Chrs.*, no. 5; *Abdn. Chrs.*, nos 6, 8; Mackenzie, *Burghs*, 160-1.
42. *Abdn. Recs.*, 91-2; Andrew Gibb, *Glasgow, The Making of a City* (Beckenham, 1983), 32; *Peebles Recs.*, 27. See map in Gibb, *Glasgow*, 27.
43. *Moray Reg.*, no. 232; Gibb, *Glasgow*, 29-31; *Glas. Friars*, no. 14.
44. *RRS*, vi, no. 260; map in *Abdn. Chrs.*; *Abdn. Friars*, 18; AUL, MS. M. 390, Mass 16/8; *Ayr Friars*, no. 12.
45. AUL, MS. M. 390, Mass 1/11; *Glas. Friars*, no. 14.
46. *Abdn. Recs.*, 169-71, 84. Leasing to individual burgesses continued until 1551, *Municipal Corporations (Scotland), Local Reports*, i (London, 1835), 14.
47. *Art. Inq.*, c. 42; Mackenzie, *Burghs*, 165; *Abdn. Recs.*, 167.
48. Duncan, *Scotland*, 503; David Nicholas, *Town and Countryside Social, Economic and Political Tensions in Fourteenth-Century Flanders* (Brugge, 1971), 12.
49. Georges Duby, *Rural Economy and Country Life in the Medieval West* tran. Cynthia Postan (London, 1968), 150.
50. *Scone Liber*, no. 177; NLS, Adv. MS. 30. 5. 26, f. 15; *Abdn. Reg.*, i, 171; *Chron. Lanercost*, 234-5; Fraser, *Southesk*, ii, no. 31.
51. *Chron. Perth*, 1; NLS, Adv. MS. 80. 4. 15, f. 82.
52. *RMS*, i, no. 846.
53. *AB Ill.*, ii, 73-4; Fraser, *Sutherland*, iii, no. 16; *RMS*, ii, no. 187; SRO, GD52/1031. For the Spens marriage, see D. Sellar, 'Spens Family Heraldry', *Notes and Queries of the Society for West Highland and Islands Historical Research*, no. xxii (Dec. 1983).
54. SRO, GD52/1031, 1032, 1033; *AB Coll*, 272; SRO, GD33/36/3; *Abdn. Reg.*, ii, 286-7.
55. *HMC, Milne Home*, 272(2); NLS, Adv. MS. 80. 4. 15, f. 82.
56. *RRS*, vi, no. 224; AUL, MS. M. 390, Mass 10/27.
57. Fraser, *Southesk*, ii, no. 31; *HMC, Milne Home*, 272(1); Fraser, *Frasers of Philorth*, no. 2; Fraser, *Grant*, iii, no. 15.
58. *Scone Liber*, no. 177; *Abdn. Reg.*, i, 183; *RMS*, i, no. 834.
59. *St Giles Reg.*, nos 8, 14.
60. *Lanark Recs.*, no. 2; *RRS*, ii, no. 475; Duncan, *Scotland*, 480.
61. *RMS*, i, no. 164.
62. *Abdn. Recs.*, 15-16.
63. *ER*, i, 593.

CHAPTER FIVE: THE BURGH IN THE KINGDOM
1. Adolphus Ballard, 'The Theory of the Scottish Burgh', *SHR*, xiii (1916), 16, 17; Mackenzie, *Burghs*, 38-9; George Neilson, 'On Some Scottish Burghal Origins', *Juridical Review*, xix (1902), 132; Ennen, *Medieval Town*, 1. The former picture of sharp dichotomy between town and country in medieval Europe is being modified, Nicholas, *Town and Countryside*, 9-10; Mundy, *Medieval Town*, 14-15. A more complex view of the town-country relationship is set forth in Hohenberg,

Urban Europe, 22.

2. Gottfried, *Bury St Edmunds*, 68 n. 46; Platt, *English Town*, 98-9; Rörig, *Medieval Town*, 114.
3. Alexander Fenton, 'Sickle, Scythe and Reaping Machine. Innovation Patterns in Scotland' in *Ethnologie Europaea*, vii, no. 1 (1973-4), 5. In Europe, burgesses often contributed capital to stockraising, Duby, *Rural Economy*, 48-9. For some local surnames see G. F. Black, *The Surnames of Scotland: their origin, meaning and history* (New York, 1948) and Ewan, 'Burgesses', 252 n. 4.
4. *Dundee Chrs.*, 12; J. C. Murray, 'Conclusions', 248; Spearman, 'Canal Street II', 59; Wordsworth, 'Castle Street', 322; Dickinson, *European City*, 322; Mundy, *Medieval Town*, 13; Duby, *Rural Economy*, 128.
5. H. Murray, 'St Paul Street', 81; Robinson, 'Botanical Remains', 206; Fraser, 'Plant Remains', 239-40.
6. Stones, '67-71 Green', 95.
7. *Statuta Gilde*, c. 21. See safe-conducts in *Rot. Scot.*
8. H. Murray, 'St Paul Street', 81; Robinson, 'Botanical Remains', 205; *Abdn. Recs.*, 191.
9. Hodgson, 'Three Burghs', 3, 10.
10. H. Murray, 'Aberdeen Bldgs', 228; J. C. Murray, 'Conclusions', 248; Crone and Barber, 'Structural Timbers', 88.
11. Wordsworth, 'Castle Street', 385-6; Fraser, 'Plant Remains', 240.
12. Spearman, 'Workshops', 134. It is possible that, as in Europe, the demands of the burghs stimulated more intense agricultural production in their hinterlands, Ennen, *Medieval Town*, 158-9. This point would be worth further research.
13. *Newb. Reg.*, no. 271.
14. AUL, MS. M. 390, Mass 10/5; MA, Brechin Doc. no. 3. For an argument downplaying this connection, see Mackenzie, *Burghs*, 38, 163-4.
15. *ER*, ii, 80, 115; Pirenne, *Medieval Cities*, 231-2.
16. *ER*, ii, 81.
17. *Ibid*, i-iii, sub indicibus.
18. *Ibid*, ii, 175, i, 493.
19. *ER*, iii, 652, ii, 114; *APS*, i, 508, although this apparent decrease may be due to the nature of the records. Debts were recorded only when they were partially or wholly repaid, making it difficult to determine if the decrease was a result of fewer loans or fewer repayments. Moreover, some of the records for the 1370s are missing.
20. *ER*, iii, *passim*; Duncan, 'Perth', 39.
21. *CDS*, iv, no. 122; Carus-Wilson, *Medieval Merchant*, 265-71; Duncan, *Scotland*, 509; ER, ii, iii, sub indicibus; *ER*, iii, 3; *Dunf. Gd. Bk.*, passim.
22. *ER*, iii, 428.
23. *Rot. Scot.*, i, 930; *CDS*, iii, no. 960; *ER*, ii, 168-9.
24. ER, ii, 32, iii, 189-90, ii, 50, 51, iii, 178.
25. *Ibid*, ii, 168, i, 532, 477.
26. *Ibid*, i, 531, iii, 37, 672. David H. Caldwell, 'Royal Patronage of Arms and Armour in Fifteenth and Sixteenth-Century Scotland' in *Scottish Weapons and Fortifications 1100-1800*, ed. D. Caldwell (Edinburgh, 1981), 74.
27. *ER*, ii, 346-7, p. lxxiv. This type of commission suggests that there may have been some family connection between Crab and his namesake from Berwick who helped fortify that burgh against the English. See below, p. 123 (in this text). For the earlier confusion of the two, see E. W. M. Balfour-Melville, 'Two John Crabbs' in *SHR*, xxxix (1960).
28. *ER*, iii, 175, ii, 134.
29. *Ibid*, ii, 6, 65, iii, 46, 113, ii, 168, i, 493.
30. *Ibid*, ii, 520, 308, 79, iii, 89, 665, 117, ii, 85.
31. *Ibid*, i, 64; Lucas, 'John Crabbe', 342-5; *ER*, i, 339.
32. *ER*, ii, 243, 329; *Rot. Scot.*, i, 959; *ER*, ii, 622.

33. *ER*, i, 169, iii, 59, i, 616.
34. *Chron. Wyntoun* (Laing), Bk 8, ch. 38; *ER*, i, pp clvi-ii.
35. *CDS*, iv, nos 490, 510, 520; Nicholson, *Scotland*, 219; *Rot. Scot.*, i, 718, 721; *ER*, ii, 55, iii, 99.
36. Rooseboom, *Staple*, 5; *ER*, ii, 261; Annie I. Dunlop, *Scots Abroad in the Fifteenth Century.* Hist. Assn. Pamphlet no. 124 (London, 1942), 3-4
37. *ER*, iii, 219, 613, 33-4.
38. *Ibid*, i, 594, iii, 175.
39. *Ibid*, sub indicibus, ii, 511.
40. *Ibid*, ii, 159-60, 430; Stewart, *Coinage*, 26-7.
41. *ER*, ii, 54-6, 432, 502, 582; *Nat. MSS. Scot.*, i, no. 45. A receipt issued by Mercer in Bruges in 1360 survives, SRO, AD1/17.
42. *RMS*, i, no. 100; *ND*, no. 326; *Abdn. Reg.*, i, 141; *RMS*, i, no. 803; *ER*, ii, iii, sub indicibus.
43. *ER*, i, 426, ii, 373.
44. *Ibid*, i, 425, iii, 411, 434. For the Rollos see *ER*, ii-iv sub indicibus.
45. *APS*, i, 496; *ER*, iii, 50, 71, 97, 301.
46. *Ibid*, iii, 111, 67, ii, 469, iii, 617.
47. *Ibid*, i, 76, 316; SRO, GD76/149.
48. *Ibid*, iii, 549.
49. *Ibid*, ii, 360-1.
50. *Ibid*, iii, 6, 355.
51. *Ibid*, i, 172.
52. *Ibid*, iii, 76, 87.
53. *Ibid*, iii, *sub indicibus*.
54. *Abdn. Reg.*, i, 171; NLS, Adv. MS. 30. 5. 26, f. 15; *Invernessiana*, 88-90.
55. *Rot. Scot.*, i, 898.
56. For town-church conflict see Gottfried, *Bury St Edmunds*, ch. 6; Pirenne, *Medieval Cities*, 178-90; *Lind. Liber*, no. 10; *Abdn. Reg.*, i, 145, 183.
57. *RRS*, vi, no. 152; *Camb. Reg.*, no. 55.
58. D. E. R. Watt, *Biographical Dictionary of Scottish Graduates to AD 1410* (Oxford, 1977); D. E. R. Watt, 'Scotsmen at Universities between 1340 and 1410 and their Subsequent Careers: a Study of the Contribution of Graduates to the Public Life of their Country', DPhil thesis (Oxford, 1957) 128, 134, 340; J. Dowden, *The Bishops of Scotland* (Glasgow, 1912), 152, n. 4; SRO, GD52/395; RMS, i, no. 563.
59. *Chron. Fordun*, i, 360-1; *St Nich. Cart.*, i, 12-20.
60. AUL, MS. M. 390, Mass 10/22.
61. *Rot. Scot.*, ii, 2; *CDS*, iii, no. 1639.
62. SRO, GD16/24/169; *Scone Liber*, no. 186; *Yester Writs*, no. 31; ER, i, 107, 470.
63. Nicholson, *Scotland*, 216; *ER*, iii, sub indices.
64. *Invernessiana*, 86; *Camb. Reg.*, no. 181; Fraser, *Grandtully*, no. 79.
65. *CDS*, ii, no. 922; Nicholson, *Scotland*, 54-5; Evan M. Barron, *Inverness in the Middle Ages* (Inverness, 1907), 56-7, 67-8; Fischer, *Germany*, 238.
66. *Chron. Walsingham*, i, 369.
67. Alexander Grant, 'The development of the Scottish peerage' in *SHR*, lvii (1978), 1. Links between burgesses and their baronial relations probably remained close. In 1338 Sir John de Crichton witnessed a grant by the son and heir of Thomas de Crichton, burgess of Berwick, *Newb. Reg.*, no. 207.
68. SRO, GD79/5/2, GD79/5/3; *Edin. Chrs.*, no. 14; *ER*, iii, 378; *AB Coll.*, 272; SRO, GD33/36/2; Fraser, *Southesk*, ii, no. 47; *Abdn. Recs.*, 21, 100.
69. *ER*, iii, 564, 622; Rooseboom, *Staple*, app. no. 12; *ER*, iii, 119.
70. *Abdn. Reg.*, i, 183; *RRS*, vi, no. 224; *RMS*, i, no. 754.

CHAPTER SIX: THE COMMUNITY

1. Reynolds, *Kingdoms and Communities*. This is the theme of her book.
2. Reynolds, *English Towns*, 66-7; Robert Hunter, 'Corporate Personality and the Scottish Burgh: An Historical Note' in *The Scottish Tradition: Essays in Honour of Ronald Gordon Cant*, ed. G. W. S. Barrow (Edinburgh, 1974), 226; Ewan, 'Community of Burgh', 228; Hohenberg, *Urban Europe*, 34.
3. *Leges Burgorum*, c. 15.
4. *Ayr Chrs.*, nos 1, 17; *Irvine Muniments*, no. 3; *Hadd. Chrs.*, 1-3; *Lanark Recs.*, no. 2; *Banff Annals*, ii, 375-6; *Dundee Chrs.*, 12.
5. See discussion in Hunter, 'Corporate Personality'.
6. J. C. Murray, 'Conclusions', 247.
7. Reynolds, *English Towns*, 88; Hohenberg, *Urban Europe*, 45; Maryanne Kowaleski, 'The history of urban families in medieval England', *Journal of Medieval History*, xiv (1988), 49, 56; Ewan, 'Community of Burgh', 236. See Gibb's plan of medieval burghal zones in Glasgow, Gibb, *Glasgow*, 24.
8. Barrow, *Kingship and Unity*, 129.
9. Reynolds, *English Towns*, 138; *Camb. Reg.*, nos 54, 55.
10. Sir James Marwick, *Edinburgh Guilds and Crafts* (SBRS, 1909), 23.
11. W. C. Dickinson, *Scotland from the Earliest Times to 1603* 3rd ed. rev. A. A. M. Duncan (Oxford, 1977), 282; *Statuta Gilde*, c. 15; *Leges Burgorum*, c. 72, 67, 68; *Statuta Gilde*, c. 12, 14; *Juramenta Officiariorum*, 127-30.
12. Reynolds, *Kingdoms*, 34-6; Grant, *Independence*, 158.
13. For example, *Moray Reg.*, no. 235. Reynolds discusses such non-burgess participation in *Kingdoms*, 187-8.
14. Hunter, 'Corporate Personality', 229, 232; Reynolds, *Kingdoms*, 59-64.
15. Reynolds, *Kingdoms*, 63-4; AUL, MS M. 390, Mass 1/11, 8/3, 10/11.
16. *St A. Lib.*, 284-5; BL, MS. Add. 33245, f. 80r; *Pais. Reg.*, 385-6.
17. SRO, RH6/199; *RMS*, i, no. 266; AUL, MS M. 390, Mass 10/5.
18. In 1289 the *prepositi* and the rest of the burgesses of the community of Banff petitioned the Guardians. The Guardians in their reply also used the term community, *Abdn. Chrs.*, 290-1; *A B Ill*, ii, 129.
19. *Irvine Muniments*, no. 1; *Ayr Friars*, no. 27.
20. *Familie of Innes*, 57-9; *Ayr Friars*, nos 17-21, 24, 26, 27.
21. *Spald. Misc.*, v, 250; AUL, MS M. 390, Mass 10/5.
22. Reynolds, *Kingdoms*, 98-9.
23. *Glas. Reg.*, i, nos 280, 282; *St Giles Reg.*, nos 8, 14, 19, 1.
24. Ronald G. Cant, *Historic Elgin and its Cathedral* (Elgin, 1974), 13; Henry Gordon Slade, 'Aberdeen: The Burgh Kirk of St. Nicholas', *The Deeside Field*, 3rd ser (1978), 64; *St Nich. Cart.*, i, 16-17; *Edin. Chrs.*, no. 14; *Edin. Recs.*, 1; *St Giles Reg.*, no. 163.
25. *Statuta Gilde*, preamble; Reynolds, *Kingdoms*, 72-3.
26. Nicholson, *Scotland*, 17.
27. Mackenzie, *Burghs*, 72. Although in general stressing the strength of burghal solidarity in the Wars of Independence, Barrow also suggests that inter-burghal conflicts might influence two burghs to take opposing sides, G. W. S. Barrow, *Robert Bruce and the Community of the Realm of Scotland*, 3rd ed. (Edinburgh, 1988), 300.
28. *Abdn. Chrs.*, 290-1, 289-90; *A B Ill*, ii, 129.
29. *RMS*, i, no. 308; MA, M/W1/1. The fact that Montrose and Dundee were united in fighting the Brechin privileges may be the source of Mackenzie's error in ascribing the Montrose-Forfar agreement to Montrose and Dundee, Mackenzie, *Burghs*, 103. In Germany, the craft guilds of some towns made alliances with each other to protect their trade, Rörig, *Medieval Town*, 159-60.
30. *RRS*, vi, nos 120, 121.
31. *Abdn. Chrs.*, nos 1, 3; *RRS*, vi, no. 483; *RMS*, i, no. 340.
32. *RRS*, vi, nos 136, 462.

33. *RCRB*, i, 538; *Irvine Muniments*, no. 4.
34. *Hans. Urk.*, iii, nos 127, 131; *Rot. Scot.*, i, 948. In England it was common for merchants from several cities to form fellowships to pursue common interests or negotiate concessions, Carus-Wilson, *Medieval Merchant*, xiii.
35. DA, TC/CC1/14A.
36. *RMS*, i, no. 340; *Irvine Muniments*, no. 4.
37. *RMS*, i, no. 379; SRO, GD190/2/2; *ER*, iii, 111, 137. The five witnesses' names are followed by the phrase 'burgesses of Aberdeen' but it is possible that this may only refer to the last two or three names as those appearing first, unless they had namesakes in Aberdeen, were prominent burgesses of Inverness.
38. SRO, GD79/5/4.
39. *RMS*, i, no. 760; *ER*, ii, 415; *Rot. Scot.*, i, 885, 905; SRO, GD124/1/411; *ER*, iii, 673, 682.
40. SRO, GD215/1705; *ER*, iii, 128. In England, some merchants of Bury St Edmunds became freemen of King's Lynn from where they exported their goods, Gottfried, *Bury St Edmunds*, 92, n. 61. There was some trade with Ireland but as the two countries produced similar goods it was probably limited. Nor did Edward Bruce's devastating invasion of Ireland in the early fourteenth century help Ireland's economy, B. J. Graham, 'The Towns of Medieval Ireland' in *The Development of the Irish Town* ed. R. A. Butlin (London, 1977), 39, 50.
41. *Abdn. Chrs.*, no. 3; *RMS*, ii, no. 2387; *Dundee Chrs.*, 9-11.
42. *Art. Inq.* sets out guidelines for the conduct of the ayre. The chamberlain became even more associated with the burghs after 1424 when his other royal duties were given to new officials. By the late fourteenth century, the chamberlains increasingly used deputies, often burgesses, to carry out their duties and it may have been this practice which decided James I to limit their duties, Grant, *Independence*, 149.
43. *Frag. Coll.*, c. 16-20.
44. *Curia Quatuor Burgorum* in *Ancient Burgh Laws*, 156; *RCRB*, i, 541-2.
45. *APS*, i, 67, 514-5; *APS*, ii, 179; Nicholson, *Scotland*, 264-5; Theodora Pagan, *The Convention of the Royal Burghs of Scotland* (Glasgow, 1926), 8-9. By the fourteenth century it was becoming common throughout northwest Europe to base the political nation on separate estates, Ennen, *Medieval Town*, 161.
46. *APS*, i, 451-3; Robert S. Rait, *The Parliaments of Scotland* (Glasgow, 1924), 238-9; A. A. M. Duncan, 'The Early Parliaments of Scotland', *SHR*, xlv (1966), 51; *CDS*, ii, no. 823.
47. Dickinson, *Scotland to 1603*, 186-7; Barrow, *Bruce*, 300.
48. *APS*, i, 475-6. Rait, *Parliaments*, 3, 239-40 suggests that the indenture was made outside parliament, but this is convincingly refuted by Duncan, 'Parliaments', 51, and E. W. M. Balfour-Melville, 'Burgh Representation in Early Scottish Parliaments', *English Historical Review*, lix (1944), 82-3.
49. *APS*, i, 484-7; *Formulary E*, no. 77; Dickinson, *Scotland to 1603*, 187-8.
50. The older idea is expressed in Rait, *Parliaments*, 3.
51. *APS*, i, 515; *Edin. Chrs.*, no. 6; Rait, *Parliaments*, 242.
52. Dickinson, *Scotland to 1603*, 188-9.
53. Grant, *Independence*, 162-3.
54. Ranald Nicholson, 'Crown in Jeopardy' in *The Scottish Nation* ed. Gordon Menzies (BBC, 1972), 34. Unlike England, the lairds were in the second estate with the nobility.
55. *APS*, i, 492-3, 494-5.
56. *APS*, i, 497-8, 501-3, 507-9; Grant, *Independence*, 168. The minutes of the Lords of the Articles are printed in *The Acts of the Lords Auditors of Causes and Complaints* ed. T. Thomson (Edinburgh, 1839).
57. *APS*, i, 507, 555, 573-4; *Nat. MSS. Scotland*, ii, no. 50; *Abdn. Recs.*, 80, ; *Abdn. Counc.*, i, 393-4. That burgess attendance was expected by the mid-fifteenth century is shown by an attempt to regulate the dress of burgh commissioners, *APS*, ii, 43.

58. Nicholson, *Edward III*, 59; A. A. M. Duncan, 'Taxation of Burghs 1326-1331, 1424-1425, 1535' in *Historical Atlas*, 64, Map 70.
59. *ER*, ii, p. xli; Lloyd, *Wool Trade*, 174; Nicholson, *Scotland*, 194, 176.
60. *ER*, ii, pp xxxviii-xxxix, 8.
61. *Ibid*, p. xli.
62. *Ibid*, 10, 55.
63. *Chron. Walsingham*, i, 369; Donald L. Galbreath, 'Scottish Seals from the Continent', *SHR*, xxvii (1948), 136; *ER*, ii, 55.
64. *ER*, ii, pp lxvii-lxviii, 219.
65. *Ibid*, pp lxxi-lxxii; Nicholson, *Scotland*, 176-7. The diversion of the money away from the ransom was noted by a contemporary chronicler, Sir Thomas Grey, *Scalachronica*, 174.
66. *CDS*, ii, no. 823; *Chron. Lanercost*, 173. Some burgesses of Berwick later gave support to the disinherited, G. W. S. Barrow, 'The Aftermath of War: Scotland and England in the Late Thirteenth and Early Fourteenth Centuries', *TRHS*, 5th ser., xxviii (1978), 108.
67. Evan Macleod Barron, *The Scottish War of Independence: A Critical Study*, 2nd ed. (Inverness, 1934), 229; Palgrave, *Docs. Hist. Scot.*, i, 310.
68. Lynch, 'Introduction', 4. Barrow points out that the resilience of the burgesses is suggested in the activities of Thomas of Coldingham, burgess of Berwick, who kept up his wool trade business right through the war, Barrow, *Bruce*, 302.
69. Ewan, 'Bon Accord', 32-3.
70. Barrow, *Bruce*, 301.
71. *Ibid*, 301-2 for royal help to Berwick by Robert I after 1318.
72. Nicholson, *Scotland*, 82.
73. *Formulary E*, no. 59; *APS*, ii, 10-11, 14, 9.
74. *Rot. Scot.*, i, 718; *CDS*, iv, no. 510; *Hans. Urk.*, iii, no. 131; Rooseboom, *Staple*, app. no. 12.
75. Pryde, 'Origin of the Burgh', 276; *ER*, i, 470; *SL*, B59/23/6.
76. Gordon Donaldson, 'The Church Courts' in *Introduction to Scottish Legal History* (Stair Society, 1958), 363.
77. *RRS*, vi, no. 85; *Ayr Chrs.*, nos 14, 42.
78. *Kel. Lib.*, ii, no. 397; *BL*, MS. Add. 33245, ff 53v-54r; *Ayr Friars*, no. 21.
79. M. Lynch, 'Scottish Towns 1500-1700' in *The Early Modern Town in Scotland* ed. M. Lynch (London, 1987), 17-20.
80. *Banff Annals*, ii, 377-8; *Peebles Chrs.*, no. 2.
81. Grant, *Independence*, 73-5; *Abdn. Recs.*, 211. See Audrey-Beth Fitch, 'Assumptions about Plague in Late Medieval Scotland', *Scotia*, xi (1987).
82. *Rot. Scot.*, i, 859, 874, 978, ; David McRoberts, 'Scottish Pilgrims to the Holy Land', *Innes Review*, xx (1969), 81-2; David McRoberts, *The Pilgrimage to Whithorn* (Glasgow, n. d.), 2, 4; *Angels, Nobles*, 44-5.
83. Lynch, 'Scottish Towns 1500-1700', 3, 27.

Bibliography

The following bibliography is selective and includes only works cited in the footnotes to the text. Most secondary works cited only once have not been included. Where appropriate, abbreviations are indicated by square brackets.

PRIMARY: MANUSCRIPT
Aberdeen University Library
MS.M.390, Mass 1-19 Marischal College Charters

British Library
MS. Add. 33245   Registrum de Aberbrothock

Dundee City Archives
TC/CC 10   Burgh Writs
TC/CC 14A   Return to royal enquiry re Dundee privileges 1325
TC/CC 15   Tolbooth Charter 20 Oct.1325
TC/CC 17   Charter of privileges 1360

Montrose Archives
M/W1   Burgh Writs
M/WC   Royal Charters
Brechin doc.   Brechin Writs and Charters

National Library of Scotland
Adv. MS. 9A.1.10   Hutton transcripts
Adv. MS. 20.3.9   Hutton transcripts (E. & N. Scot)
Adv. MS. 30.5.26   Extracts from charters in registers
                        in Lower Parliament House
Adv. MS. 80.4.15   Transcripts of charters relating to
                        estate and family of Dundas
MS. 6485   Inventory of Pitfirrane Papers

St Andrews University Library
B65   St Andrews burgh charters
SL110   St Andrews charters to 1450
Skene of Halyards papers

Sandeman Library, Perth
B59   Perth burgh charters

Scottish Record Office
AD1   Advocate's Department
GD1/5   James Wright's Antiquarian Notes
GD1/17   John C.Brodie and Sons,W.S., Edin.
GD4   Benholme Hedderwick Writs
GD16   Airlie Muniments
GD33   Haddo Muniments
GD52   Lord Forbes Collection
GD76   Henderson Collection
GD79   King James VI Hospital, Perth

GD83	Bamff Charters
GD103	Society of Antiquaries Charters
GD111	Curie Collection
GD124	Mar and Kellie
GD150	Morton Papers
GD190	Smythe of Methven
GD198	Haldane of Gleneagles
GD215	Beveridge Papers
RH1	Register House Charters
RH6	Register House Charters

PRIMARY: PRINTED

Aberdeen Friars: Red, Black, White, Grey. ed. P. J. Anderson (Aberdeen, 1909). [*Aberdeen Friars*]

Ane Account of the Familie of Innes. ed. Cosmo Innes (Spalding Club, 1864). [*Familie of Innes*]

The Acts of the Parliaments of Scotland. eds. T. Thomson and C. Innes (Edinburgh, 1844-75). [*APS*]

Ancient Laws and Customs of the Burghs of Scotland 1124-1424. ed. C. Innes (SBRS, 1868). [*Ancient Burgh Laws*]

The Annals of Banff (New Spalding Club, 1891-93). [*Banff Annals*]

Bower, Walter. *Scotichronicon*, viii. ed. and tran. D. E. R. Watt (Aberdeen, 1987). [Watt, *Bower*]

Calendar of the Close Rolls preserved in the Public RecordOffice (London, 1902-63) [*CCR*]

Calendar of Documents relating to Scotland. ed. J. Bain (Edinburgh,1884-8). [*CDS*]

Calendar of Documents relating to Scotland, supplementary volume (E d i n - burgh, 1987). [*CDS*]

Calendar of the Fine Rolls preserved in the Public RecordOffice (London, 1911-62) [*CCR*]

Calendar of Inquisitions Miscellaneous (Chancery) preserved in the Public Record Office (London, 1916-68)

Calendar of the Patent Rolls preserved in the Public Record Office (London, 1895-1982) [*CPR*]

Calendar of Writs preserved at Yester House 1166-1503. eds. C. C. H. Harvey and J. Macleod (SRS, 1930). [*Yester Writs*]

Cartularium Ecclesiae Sancti Nicolai Aberdonensis (New Spalding Club, 1888). [*St Nich. Cart.*]

Charters of the Abbey of Crosraguel. ed. F. C. Hunter-Blair (AHCAG, 1886). [*Cross. Chrs.*]

Charters and Documents relating to the Burgh of Peebles. ed. William Chambers (SBRS,1872). [*Peebles Chrs.*]

Charters and other Documents relating to the City of Edinburgh. ed. J. D. Marwick (SBRS, 1871). [*Edin. Chrs.*]

Charters and other Documents relating to the Royal Burgh of Stirling. ed. R. Renwick (Glasgow, 1884). [*Stirling Chrs.*]

Charters of the Friars Preachers of Ayr. ed. R. W. Cochran-Patrick (AHCAG, 1881). [*Ayr Friars*]

Charters and other Writs illustrating the History of the Royal Burgh of Aberdeen. ed. P. J. Anderson (Aberdeen, 1890). [*Aber. Chrs.*]

Charters of the Royal Burgh of Ayr. ed. W. S. Cooper (AHCAG,1883). [*Ayr Chrs.*]

Charters and Writs Concerning the Royal Burgh of Haddington 1318-1543. ed.

J. G. Wallace-James (Haddington, 1895) [*Hadd. Chrs.*]
Charters, Writs and Public Documents of the Royal Burgh of Dundee ed. W.
  Hay (Dundee, 1880) [*Dundee Chrs.*]
Chronicle of Walter de Guisborough. ed. Harry Rothwell(Camden Society,
  1957) [*Chron. Guis.*]
Chronicon de Lanercost. ed. Joseph Stevenson (MaitlandClub, 1839).[*Chron.
  Lanercost*]
Collections for a History of the Shires of Aberdeen and Banff. ed. Joseph
  Robertson (Spalding Club, 1843). [*AB Coll.*]
Davidson, John and Gray, Alexander. *The Scottish Staple at Veere.* (London,
  1909).
Early Records of the Burgh of Aberdeen, 1317, 1398-1407. ed. W. C. Dickin-
  son (SHS, 1957) [*Abdn. Recs.*]
Early Scottish Charters prior to 1153. ed. A. C. Lawrie(Glasgow, 1905)
  [*ESC*]
Early Travellers in Scotland. ed. P. Hume Brown (Edinburgh,1891).
The Exchequer Rolls of Scotland. eds. J. Stuart et al. (Edinburgh,1878-80).
  [*ER*]
Extracts from the Council Register of the Burgh of Aberdeen 1398-1570. ed.
  John Stuart (Spalding Club, 1844). [*Abdn. Counc.*]
Extracts from the Records of the Burgh of Edinburgh A. D. 1403-1528. ed. Sir
  James D. Marwick (SBRS, 1869). [*Edin. Recs.*]
Extracts from the Records of the Burgh of Peebles. ed. R. Renwick (SBRS,
  1910). [*Peebles Recs.*]
Extracts from the Records of the Royal Burgh of Lanark. ed. R. Renwick
  (Glasgow, 1893). [*Lanark Recs.*]
Facsimiles of the National Manuscripts of Scotland (London,1867) [*Nat.
  MSS. Scot.*]
Fischer, Thomas. *The Scots in Germany.* (Edinburgh, 1902)
Foedera, Conventiones, Litterae et Cuiuscunque Generis Acta Publica. ed. T.
  Rymer, Hague edn. (The Hague, 1839-45). [*Foedera (H)*]
Formulary E. Scottish Letters and Brieves 1286-1424 ed. A. A. M. Duncan
  (Glasgow, 1976).
Fraser, W. *The Chiefs of Colquhoun and their Country* (Edinburgh, 1869).
  [Fraser, *Colquhoun*]
Fraser, W. *The Chiefs of Grant* (Edinburgh, 1883). [Fraser, *Grant*]
Fraser, W. *History of the Carnegies, Earls of Southesk, and of their Kindred*
  (Edinburgh,1867). [Fraser, *Southesk*]
Fraser, W. *Memorials of the Montgomeries Earls of Eglinton* (Edinburgh,
  1859). [Fraser, *Eglinton*]
Fraser, W. *The Red Book of Grandtully* (Edinburgh, 1868). [Fraser,
  Grandtully]
Fraser, W. *The Sutherland Book* (Edinburgh, 1892). [Fraser, *Sutherland*]
Fraser-Mackintosh, Charles. *Invernessiana. Contributions toward a history of
  the town and parish of Inverness, from 1160 to 1599* (Inverness, 1875).
The Frasers of Philorth. ed. A. Fraser, Lord Saltoun(Edinburgh, 1879).
  [*Frasers of Philorth*]
Froissart, Jean. *Chronicles of England, France, Spain and the Adjoining
  Countries.* tran. Thomas Johnes (London,1849) [*Chron. Froissart*]
A Genealogical Deduction of the Family of Rose of Kilravock. ed. C. Innes
  (Spalding Club, 1848). [*Family of Rose*]
The Gild Court Book of Dunfermline 1433-1597. ed. Elizabeth P. D. Torrie
  (SRS,1986) [*Dunf. Gd. Bk.*]
Gordon of Rothiemay, James. *Abredoniae Utriusque Descriptio: A Description*

of Both Towns of Aberdeen (Spalding Club,1842).

Hansisches Urkundenbuch. eds. K. Hohlbaum, K. Kunze and W. Stein (Halle, 1879-96) [*Hans. Urk.*]

Illustrations of the Topography and Antiquities of the Shires of Aberdeen and Banff. eds. George Grub et al. (Spalding Club,1847-69) [*A B Ill*]

Joannis de Fordun. *Chronica Gentis Scotorum.* ed. W. Skene (Edinburgh, 1871) [*Chron. Fordun*] *Joannis de Fordun Scotichronicon cum Supplementis etContinuatione Walteri Bower.* ed. W. Goodall (Edinburgh, 1759). [*Chron. Bower*]

Liber Cartarum Prioratus Sancti Andree in Scotia. ed. Thomas Thomson (Bannatyne Club, 1841). [*St A. Lib.*]

Liber Collegii Nostre Domine: Munimenta Fratrum Predicatorum de Glasgu. ed. Joseph Robertson (Maitland Club, 1846). [*Glas. Friars*]

Liber Ecclesie de Scon (Bannatyne and Maitland Clubs,1843). [*Scone Liber*]

Liber Pluscardensis. ed. F. J. H. Skene (Edinburgh, 1877-80). [*Chron. Pluscarden*]

Liber S. Marie de Calchou. ed. Cosmo Innes (Bannatyne Club,1846). [Kel. Lib.]

Liber Sancte Marie de Lundoris (Abbotsford Club,1841). [*Lind. Lib*]

Liber Sancte Marie de Melros. ed. Cosmo Innes (BannatyneClub, 1837). [*Melr. Lib.*]

Liber S. Thome de Aberbrothoc (Bannatyne Club, 1848-56). [*Arb. Lib.*]

Livingstone, Matthew. 'A Calendar of Charters and Other Writs Relating to Lands or Benefices in Scotland in Possession of the Society of Antiquaries of Scotland', *PSAS*, xli (1906-7).

Miscellany of the Spalding Club, v. ed. John Stuart (Spalding Club, 1852). [*Spalding Misc.*]

Muniments of the Royal Burgh of Irvine (AHCAG, 1890). [*Irvine Muniments*]

Palgrave, F. ed. *Documents and Records illustrating theHistory of Scotland* (London, 1837) [Palgrave, *Docs. Hist. Scot.*]

Pegolotti, Francesco Balducci. *La Pratica Della Mercatura.* ed. Allen Evans (Camb., Mass., 1936).

Raine, J. *The History and Antiquities of North Durham* (London, 1852). [*ND*]

Records of the Convention of the Royal Burghs of Scotland. ed. J. D. Marwick (Edinburgh, 1866) [*RCRB*]

The Records of Elgin (New Spalding Club, 1903-8) [*Elgin Recs.*]

Regesta Regum Scottorum. eds. G. W. S. Barrow et al. (Edinburgh, 1960-88) [*RRS*]

The Register of Brieves. ed. Lord Cooper (Stair Society,1946). [*Reg. Brieves*]

Registrum Cartarum Ecclesie Sancti Egidii de Edinburgh. ed. David Laing (Bannatyne Club, 1859). [*St Giles Reg.*]

Registrum de Dunfermlyn. ed. Cosmo Innes (Bannatyne Club,1842). [*Dunf. Reg.*]

Registrum Episcopatus Aberdonensis. ed. Cosmo Innes (Spalding and Maitland Clubs, 1845). [*Abdn. Reg.*]

Registrum Episcopatus Brechinensis (Bannatyne Club, 1856). [*Brech. Reg.*]

Registrum Episcopatus Glasguensis. ed. Cosmo Innes(Bannatyne and Maitland Clubs, 1843). [*Glas. Reg.*]

Registrum Episcopatus Moraviensis. ed. Cosmo Innes(Bannatyne Club, 1837). [*Moray Reg.*]

Registrum Honoris de Morton. ed. Thomas Thomson (BannatyneClub, 1853). [*Mort. Reg.*]

Registrum Magni Sigilli Regum Scotorum. eds. J. M. Thomson et al. (Edinburgh, 1882-1914). [*RMS*]

Registrum Monasterii S. Marie de Cambuskenneth. ed. Sir William Fraser (Grampian Club, 1872). [*Camb. Reg.*]

Registrum Monasterii de Passelet. ed. Cosmo Innes (Maitland Club, 1832). [*Pais. Reg.*]

Registrum S. Marie de Neubotle. ed. Cosmo Innes (BannatyneClub, 1849). [*Newb. Reg.*]

Report of the Royal Commission on Historical Manuscripts, Colonel David Milne Home (London, 1902). [*HMC, Milne Home*]

Rooseboom, Matthijs D. *The Scottish Staple in the Netherlands* (The Hague, 1910). [Rooseboom, *Staple*]

Rotuli Scotiae in Turri Londinensi et in Domo CapitulariWestmonasteriensi Asservati. eds. D. Macpherson et al (London,1814-19). [*Rot. Scot.*]

Scalacronica, by Sir Thomas Gray of Heton, Knight. ed. Joseph Stevenson (Maitland Club, 1836). [*Scalacronica*]

Smit, H. J. *Bronnen Tot de Geschiedensis van den handel mit Engeland, Schotland en Ierland* ('S-Gravenhage, 1928) [Smit]

Stevenson, J. *Documents Illustrative of the History of Scotland* (London, 1870). [Stevenson, *Documents*]

Stones, E. L. G. *Anglo-Scottish Relations 1178-1328* (London,1965).

Walsingham, Thomas. *Historia Anglicana.* ed. T. H. Riley (Rolls Series, 1863) [*Chron. Walsingham*]

Wyntoun, Andrew of. *The Orygynale Cronykil of Scotland.* ed. D. Laing (Edinburgh, 1872-79) [*Chron. Wyntoun* (Laing)]

Yair, James. *An Account of the Scotch trade in the Netherlands* (London, 1776).

SECONDARY SOURCES

Adams, Ian H. *The Making of Urban Scotland* (London, 1978).

Atkin, Malcolm and Evans, D. H. 'Population, Profit and Plague:The Archaeological Interpretation of Buildings and Land Use in Norwich', *Scottish Archaeological Review*,iii (1984).

Balfour-Melville, E. W. M. 'Burgh Representation in Early Scottish Parliaments', *English Historical Review*, lix (1944).

Ballard, Adolphus. 'The Theory of the Scottish Burgh', *SHR*, xiii (1916).

Barber, John. 'Medieval Wooden Bowls' in *Studies in Scottish Antiquity presented to Stewart Cruden*, ed. David J. Breezě (Edinburgh, 1984).

Barley, M. W. ed. *European Towns, Their Archaeology and Early History* (London, 1977).

Barron, Evan M. *Inverness in the Middle Ages* (Inverness,1907).

Barrow, G. W. S. 'The Aftermath of War: Scotland and England in theLate Thirteenth and Early Fourteenth Centuries', *Transactions of the Royal Historical Society*, 5th ser., xviii (1978).

Barrow, G. W. S. *Kingship and Unity: Scotland 1000-1306* (London, 1981).

Barrow, G. W. S. 'Land Routes: The Medieval Evidence' in *Loads and Roads in Scotland and Beyond*, eds. Alexander Fenton and Geoffrey Stell (Edinburgh, 1984).

Barrow, G. W. S. *Robert Bruce and the Community of the Realm of Scotland*, 3rd ed. (Edinburgh, 1988).

Bennett, H. 'Textiles' in *Aberdeen Excavations* ['AberdeenTextiles']

Bennett, H. 'Textiles' (PHSE, forthcoming).

Blake, J. B. 'Medieval Smuggling in the North-east: Some Fourteenth-century Evidence', *Archaeologia Aeliana*, 4th ser., xliii (1965)

Blanchard, Linda. 'The Excavated Buildings' in *Perth Excavations*.

188 *Bibliography*

Blanchard, Linda. 'An Excavation at 45 Canal Street Perth' in *Perth Excavations*.

Blanchard, Linda. 'Kirk Close, 86-100 High Street' in *Perth Excavations*.

Blanchard, Linda, 'Kirk Close – a Backland Excavation' in *Town Houses and Structures*.

Bogdan, N. Q. and Wordsworth, J. W. *The Medieval Excavations at the High Street Perth 1975-76. An Interim Report* (Perth, 1978).

Booton, Harold. 'Burgesses and Landed Men in North-East Scotland in the Later Middle Ages: A Study in Social Interaction' PhD thesis (Aberdeen, 1988).

Booton, Harold. 'Inland Trade: A Study of Aberdeen in the Later Middle Ages' in *Scottish Town*.

Brooks, N. P. and Whittington, G. 'Planning and growth in the medieval Scottish burgh: the example of St Andrews', *Transactions of the Institute of British Geographers*, new series, ii, no. 2 (1977).

Brooks, N. P. 'Urban Archaeology in Scotland' in *European Towns*.

Campbell, James. 'England, Scotland and the Hundred Years War in the Fourteenth Century' in *Europe in the Late Middle Ages*, eds. J. R. Hale, J. R. L. Highfield and B. Smalley (London, 1965).

Cant, R. G. *St Andrews*. The Preservation Trust Handbook, rev. ed. (St Andrews, 1971).

Carus-Wilson, Eleanora. *Medieval Merchant Venturers* (London, 1954).

Clanchy, M. T. *From Memory to Written Record: England 1066-1307* (London, 1979).

Cowan, Ian B. 'The Emergence of the Urban Parish' in *Scottish Town*.

Cripps, J. 'Establishing the Topography of Medieval Aberdeen: An Assessment of the Documentary Sources' in *New Light on Medieval Aberdeen*.

Crone, A. and Barber, J. 'Structural Timbers' in *Perth Excavations*.

Crossley, D. W. ed. *Medieval Industry* (London, 1981)

Curteis, A. 'The Worked Wood' (PHSE, forthcoming).

de Vries, Jan. *European Urbanization 1500-1800* (Camb., Mass., 1984).

Dickinson, Robert E. *The West European City* (London, 1961).

Dickinson, W. Croft. 'Burgh Life from Burgh Records', *Aberdeen University Review*, xxxi (1946).

Dickinson, W. Croft. introduction to *Early Records of the Burgh of Aberdeen, 1317, 1398-1407* (SHS, 1957) [*Abdn. Recs.*].

Dickinson, W. C. *Scotland from the Earliest Times to 1603*, 3rd ed., rev. ed. A. A. M. Duncan (Oxford, 1977).

Dickinson, W. C. ed. *The Sheriff Court Book of Fife 1515-22* (SHS,1928) [*Fife Ct. Bk.*].

di Folco, John A. 'Roof Furniture and Floor Tiles' (PHSE, forthcoming).

Dilley, James. 'The German Merchants and Scotland, 1295-1327',PhD thesis (UCLA, 1946).

Dilley, James 'German Merchants in Scotland, 1297-1327', *SHR*, xxvii (1948).

Ditchburn, David. 'Trade with Northern Europe, 1297-1540' in *Scottish Town*.

Dodd, William. 'Ayr A Study of Urban Growth', *CAAS*, 2nd ser., x, (1972).

Donnelly, J. 'Thomas of Coldingham, merchant and burgess of Berwick upon Tweed (died 1316)', *SHR*, lix (1980).

Duby, Georges. *Rural Economy and Country Life in the MedievalWest*. tran. Cynthia Postan (London, 1968).

Duncan, A. A. M. 'The Early Parliaments of Scotland', *SHR*, xlv (1966).

Duncan, A. A. M. 'Perth. The First Century of the Burgh', *Transactions of the Perthshire Society of Natural Science, Special Issue* (1974).

Duncan, A. A. M. *Scotland: The Making of the Kingdom* (Edinburgh, 1975).

Dunlop, Annie I. ed. *The Royal Burgh of Ayr* (CAAS, 1953).

Ennen, Edith. *The Medieval Town.* tran. Natalie Fryde (Amsterdam, 1979)

Evans, Dave. *Digging up the 'Coopie'. Investigations in the Gallowgate and Lochlands* (Aberdeen, 1987).

Ewan, E. 'The Age of Bon-Accord: Aberdeen in the Fourteenth Century' in *New Light on Medieval Aberdeen.*

Ewan, E. 'The Burgesses of Fourteenth-century Scotland: a Social History', PhD thesis (Edinburgh, 1985).

Ewan, E. 'The Community of the Burgh in the Fourteenth Century' in *Scottish Town.*

Fischer, Thomas. *The Scots in Germany* (Edinburgh, 1902).

Flett, Iain and Cripps, J. 'The Documentary Sources' in *Scottish Town.*

Fox, R. 'Urban Development, 1100-1700' in *An Historical Geography of Scotland.*

Fraser, M. and Dickson, J. M. 'Plant remains' in *Aberdeen Excavations.*

Gibb, Andrew. *Glasgow – The Making of a City* (London,1983).

Gies, Joseph and Frances. *Life in a Medieval City* (NewYork, 1969).

Gordon, George and Dicks, Brian eds. *Scottish Urban History* (Aberdeen, 1983).

Gottfried, Robert S. *Bury St Edmunds and the Urban Crisis:1290-1539* (Princeton, 1982).

Graham, Angus. 'Archaeological Notes on Some Harbours in Eastern Scotland', *PSAS*, ci (1968-69).

Grant, Alexander. *Independence and Nationhood: Scotland 1306-1469* (London, 1984).

Grant, I. F. *The Social and Economic Development of Scotland before 1603* (Edinburgh, 1930).

Hall, Derek W. *Excavations at Market Street St Andrews 1985 Interim Report* (SUAT, 1985).

Hall, Derek. *Excavations at St Nicholas Farm St Andrews 1986-87. Interim Report* (SUAT, 1987).

Hanham, Alison. 'A medieval Scots merchant's handbook', *SHR*, xxi, (1971).

An Historical Atlas of Scotland rev. ed. (forthcoming).

Hodgson, G. W. I. and Smith, C. 'The Animal Remains' in Wordsworth'Castle Street, Inverness'. ['Inverness Animal']

Hodgson, G. W. I. 'The Animal Remains from Medieval Sites WithinThree Burghs on the Eastern Scottish Seaboard' in *Site Environment and Economy* ed. Bruce Proudfoot (British Archaeological Reports International Series 173, 1983).

Hodgson, G. W. I. 'Report on the animal remains excavated during1975-76 from the mediaeval levels at the High Street, Perth' (PHSE, forthcoming).

Hohenberg, Paul M. and Lees, Lynn Hollen. *The Making of Urban Europe 1000-1950* (Camb., Mass., 1985).

Holdsworth, Philip ed. *Excavations in the Medieval Burgh of Perth 1979-1981* (Edinburgh, 1987).

Holmes, Nicholas M. McQ. 'Excavation south of Bernard St., Leith,1980', *PSAS*, cxv (1985).

Houston, J. M. 'The Scottish Burgh', *Town Planning Review*, xxv (1954-55).

Hunter, Robert. 'Corporate Personality and the Scottish Burgh: AnHistorical Note' in *The Scottish Tradition, Essays in Honour of Ronald Gordon Cant*, ed. G. W. S. Barrow (Edinburgh, 1974).

Introductory Survey to the Sources and Literature of Scots Law (Stair Society, 1936).

Keith (also Pagan), Theodora. 'The Trading Privileges of the Royal Burghs of Scotland', *English Historical Review*, xcviii (1913).

Kenworthy, M. 'Analysis of the Fabrics' in *Aberdeen Excavations*.

Laing, Lloyd. 'Cooking-Pots and the Origins of the Scottish Medieval Pottery Industry', *The Archaeological Journal*,cxxx (1973).

Laing, Lloyd R. and Talbot, Eric. 'Some Medieval and Post Medieval Pottery from S. W. Scotland', *Glasgow Archaeological Journal*, iii (1974).

Lloyd, T. H. *The English Wool Trade in the Middle Ages* (Cambridge, 1977).

Lucas, H. S. 'John Crabbe, Flemish Pirate, Merchant, and Adventurer', *Speculum*, xx (1945).

Lynch, M. 'Scottish Towns 1500-1700' in *The Early ModernTown*, ed. M. Lynch (London, 1987).

Lynch, M. 'Towns and Townspeople in Fifteenth-Century Scotland' in *Towns and Townspeople in the Fifteenth Century*, ed. J. A. F. Thomson (London, 1988).

Lynch, M. 'Whatever happened to the medieval burgh?', *Scottish Economic and Social History*, iv (1984).

Lynch, M., Stell, G., and Spearman, R. M. eds. *The Scottish Medieval Town* (Edinburgh, 1988).

MacAskill, Norman. 'Pottery' in *Perth Excavations*. ['Perth Pottery']

MacAskill, Norman. 'Small Finds in Inverness' in Wordsworth 'Castle Street, Inverness'.

MacAskill, N. et al. 'Pottery' (SUAT, unpublished report).

McGavin, Neil A. *Excavations at Mill Street, Perth, 1979-80. An Interim Report* (Urban Archaeology Unit, Perth, n. d.).

MacGregor, A. C. 'A Report on Worked Bone, Antler and Ivory' (PHSE, forthcoming).

Mackenzie, William Mackay. *The Scottish Burghs* (Edinburgh,1949).

McNeill, Peter and Nicholson, Ranald eds. *An Historical Atlas of Scotland c.400-c. 1600* (St Andrews, 1975)

MacQueen, Hector and Windram, William. 'Laws and Courts in the Burghs' in *Scottish Town*.

Martin, C. 'The Boat Timbers' (PHSE, forthcoming).

Martin, G. H. 'New Beginnings in North-Western Europe' in *European Towns*.

Marwick, Sir James D. *Edinburgh Guilds and Crafts* (SBRS,1909).

Marwick, Sir James D. *List of Markets and Fairs* (Glasgow,1890).

Moorhouse, S. A. 'The medieval pottery industry and its markets' in *Medieval Industry*

Munby, Julian. 'Medieval domestic buildings' in *Urban Archaeology*.

Mundy, John and Reisenberg, Peter. *The Medieval Town* (Huntington, 1958).

Municipal Corporations (Scotland), Local Reports, i (London, 1835).

Murray, David. *Early Burgh Organization in Scotland* (Glasgow, 1924-32).

Murray, Hilary. 'The Excavated Secular Buildings' in *Aberdeen Excavations*. ['Aber. Bldgs']

Murray, Hilary. 'Excavation at 45-47 Gallowgate, Aberdeen', *PSAS*, cxiv (1984).

Murray, Hilary. 'Medieval Wooden and Wattle Buildings Excavated in Perth and Aberdeen' in *Town Houses and Structures*. ['Medieval Bldgs']

Murray, Hilary. '42 St Paul Street 1977-8' in *Aberdeen Excavations*.

Murray, Hilary. 'Wooden and Clay Buildings from Perth High Street Excavations' (PHSE, forthcoming). ['Perth Bldgs']

Murray, J. C. 'The Archaeological Evidence' in *New Light on Medieval Aberdeen*.

Murray, J. C. 'Conclusions' in *Aberdeen Excavations*.

Murray, J. C. *The Deserted Medieval Burgh of Rattray,Aberdeenshire. Interim Report on the Excavations*. (Aberdeen,1986).

Murray, J. C. ed. *Excavations in the Medieval Burgh of Aberdeen1973-81* (Edinburgh, 1982).

Murray, J. C. and Stones, Judith. '45-59 Green, 1976' in *Aberdeen Excavations*.

National Museum of Antiquities of Scotland, *Angels, Nobles and Unicorns*, exhibition catalogue (Edinburgh, 1982).

Neilson, George. 'On Some Scottish Burghal Origins', *Juridical Review*, xiv (1902).

Nicholas, David. *Town and Countryside: Social, Economic and Political Tensions in Fourteenth-Century Flanders* (Brugge,1971).

Nicholson, Ranald. *Edward III and the Scots* (London, 1965).

Nicholson, Ranald. *Scotland: The Later Middle Ages* (Edinburgh, 1974).

Pagan (formerly Keith), T. *The Convention of the Royal Burghs of Scotland* (Glasgow,1926).

Palliser, D. 'The Medieval Period' in *Urban Archaeology*.

Pirenne, Henri. *Medieval Cities: Their Origins and the Revival of Trade* tran. F. D. Halsey (Princeton, 1925).

Platt, Colin. *The English Medieval Town* (London, 1978).

Postan, M. M. *Medieval Trade and Finance* (Cambridge, 1973).

Pryde, George. *The Burghs of Scotland: a critical list* (Oxford, 1965).

Pryde, George. 'The Origin of the Burgh in Scotland', *Juridical Review*, xlvii (1935).

Pryde, George. 'The Scottish Burgh', *SHR*, xxxviii (1959).

Rait, Robert S. *The Parliaments of Scotland* (Glasgow,1924).

Reid, W. Stanford. 'Sea-Power in the Anglo-Scottish War, 1296-1328', *The Mariner's Mirror*, xlvi (1960).

Reid, W. Stanford. 'Trade, Traders, and Scottish Independence', *Speculum*, xxix (1954).

Reynolds, Susan. *An Introduction to the History of English Medieval Towns* (Oxford, 1977).

Reynolds, Susan. *Kingdoms and Communities in Western Europe,900-1300* (Oxford, 1984).

Robinson, D. 'Botanical Remains' in *Perth Excavations*.

Rodger, R. G. 'The Evolution of Scottish Town Planning' in *Scottish Urban History*.

Rörig, Fritz. *The Medieval Town* (Berkeley, 1967).

Schofield, John. 'Excavations south of Edinburgh High Street,1973-4', *PSAS*, cvii (1975-76).

Schofield, John. 'Recent approaches in urban archaeology' in *Urban Archaeology*.

Schofield, John and Leech, Roger eds. *Urban Archaeology in Britain* (London, 1987).

Shead, Norman. 'Glasgow: An Ecclesiastical Burgh' in *Scottish Town*.

Shirley, G. W. *The Growth of a Scottish Burgh: A Study in the Early History of Dumfries* (Dumfries, 1915).

Simpson, Anne Turner et al. *Scottish Burgh Survey reports* (Glasgow, 1977-82).

Simpson, Anne Turner and Stevenson, Sylvia eds. *Town Houses and Structures in Medieval Scotland: a Seminar* (SBS, 1980).

Simpson, G. G. ed. *Aberdeen's Hidden History* (Aberdeen,1972).

Simpson, G. G. 'The Use of Documentary Sources by the Archaeologist. A Viewpoint from Scotland', *Archives*, xiii, no. 60 (1978).

Smith, J. S. ed. *New Light on Medieval Aberdeen* (Aberdeen,1985).

Society of Antiquaries of Scotland. *Scotland's Medieval Burghs:an archaeological heritage in danger.* ed. Grant G. Simpson (Edinburgh, 1972).

Spearman, R. M. '29-30 South Methven Street' in *Perth Excavations.*

Spearman, R. M. 'Canal Street II' in *Perth Excavations.*

Spearman, R. M. 'The Medieval Townscape of Perth' in *Scottish Town.*

Spearman, R. M. 'Workshops, Materials and Debris – Evidence of Early Industry' in *Scottish Town.*

Stell, G. 'The earliest tolbooths: a preliminary account', *PSAS*, cxi, (1981).

Stell, G. 'Urban Buildings' in *Scottish Town.*

Stevenson, Carl. *Borough and Town* (Camb., Mass., 1933).

Stevenson, Alexander W. K. 'Trade between Scotland and the LowCountries in the Later Middle Ages', PhD thesis (Aberdeen, 1982).

Stevenson, A. 'Trade with the South 1070-1513' in *Scottish Town.*

Stevenson, Wendy B. 'The monastic presence in Scottish burghs in the twelfth and thirteenth centuries', *SHR*, lx (1981).

Stewart, I. H. *The Scottish Coinage* (London, 1955).

Stones, J. 'Iron Objects' in *Aberdeen Excavations.*

Stones, J. 'The Small Finds' in *Aberdeen Excavations.*

Stones, J. *A Tale of Two Burghs. The Archaeology of Old and New Aberdeen* (Aberdeen, 1987).

Thomas, C. 'Leather' in *Perth Excavations.*

Thoms, Lisbeth. 'Trial Excavation at St. Ann's Lane, Perth', *PSAS*, cxi (1982).

Torrie, E. P. 'The Gild of Dunfermline in the Fifteenth Century' PhD thesis (Edinburgh, 1984).

Torrie, E. P. 'The Guild in Fifteenth-Century Dunfermline' in *Scottish Town.*

Watt, D. E. R. *A Biographical Dictionary of Scottish Graduates to A. D. 1410* (Oxford, 1977).

Whitehand, Jeremy W. R. and Alauddin, Khan. 'The Town Plans of Scotland: Some Preliminary Considerations', *Scottish Geographical Magazine*, lxxxv (1969).

Whittington, G. et al. 'Discovery of Mediaeval Plough-Marks in St Andrews', *Scottish Studies*, xx (1976).

Whittington, G. and Whyte, I. D. *An Historical Geography of Scotland* (London, 1983).

Wood, Margaret. *The English Medieval House* (New York,1965).

Wordsworth, Jonathan et al.'Excavation of the settlement at 13-21 Castle Street, Inverness, 1979', *PSAS*, cxii (1982).

Wordsworth, Jonathan. 'The Archaeological Investigation of Medieval Inverness' in *The Middle Ages in the Highlands* (Inverness Field Club, 1981).

Wright, D. 'The Baskets' (PHSE, forthcoming).

Index